A Man of Letters

Thomas Sowell

Composition by Na Liu
editing by Elizabeth Costa,
and book design by Thomas Sowell

CONTENTS

First edition published in 2007 by Encounter Books, an activity of Encounter for Culture and Education, Inc., a nonprofit, tax exempt corporation.

Encounter Books website address: www.encounterbooks.com

Manufactured in the United States and printed on acid-free paper.

The paper used in this publication meets the minimum requirements of ANSI/NISO Z39.48-1992 (R 1997)(Permanence of Paper).

Library of Congress Cataloging-in-Publication Data

Sowell, Thomas, 1930–
    A man of letters / Thomas Sowell.
    p.   cm.
    Includes index.
    ISBN-13: 978-1-59403-196-0 (hardcover : alk. paper)
    ISBN-10: 1-59403-196-7 (hardcover : alk. paper)
    1. Sowell, Thomas, 1930–   2. African American intellectuals—Biography.   3. Intellectuals—United States—Biography.   4. African Americans—Intellectual life—20th century.   5. African Americans—Civil rights—History—20th century.   I. Title.
E185.97.S69A3 2007
973'.04960730794092—dc22
[B]
2007000131

10 9 8 7 6 5 4 3 2

PREFACE

When looking back over our lives, memories may fade or be fickle, but letters don't change with time. Letters served as an anchor in reality when I was writing my little memoir, *A Personal Odyssey*. Now the four filing cabinets in my garage, full of letters going back more than half a century, permit a more in-depth look at a long life that has now spanned about a third of the entire history of the United States. Many of these letters dealt with landmark events in the country and in the world, not just those in my personal life. They now permit a look back at the history of an era as well as the life of an individual.

This was an era of enormous changes in the world around me. When I was born on June 30, 1930, most Americans did not have a telephone or a refrigerator. My own family did not have electricity, central heating, or hot running water. The Great Depression of the 1930s was just getting under way. Franklin D. Roosevelt was still governor of New York, Winston Churchill was just a largely ignored backbencher in the British Parliament, and Adolf Hitler's National Socialist Party was still only the second-largest party in Germany. Who could have predicted at that time the world-shattering events in which they would all play major roles?

Who could have predicted even the more mundane story of a black child born to a maid in the Jim Crow South, his father having died before his birth? The world I grew up in changed beyond recognition during my lifetime and these changes could not leave me unchanged. I often wonder what my mother, who died giving birth to my younger brother, would have made of our lives if she could see them unfolding. How could she have dreamed that the child she brought into the world at the cost of her life would someday be a jet propulsion engineer at NASA? Could she even have imagined rockets taking people to the moon? And would she have been much less surprised by my life? Once, as a young man in my early twenties, I sat in my little studio apartment with another brother who had stopped by. We were commiserating with each other over the rough times we were going through. We both held entry-level jobs in the government and things were not going well, either on those jobs or in our personal lives. However, at one point my brother straightened up, looked directly at me and said: "If our mother were alive, she would think that we had succeeded beyond her wildest dreams."

Even at that point, neither I nor anyone else could have predicted the course my life would take—that I would end up in a profession of which I had no conception at the time and in institutions I did not know existed. Looking back on it all now, I am struck by how easily things could have taken a different path at many points along the way, with many of those paths leading into blind alleys or even into death. The story of the path that they did take, and that the world around me took, is told in these letters.

INTRODUCTION

Having been born in North Carolina and having grown up in Harlem, I had dropped out of high school in 1946 at age 16 and left home at age 17 to go live on my own, usually in a rented room. I discovered the hard way that there was no great demand for a high-school dropout with no skills or experience. I had no clear indication of where I was heading, if anywhere beyond the string of low-level, poorly-paying jobs I held. After nearly three tough years on my own, it was a major advance when I received an offer of a job as an entry-level clerk with the government in Washington in September 1950.

Washington was a new experience, going beyond a change of jobs and cities. In Washington lived a sister named Mary Frances and two brothers, William and Charles. A younger brother lived in North Carolina and another brother in Detroit. I never knew that any of them existed while I was growing up. I had been adopted in infancy and was not told that I had been adopted until I was nearly grown. Having left the family in which I had grown up when I was 17, I now had a new family and that was a good feeling. Washington itself was not a good experience, however, when I arrived there in 1950. Racial barriers made downtown restaurants and most movie houses off-limits. The schools were racially segregated. Washington was a typical Southern town in every way except that blacks did not have to ride in the back of buses and trolleys.

The Korean war was raging and my military draft status made it clear that my civilian days were numbered. After several months in Washington, I decided to spend my remaining time as a civilian back in New York. About five months after I returned to New York, I was drafted in October, 1951—and was surprised to find myself assigned to the Marine Corps instead of the Army. Heavy casualties among Marines in Korea had led the Marine Corps to take a share of the draftees to replenish their ranks. Dismayed as I was at the time to be in the Marines, which meant going back to the South again, to boot camp at Parris Island, South Carolina, in retrospect my two years of military service contributed much to my future, both financially and in terms of personal maturity. The G.I. Bill enabled me to go to college and college opened up new worlds for me.

While in the Marine Corps, I was sent to the photography school at the Naval Air Station in Pensacola, Florida. It was not only the best assignment during my military service, it gave me a marketable skill and a greater ability to enjoy photography—and photography remained a major interest for the rest of my life.

After being released from active military duty, I returned briefly to New York and then resumed my job as a government clerk in Washington, using the G.I. Bill to finance some evening courses at Howard University, a local black institution. This arrangement lasted about a year and a half, during which time I grew increasingly dissatisfied with Howard and finally took the desperate gamble of applying to higher powered and more expensive universities, including Harvard, even though this would require me to spend every dime I had, or could borrow, to finance my first year, in the hope of doing well enough that year to earn a scholarship that would supplement the G.I. Bill to finance the rest of the way.

It is doubtful whether I would have done so if I had had any realistic understanding of the odds against all this. But, despite some rocky times, it somehow worked out. I was admitted to Harvard on the strength of my test scores and some very strong letters of recommendation from my two favorite teachers at Howard University, the distinguished writer and poet Sterling Brown and a remarkable lady who taught me freshman English, Dr. Marie Gadsden. "Mrs. G," as I came to call her, also arranged for me to meet a lovely young lady who was attending Radcliffe, the women's college at Harvard in those days, though nothing came of it. But I remained in touch with Mrs. G, usually by letter, in the years ahead. A wise confidante, she became in fact the person with whom I exchanged the most letters over the next several decades.

After graduating from Harvard in 1958 with a degree in

economics, I went on to a year of postgraduate study in economics at Columbia University, where I received a master's degree, and then on to the University of Chicago to work toward a Ph.D. in economics. This is where I was at the time when the first of these letters was written in 1960.

A fuller account of these years can be found in my book *A Personal Odyssey*. The abbreviated account here is just to set the stage for the letters that follow.

EDITORIAL NOTE: Many, if not most, of the letters that follow are excerpts rather than the complete originals. Only where there are passages missing within these excerpts are ellipses used. Addresses are usually omitted to conserve space and, for the same reason, my own closings are usually omitted, except where they are included to indicate a special relationship to the person to whom I was writing. Closings in letters from other people are usually included only to the extent needed to indicate who the sender was. Therefore, for example, a letter signed "Bill Proxmire" will not include the formal name typed underneath, "William Proxmire" or whatever title the sender might have typed under that. In some places, names have been replaced by asterisks to protect the innocent or, in some cases, the guilty. While most letters are in chronological order, sometimes letters that fit together in subject matter are put together, even if another letter on a different subject would belong in their midst chronologically.

The 1960s

In many ways, the decade of the 1960s was a turning point in the history of American society, though few of us foresaw what it was turning to.

As 1960 began, I was enrolling in my second quarter as a graduate student at the University of Chicago. My life was economically grim and socially barren but intellectually challenging, as I studied economics in a tough program leading toward the Ph.D. Ideologically, I was a Marxist but the University of Chicago was nevertheless my first choice, despite its having the most conservative economics department of any top university. I had respect for its intellectual caliber and went there specifically to study the history of economic thought under Professor George J. Stigler, the leading authority on that subject. In fact, I had gone to Columbia University to study under Professor Stigler the year before, only to discover when I arrived there that he had just left for the University of Chicago. I followed him in the fall of 1959.

My personal life was cramped, both literally and figuratively. I lived in a small room in the International House, a few blocks down the street from the university, but this was just a place to sleep and eat. Its activities were more social than intellectual, and rather shallow and pretentious. The only activity there that I took part in regularly was joining other students watching the evening news on television. Most of my family and friends were back east and I made few new friends in Chicago. I always felt better going to the university than returning to the International House. My limited social life was especially hard to take because, a few years earlier, I had had my own little studio apartment in Washington with my own photographic darkroom in a walk-in closet. Now my occasional photographic jaunts led only to rolls of film to be put aside to be developed in later years when I could resume a more normal life.

In March 1960, my first article was published in the *American Economic Review*, the leading journal of the profession, where it was very unusual for a graduate student's work to appear. This buoyed my spirits and gave me some much-needed encouragement to persist in the task of completing my education. It was a task that was becoming more wearisome after a dozen years of struggle—in both civilian and military life—since leaving home at age 17, and with still with no real sign of light at the end of the tunnel.

Other things were happening elsewhere that attracted my attention. Sit-ins by young blacks protesting racial segregation in a restaurant in Atlanta were one of the early signs of the new civil rights movement. A friend who was teaching at Tuskegee Institute sent me clippings about it and I responded in a letter.

March 22, 1960

Dear Hildred,

Received the clippings you sent. Found them very interesting and was very proud of the way our people have sprung to life and the good judgment with which things have been handled. I found myself wishing I were down there in the midst of it all, but then perhaps it is best that I am not, since I might do something foolish that would undermine the whole operation. It was particularly interesting that 18 of the 21 Negro restaurant workers in Atlanta refused to help the owner clear the steam table. Who would have believed this possible ten years ago?

With hindsight, I can see legal, moral, and other problems with this approach, but at the time I thought it was good. A month later I wrote to her again, this time discussing different approaches to education and condemning those at the black colleges. In short, even at this early date, I saw the obstacles to the advancement of blacks as involving more than discrimination by whites.

April 21, 1960

Dear Hildred,

Here at the University of Chicago one of the profs told me, "If you could see the grades that students from Negro colleges get here in the graduate school, you would swear we were discriminating." Note that this is not Negro students, but students from Negro colleges. Negro students who don't come from

> Negro colleges do all right. I knew that these colleges get poor material but I also know that they do a damn poor job when they get good material. The "poor material" business gives them a ready excuse for all their backward, narrow, inbred ideas.

Despite my dismay at the low quality of the black colleges, I thought they could be improved and wanted to teach at one of these colleges when I finished graduate school, in hopes of being able to contribute toward that improvement. Whether or not that was possible could only be determined by experience and I wanted to preview the possibilities by teaching at some black college during the summer while still in graduate school. However, my efforts to find a summer teaching post at a black college came to nought, so I found my first professional work as a summer intern in economics at the U.S. Department of Labor in Washington.

The job paid more than I had ever made before, enabling me to enjoy a few of the amenities of life. Inadvertently, it also played a role as a turning point in my ideological orientation. After a year at the University of Chicago, including a course from Milton Friedman, I remained as much of a Marxist as I had been before arriving. However, the experience of seeing government at work from the inside and at a professional level started me to rethinking the whole notion of government as a potentially benevolent force in the economy and society. From there on, as I learned more and more from both experience and research, my adherence to the visions and doctrines of the left began to erode rapidly with the passage of time. But because this was an erosion, rather than a sudden "road to Damascus" conversion, I was spared the shock that some others went through in disengaging from the left.

Something else happened to me in the summer of 1960 that seemed even more important to me at the time—a lovely young woman whom I shall call Audrey. She too was a summer intern, in her case working at the *Washington Post*. She was my all-consuming passion for the summer and, I hoped, for much longer than the summer.

There were complications, however. Audrey was a senior in college in Pittsburgh and I was in graduate school in Chicago, so we would not be able to see much of each other during the coming academic year. More fundamental complications were that Audrey was not only a decade younger than me, she was from a very different background—a family that was part of the black elite. Her father was a doctor and also owned rental property. Personally she was someone who liked to keep her emotions under control, so I was taken completely by surprise one night near the end of the summer when she suddenly began to cry. When I asked her what was wrong, she said: "You are going to go back to Chicago and forget all about me!"

"I will never forget you, Audrey," I said. And I never have.

We decided informally that we would get married after we had completed our education, though I would have married her then and there.

I wrote about Audrey to a number of people, including Norton, my former room mate at Harvard, and Mrs. Gadsden, who had taught me freshman English at Howard University. After the summer was over and I was back at the University of Chicago for my last year in residence, I wrote to Norton.

October 9, 1960

Dear Nort,

Back in harness again with mixed feelings. This has been a hell of a summer. Didn't accomplish *anything* intellectually or academically. My summer was essentially Audrey; economics receded into the dim background. Audrey, as I may have mentioned before, is only twenty (20) years old. But she is quite mature in many ways, though of course not evenly so across the board. We have already had our ups and downs, but I think we will muddle through together. Stopped by to see her last week in Pittsburgh on my way out here. She attends ****** ****** there. I'd like you and Irene to meet her sometime, and vice-versa. . . .

This should be my last year in residence, with all unfulfilled requirements to be taken care of in absentia. Don't know just what kind of work I will go into next June. There are serious objections to all the possibilities I have seen open as of now. The Labor Department was a big disappointment. It was a congenial place to work and the pay was good, but the work and the people were as pedestrian as hell. My boss, ****** ******, was intellectually pitiful. And this was not some senile old man in whom you see the ruins of a once sharp mind; ****** is still in the full vim and vigor of his late thirties. Moreover, he is not just an isolated instance. The program I was in exposed me to many (if not most) of the top people in the Department, who gave lectures with discussions afterwards. Most of them were genial mediocrities, real organization men. . . .

Spent a very pleasant summer in Washington. Went to concerts, ballet, beisbol, etc. and became acquainted with a number of eateries around town. Really hated to leave from that standpoint. However, the long vacation from the books made me anxious to get on with my work. It may have been a good thing. Last summer [1959] I logged in much grinding time and got sick of it all halfway through the [following] academic year. This year going stale shouldn't be a problem, although getting back in gear may be.

Although Audrey wanted me to visit her family in upstate New York during the Christmas holidays, I knew that I would need a job after finishing my studies at the University of Chicago the following June, and the place to look for a job was at the annual meetings of the American Economic Association, which were held during the Christmas holidays, and in 1960 were held in St. Louis. Audrey was hurt and this may have been the beginning of the unraveling of our relationship. I wrote to Mrs. Gadsden about the situation on the train taking me back to Chicago after the A.E.A. convention. Mrs. G was no longer at Howard University but was working in various countries overseas.

December 30, 1960

Dear Mrs. G,

Your last letter was even more welcome than usual, because it was a tonic at a time when my spirits were low over one of my recurrent crises with Audrey. In many ways she is a very insightful woman, but in others a complete infant. Incidentally, I took the liberty of showing her your previous letter and she was enormously impressed (of course) and is anxious to meet you. . . .

Among the people I talked with at the convention was the new chairman of the economics department at Howard. . . . He seems anxious to have me come there, but everything he says has the net effect of making me doubt him, the situation and the possibility of achieving anything worthwhile. First impressions may be misleading, but he struck me as low and oily. He tended to deprecate teaching, which the students desperately need, in favor of newsy "research" and grant-grabbing projects. He seems to be one of those philistines who automatically assumes that everyone else is a philistine, and makes his pitch accordingly. . . . He seemed genuinely unable to reconcile my going to Chicago with my coming from liberal Harvard. I don't think it really occurred to him that I have a mind of my own and did not regard myself as a "product" of either institution. . . .

Had an interview with the chairman of the economics department of Western Michigan University, who was in sharp contrast with our academic "operator" from Howard. He was sincere, interested in teaching and regarded my questions and qualms as reasonable doubts understandable in the circumstances rather than as impediments to be of-coursed aside. Unfortunately, the location more or less rules it out. I want to begin work on the east coast because Audrey is going to law school at either Harvard, Columbia or Georgetown. She has a brilliant academic record and can probably get in at any of these places. Unfortunately, she has some of the shortcomings that Sterling Brown once elaborated as typical of straight-A students, the principal one being an uncritical absorption of the general framework of ideas within which they receive the information they absorb and feed back. She does not seem to have an intellectual or moral center of gravity within herself, and seems unable to shake loose from the superstition that there is something "natural" about the conventional.

Nevertheless, I told Mrs. G "Audrey and I are planning to get married in about 18 months."

1961

I returned from the American Economic Association without either a job offer or a clear sense of which kinds of jobs I wanted. I had accomplished nothing—and at the high cost of failing to go meet Audrey's parents. Her mother especially seemed to have had misgivings about our relationship, even back during the summer of 1960. Near the end of that summer Audrey had phoned her mother and, after a while, told her that she had to end the call because she was going to go to a movie with me. When she mentioned my name, her mother asked if this was the same Tom she had talked about back in June—and was by no means happy when Audrey said that it was. Apparently Audrey did not usually go out with the same guy this long before.

There was another aspect to this. Even though I was trying to coordinate my job search with Audrey's postgraduate plans, she neglected to keep me up to date on those plans and seemed inexplicably hurt when I complained of her irresponsibility when so much was at stake. Two months after the A.E.A. convention, I wrote to Mrs. Gadsden about how things had deteriorated further.

March 5, 1961

Dear Mrs. G,

Audrey's mother seems to be a factor of unknown proportions in our problems. At the beginning of the summer [1960] Audrey was worried over her mother's reaction to me, what with our age differences and my being a different sort of person than her mother would be expected to approve. She came back to D.C. in July after a visit home over-joyed at her mother's apparent acceptance of it all. But when she talked with her mother on the phone in September, a sour note was then introduced. Apparently she [the mother] must have expected it to blow over, for she said: "Don't get serious." Her mother has plans for Audrey's life, and apparently these leave no place for random factors like me. I don't imagine it set too well when Audrey and I were exchanging special delivery letters every couple of days when Audrey was home at Christmas. At any rate, since the holidays Audrey has been a changed person, all for the worse. I didn't hear from her for nearly two weeks after she got back to school, and on a visit to her in Pittsburgh since then, she was so impossible that I refused to see her on my last day there.

I thought this was it, but when Valentine's day came she sent me a card (I didn't send her one) with "please write." When she seems to be a hurt and foolish child I can't help wanting to do something. Yet what can I do? Certainly I can't alter the course of my life on the hope that she will come to her senses. I have neither the knowledge nor the finesse to say anything about the relationship between her and her mother, and more fundamentally there is no transplanting backbone. So there we are. It won't be as painful if it ends now as it would have been last summer, because the coming event has been casting its shadow before it for some time. . . .

Though my personal and professional future is unsettled at the moment, I can still look forward to it cheerfully and even eagerly. It is certain to be better than the present. Even an uninspiring job will mean having my own place and some of the basic luxuries of life. And even if Audrey and all she means is lost, there is a nice personable and uninhibited young lady in Washington who will keep me from feeling too lonesome. If only I could see my favorite teacher on her next visit to the states, my cup would runneth over.

That summer I returned to Washington and became an economist in the U.S. Department of Labor, where I had been an intern the previous summer. Mrs. G wasn't in Washington when I arrived, but she would be in the fall. She wrote to me and I replied.

Dear Mrs. G,

So good hearing from you at a trying time. My life is entering a new phase, the beginning of my professional career (at a modest level), though on the personal side it is back where it was: I am alone. Everything is over between Audrey and me. It has been clearly inevitable for some time, but it hurts just the same.

Right now I am sitting in the almost bare little efficiency apartment that will be my home for the coming year. What scenes will be enacted here and what personal growth will take place here I wish I knew—I think. I need some emotional borrowing to tide me over the barren present. By the time you arrive in the fall I should be more solidly settled, emotionally and otherwise, but even so your tough, resilient optimism should be a tonic.

I received a letter from Gloria, a young black woman whom I had met back in 1957, when she was a student at Mt. Holyoke College and I was a student at Harvard. My room mate Ralph had a girl friend named Sandra at Mt. Holyoke, and it was through her that Gloria and I were brought together. Gloria was a very bright, very thoughtful and idealistic person. Having been in predominantly white schools for years, she now wanted to go to a predominantly black institution for postgraduate work and so attended Meharry medical school in Tennessee. At this point, Gloria had graduated from medical school but was not yet a doctor. She had also married another medical student whom she had met at Meharry.

August 14, 1961

Dear Gloria,

You can't imagine how heart-warming it was hearing from you. I had come home early from work with a toothache, but it went away after I read your letter (you are guilty of practicing medicine without a license).

I thought it was typical of your generous nature that you wished me the same sort of happiness you have found. However, that isn't the way things have turned out. The relationship that began last summer is now over. Things sometimes happen in ironic ways. . . .

Wrote Sandra a while back to get the address of one of the offices at Columbia, and received a very nice letter from her in return. She was planning to go out to San Francisco, and I suppose she is there by now. Who could have predicted, that fall day at Mt. Holyoke, what would happen to the four of us?

1962

Mrs. Gadsden, after returning to the United States and spending a few months in Washington, went off to teach at Alcorn A & M, a black college in Mississippi.

January 12, 1962

Dear Mrs. G,

I really didn't think you were going to do it. People just don't go to Mississippi. I think I would sooner volunteer to go into orbit. Only today your friend Dr. Smith remarked that days like this (very cold) made him think about going back to Florida but "Those Crackers are too bad."

. . . Although last year seems in retrospect to have been one of an almost unbroken series of disappointments and reverses, my morale is much higher now than a year ago. Perhaps it is just the inner peace of having the little congenial things of life, or possibly the feeling of having ridden out storms that aren't likely to come again so frequently or in such strength.

I still kept in touch with a friend and fellow student named Cy from my graduate student days at Columbia, where we were both left-wingers. He was now at Berkeley and still on the far left. He sent me one of the radical publications out there with an article by a local black leftist that he thought was significant but which I viewed otherwise.

March 15, 1962

Dear Cy,

The "black Negro" article has a certain morbid fascination for me, like an ambitious experiment that ended in smoke and goo and broken glass. It is such a mixture of insights and utter nonsense that it is hard to know where to start to criticize it. I suppose going by mere page order is as good a way as any.

We are told on page 7 that "pride in his [cultural] heritage" prompted many Africans to escape from slavery. Don't *all* prisoners attempt to escape, regardless of the state of their cultural heritage? Is there even a shred of evidence that attempts to escape dropped off as the African cultural heritage faded with the passing generations? If one makes an arbitrary assertion of a functional relationship between A and B, there should be some elementary attempt to show concomitant variation. Looked at another way, one should *test* one's hypothesis, not just become hypnotized with its symmetry and plausibility. Plausibility is the most treacherous of all guides, since what will seem plausible to anyone is a function of what he already believes. . . .

Section II (p. 11) opens with the statement that "Today, the struggle of the Negro to achieve equality in American society can no longer be separated from the struggle of the colonial peoples to attain freedom and equality in the modern world." As a matter of fact, they are in causal terms almost wholly unrelated. If he means only that in non-causal *topical* terms they can be lumped together by analogy, he asserts something very piddling; whether A can be lumped together with B under the same topical heading is purely a matter of how one chooses to organize things in one's mind. It is not a fact of the external world. This is similar to the problem that arises when sociologists construct their social "classes"; any group of people can be *called* a class (*e.g.*, left-handed bus drivers), but that is very different from saying that they *function* as a class, *i.e.*, act in concert or behave differently toward each other than toward the world at large. . . .

We are asked on page 15 why Ralph Bunche has not spoken out on the Negro problem—that is, why a diplomat in a sensitive position has not injected himself into domestic controversies unrelated to his work. Why hasn't the Postmaster General "spoken out" on foreign policy? Why hasn't the Secretary of the Interior "spoken out" on the national debt?

Cy seemed to resent my disdain for his newly discovered black genius.

April 25, 1962

Dear Cy,

I am sorry that you found my comments on * * * * *'s article "snobbish and apologetic," and still more so that you were content to rest your case on this label. You might be interested to know that I mentioned this article in passing in a letter to a former Howard professor [Mrs. G], who said in reply: "I not only know ****** ******, I taught him—the same year I taught you as a freshman. Your comments indicate that he has the same difficulty today as he had in my class. He had that occasional spark, which marks exceptional ability, but he was minus any discipline and logic."

You raised intriguing questions regarding a "double

standard" in your comments on the Cuba and Ghana articles. Perhaps there can legitimately be double standards of morality, at least in the sense in which I think you mean it, but there can never be double standards of *truth*. If, for example, we are justified in saying that tyranny in Ghana is serving a noble purpose, we are still not justified in saying that it is *not* tyranny. And, incidentally, I think there ought to be a damn sight closer scrutiny of the sweeping assumption that a noble purpose is being served, just because someone is reciting our favorite catchwords while he goes around butchering people. . . . Perhaps more than anything, there is too little attention to inconvenient truths. . . . You mention, for example, the brutalities of the Batista regime and Castro's killing of ex-Batista men. . . . In fact, the shooting of ex-*Castro* men is a far more significant development as an indication of what this regime is and where it is going.

We continued to exchange letters, but less frequently, and then not at all.

———————————

Although I was no longer in residence at the University of Chicago, I kept in touch by mail with Professor George Stigler, whom I was trying to convince that I should write a doctoral dissertation on Say's Law, with him as dissertation committee chairman. He doubted that anything new and worthwhile could still be said on the subject after mountains of other writings on Say's Law over the previous century and a half. But my interpretation of the early controversies was very different from that of others—and very different from Professor Stigler's. In our correspondence back and forth he argued that I was basing my interpretation on selected *ad hoc* remarks by Malthus, rather than on what was Malthus' "standard view."

April 1, 1962

Dear Professor Stigler:

For one thing, there are no *conflicting* statements on this point by Malthus to be resolved. The views expressed in his *Principles* are the same as those expressed in his correspondence. . . . I honestly don't know what to advance as a further argument because I see nothing to argue against—just an insistence that I prove Malthus meant what he said. How many *ad hoc* statements add up to a standard view?

One of my last exchanges of letters with my old friend Cy from Columbia University days dealt with our different views of contemporary events in Cuba and Ghana. I objected both to his conclusions and to the reasoning behind them.

June 6, 1962

Dear Cy,

My objection to the rosy pictures of Castro and Nkrumah was not based on the number of persons they had killed (I have not kept up with those statistics) but on the simple, inescapable fact that organized opposition has been rendered impossible by force in both countries. When men are jailed for years without a trial, it is fatuous to speak of the government as being on the "brink" of "authoritarianism." . . . Political repression does not necessarily contribute anything to the solution of a country's economic problems, and the austerity which is said to be the price of economic development may in fact be the price of incompetent or irresponsible leadership. Questions of this sort need critical examination in specific instances, not bland repetition of blanket excuses. . . . To be meaningful a theory must be verifiable or refutable, in principle at least. A theory which implies much and says little is a trap for the author as well as for others, because the irrefutability of what is said (which may be practically nothing) tends to lend a spurious credibility to what is implied.

I also had an exchange on intellectual issues with my old room-mate Ralph.

July 31, 1962

Dear Ralph,

The quotation you cited regarding the purpose and method of social science expresses precisely the view to which I am opposed. Certainly it takes courage to be a radical at this time and place (and perhaps at all times and places), but this is not to say that those who fail to take a radical position do so from lack of courage. It does not warrant the supposition that those who ask different questions than Mr. Bernal's are trying to "dodge" what he chooses to call "the central issues." Would a physicist be considered to be dodging chemistry? Are novelists dodging poetry?

I am also skeptical of Bernal's omniscient reference to "the social reasons that have made social science what it is." The more I study the history of economic thought, the less weight I am inclined to give to the environment as an influence on the *substance* of what is said. The situation is very analogous to that regarding the influence of Hegel on Marx. In terms of the external trappings and the method of presentation, Hegel is writ large across Marxism, but in terms of the substance of what is said, the resemblance is less than what would be expected from pure chance.

As I continued to follow the civil rights struggle in the South, my initial enthusiasm began to be accompanied by a growing skepticism as to the direction the movement was taking. I also continued my interest in educational questions. Both of these were discussed in a letter to Norton.

August 6, 1962

Dear Nort,

The more I follow the integration struggles in the South, the more I am inclined to be skeptical as to the actual fruit of it all. It is awkward to stand on the sidelines and criticize people who are suffering for their ideals, and yet the question must be asked, "What is this going to *do?*" There seem to be so many other things with greater priority than equality-of-public-accommodation that the blind preoccupation with this one thing seems almost pathological. When one considers the apathy in the Negro community toward such things as the hopeless incompetence and irresponsibility of their own colleges and other institutions, the fervor generated in the fight for "integration" in all things at all costs seems more an emotional release than a sensible movement toward something that promises a worthwhile benefit. If Howard University would just tell its students about the financial aid that is available, the summer jobs that are open, etc., it would do more than integrating every hamburger joint from here to Biloxi. . . .

Your comments about watered-down courses reminded me of an incident at the University of Chicago. I received a letter of inquiry from a college in Pennsylvania about a teaching position that involved, among other things, international trade. Later on, when I mentioned this to one of my profs [H. Gregg Lewis] and told him I had declined, he lost all patience with me.

"You turned it down?!" he said. "Why?"

"Well, I don't know anything about international trade."

"What's that got to do with it? Plenty of people teach courses they don't know anything about. Read a couple of books over the summer and teach it in the fall."

My interest in educational issues went from theoretical to practical in September 1962, when I began my teaching career as an instructor at Douglass College in New Jersey, the women's college at Rutgers University. Among the people to whom I wrote after arriving there was Audrey, who was now a student at the Harvard Law School. My reference to the "Coop" is to the Harvard Cooperative Society, which ran the campus store and to which I still belonged. A little date book from them listed the schedule of events on campus. This may have been the first time that I had written to Audrey since our breakup the previous year.

September 3, 1962

Dear Audrey,

How are things going with you and the Law School? I see by my Coop book that you begin classes the same day I do (I will be on the teaching end). This is my first academic assignment, as instructor at Douglass College, the women's college at Rutgers.

Just arrived here from Washington, after a year in the government. While D.C. has little to offer as a permanent place, it was a pleasant enough way station, and probably did me a lot of good. Met a lot of new people, especially this past summer when a large contingent of summer assistants from various colleges worked in our unit. They were certainly a refreshing change from the permanent bureaucrats, and served to reassure me that I had made the right decision in leaving for the academic world even at a financial sacrifice. My job in the government wasn't so bad—I was on good terms with my immediate supervisor, and spent a substantial part of my working time in various libraries around town—but a soft life is no substitute for fulfillment.

My living quarters here in New Brunswick, which were

rented sight unseen, have proved to be a pleasant surprise. I have a little efficiency apartment, which turns out to be only ten minutes away from my office (five minutes of this being required to get down to the ground floor).

With New York so close, I will be making a number of trips up there during the coming academic year. If you are going to be down there some week-ends, perhaps we can get together some time.

We did not in fact get together that year. Meanwhile, things got off to a good start at Douglass College, as I indicated in a letter to my brother Charles in Washington.

September 20, 1962

Dear Charles,

Well, I have just about survived my first week of classes, and think I will try for two. Actually I wouldn't swap it for anything. Had a shaky beginning on Monday, but had two very enjoyable classes this morning, with a good deal of discussion. The girls seem to be very intelligent and from indications they are digging into the reading. However, the acid test will come with my first exam next week. . . .

I am working like a dog. Though I have only 7½ hours a week in the classroom, you would be surprised how much I have to do on the outside to make those 7½ hours productive.

I was, incidentally, the first black male hired to teach at this predominantly white women's college and I believe I was the only black resident in the apartment building across the street from the college. Things were nice where I lived, as I indicated in a letter to my sister, Mary Frances.

September 22, 1962

Dear Mary,

I was pleasantly surprised when I arrived here to find my name already on the apartment door and in the mailbox (in fact, there was a card for me that had been mailed August 16th). It was a little thing but it indicated an attitude very different from what I found in Washington. Another example: today I left my clothes in the washing machine and didn't come back for a couple of hours. Discovered that someone had put my clothes in the dryer and they were dry when I got there. Again it was a small thing, and only cost 20¢, but it meant a lot.

I also wrote back to another economist named Tom at the Labor Department. The "Mrs. Schloss" referred to was Clara Schloss, the head of the branch where we had worked together. She was a very tough customer. On my last day at the Labor Department, my immediate supervisor walked by my desk and whispered, "Did you get a chance to kiss Clara goodbye?"

September 22, 1962

Dear Tom,

There is a sweet, motherly lady in the office next to mine, and she sort of patted me on the head as I went off to my first classes. However, at the time, I wasn't prepared to scorn any kind of help. The first classes were pretty bad (that is, *I* was pretty bad; the classes were pretty good). However, by my second meetings with each of the three classes I had overcome my nervousness and things moved smoothly. Some of these girls pounce on questions like little tigers, though others remind you a little of Mickey Mantle trying to hit Hoyt Wilhelm.

I trust Mrs. Schloss is back from her vacation. The very thought of Research and Statistics Branch without her, even temporarily, is enough to make one reel back. Why—it is like an electric chair with the cord unplugged, if you will pardon me for being sentimental.

Unfortunately for my bowling, the alleys around here are AMF, and they take a little learning after the Brunswick lanes in Silver Spring. My average has dropped a little, but even worse, I am more erratic than ever... I had a 90 sandwiched in between a 173 and 183.

Discovered that my classroom hours are even less than I had figured: only 7½ hours a week. However, my non-classroom working time is much more than I had imagined. Every day my mail box is stuffed with mail, notices, invitations and forms. In addition, it takes a hell of a lot of preparation to hold forth for an hour and fifteen minutes, even with discussions here and there. I see now why there are so many bad courses in college. It takes a toll to give anything worthwhile. For example, I have to do all the reading, but I don't just repeat it; only selected trouble spots

> are covered in class, and something additional has to be worked up for a lecture.

Of course I also wrote to Mrs. Gadsden, saying many of the same things about my teaching experiences but also adding something about the racial situation in New Brunswick.

> September 23, 1962
>
> Dear Mrs. G,
>
> New Brunswick seems to have no Negro middle class whatsoever. I can't recall seeing a single Negro wearing a business suit and a clean white shirt since I have been here. Also, in half a dozen trips to the local bowling alley, I haven't seen one Negro roll one ball. It is really pathetic to see all stereotypes. It is also a little disheartening to see so few Negro girls at Douglass, even though this is a state university.

Not one of the 55 students in my three classes was black. It would be the spring semester before one black student enrolled.

When I heard back from Mrs. G, I learned that she was encountering problems teaching at Alcorn A & M.

> October 25, 1962
>
> Dear Mrs. G,
>
> Hearing from you produced a warm glow, as always. Please don't ever hesitate to write because you are beset with problems. I have certainly unburdened myself to you on many occasions.
>
> At present, at least, I am probably learning more than I am

teaching. More and more aspects of students, faculty and administration reveal themselves as time goes by. The students seem to have a remarkable range of extra-curricular and summertime experiences beyond the ivory towers. They are conscientious students as far as doing the reading and taking notes, but they have a highly stereotyped view of classroom education as a spectator sport. A few seem to have real resentment at my expecting them to exercise their minds. One young lady, who was not resentful in this case, was still very disconcerted and said naively, ". . . my . . . opinion?" as if I had just made an indecent proposal to her . . . .

Did I tell you of my first class? First of all, I got my directions mixed up and found it about ten minutes late. When I handed out copies of my long reading list there were audible groans. When I tried to point out that it really wasn't so much, there was a certain undercurrent of derisive laughter. And when I added on the blackboard another article that had come out since the list was mimeographed, there was a shocked silence and exchanges of glances among the students. Well, as you can imagine, I was braced for a lot of "drop" cards in the next few days. It looked like another Dunkirk in the offing. However, not one student withdrew, and a few days later another student came around to my office for a copy of the reading list and subsequently joined the course. You can see why I do not want to lightly part with a student body like this, even if they have other shortcomings. I have also been pleasantly surprised to learn that they have suggested me for a discussion program, and yesterday one young lady told me with some pique that she noticed I was not at the student-faculty picnic, because she had looked for me.

One of the things I was learning was that different classes can have very different levels of performance—a fact which convinced me that grading on a curve was wrong if you intended for your grades to have any consistency from one class to another, much less from one year to another. I mentioned these differences to a friend in Washington.

November 1, 1962

Dear Nell,

Held a couple of exams this week. In one section, the class average was 80; in another section of the same course, the class average was 57. There are a number of economics majors in the high section of the introductory course, whereas there is only one economics major out of twenty-five students in the other section. Just a handful of interested students make a great difference in the class atmosphere, so that even the non-economics students in the good section did very well. Some of those in the low section seem to want to just get by and maybe they tend to demoralize the others.

The same day I described the situation to another friend in Washington, my old colleague as an economist in the Labor Department.

November 1, 1962

Dear Tom,

Had the task this afternoon of returning exam papers in which exactly one-half the class had flunked. These girls take their grades pretty seriously, so the opening moments of the class were sort of grim, but by the end of the hour we were all laughing. I will think twice before leaving this bunch and this situation—though I have left other places after thinking twice.

1963

As the new year began, the question for me was whether I wanted to continue teaching at Douglass College. Since I was on a one-year contract, as required by institutional policy, the choice was not strictly mine to make. However, there were informal comments about what I would be teaching the following year, giving the impression that my contract would be renewed. However, I was getting feelers from American University in Washington and from Howard University.

My friend Gloria and her family were in Ethiopia. I wrote them about the racial situation in America and the civil rights movement, of which they had been a part.

January 22, 1963

Dear Gloria and Rodney,

One of my ironic experiences has been hearing from a former teacher of mine who is now teaching in a Negro college in Mississippi, and finding the students hopelessly backward and apathetic. Though this may seem a violation of the code of the hills or something, I am more and more frequently led to believe that much of our social reforming zeal is a colossal barking up the wrong tree. There is something about principles of right and wrong, and the confrontation of opposing forces, that seems to grip the imagination, whether this aspect of the problem offers much prospect of improvement or not.

At this point, I don't think I was aware of how deeply Gloria and Rodney had been involved in the Southern sit-ins and other civil rights activities. Whether I would have softened what I said if I had known is another question.

The situation at Douglass College was beginning to become clearer—and less promising.

February 5, 1963

Dear Nell,

I was a little surprised at the number of students transferring out of my class at the end of the last semester, though I suppose I shouldn't have been, considering the grades I handed out. However, it may be a lot easier to teach with most of the deadwood gone.

It is becoming increasingly clear that this is a school where they believe in coddling students and keeping them in a state of prolonged adolescence. Some of the other faculty members seemed unhappy at a meeting today when I said that I have given a low grade to a girl who did not turn in one of her assignments. I

> was asked whether I had reminded her, and said "no." I had reminded the class, but not individuals.

Apparently the disenchantment was mutual at Douglass College, as I explained in a long letter to Mrs. Gadsden.

> February 12, 1963
>
> Dear Mrs. G,
>
> If I should ever write my memoirs, this chapter will have to be called, "Coming of Age in New Brunswick." Not only have I discovered that women are different from men, at the tender age of thirty-two, it has also dawned on me, again somewhat belatedly, that the students' intellectual passivity and a touch of the spoiled brat here and there, are not wholly unrelated to faculty attitudes.
>
> Near the end of the past semester, the department chairman mentioned to me that some students had been complaining about the extra reading they had to do in my section of the introductory course, and the low grades which were common on my exams. He said, "Now I wouldn't want to suggest that you raise your grades—" and I said, "Oh, I *know* you wouldn't," very sweetly. Later on, I thought to myself, "Mrs. G. would be proud of me," because the first thing I wanted to say to him would not have been appropriate in polite society. I thought that was the end of that, but in fact it was only the beginning of a series of episodes

which culminated in a letter received today from American University.

Between semesters, there was a considerable exodus of students who had gone to the department chairman for his permission to change sections. I was called in for a couple of friendly discussions about this, and it was suggested that perhaps I was "aiming too high" or addressing myself too much to the better students who could get the work anyway without me. Since I was new at this business, I listened and tried to be reasonable and flexible. Later, after still more students had complained that I wasn't presenting them the material but expecting them to do all the work, it was suggested that I meet with one of the veteran members of the department and "exchange ideas" on the presentation of material. At first I agreed, but when it occurred to me what this would actually mean, I refused to do this on a routine basis and informed them that I would not be back next fall. Incidentally, I had told them last fall, even before your letter advising me to do so, that I might take something somewhere else in view of the uncertain situation at Douglass. However, I had not been looking very hard, and had recently turned down a good offer from San Diego State, which I hear is a good school. This was the first time I ever quit a job without having another waiting, but I felt confident that there was a market somewhere for my services, and if pride goeth before a fall, this may be a good test case.

A couple of other things might be mentioned here. At a department meeting a while back to discuss students with low grade averages, I happened to mention that one of these girls had received a low grade in my course simply because she had not turned in an assignment. Immediately I was asked if I had reminded her, and when I said I had not, there were looks of surprise, pain and, in one case, disgust on the part of a woman who was particularly fond of that student. In addition to this spontaneous feeling, there is also the fact that the student:faculty ratio in economics is lower than the dean would wish, and that economics is not a very popular subject ("as in most women's colleges," they hasten to add), both of these facts being sources of great grief to everyone other than myself.

Meanwhile, back at the ranch, I had received an unsolicited offer from the chairman of the economics department at American University, whom I had met last year. He paid my fare to Washington for an afternoon of conversations with him, a couple of deans and the president of the university. The latter was very warm and garrulous, telling me frankly that I would be the first full-time Negro to teach there. I had expected a brief chat, but we rambled on for about half an hour. He and the deans made it a point to tell me that they were prepared to rubber-stamp whatever the chairman decided. When the chairman got back to his office, he said that he might as well make his offer right now, which he did, and I told him I would write him shortly after getting back to New Brunswick. We parted on a mutually optimistic note. Incidentally, in so far as one can judge from brief acquaintance, he seems to be a very honest and conscientious person; he even volunteered to proctor my Ph.D. exams from Chicago when I was in Washington.

Just a couple of days later, I received a telegram from him withdrawing the offer, and saying that a letter would follow. The letter arrived today. The significant sentence declared that "additional information has been brought to my attention which indicates that you might be well advised to seek a post where your keen interest in research will be given greater scope than it can possibly be afforded here." We had discussed teaching and research before, and he was well aware of my publications before. Yet my loose translation of this was that I was the kind of fellow who neglected his students in order to write. Maybe I just have an evil mind, but since my academic career is not so vast that this "information" could have come to him from any great variety of sources, it immediately suggested ye olde knife in ye old back at a distance of a couple of hundred miles. My record here shows that I have had three articles accepted by scholarly journals since last September, though what it does not show is that every word of them had been written before I ever set foot in a Douglass College classroom.

I received this letter upon returning home from a local bowling alley, where I had my first recreation in a solid week of almost round-the-clock work for my classes.

At the moment my plans are to teach next year at Howard, and if it turns out, as I suspect it will, that I cannot do anything for the students there, then when I get my Ph.D. I will move on and begin my real academic career, a sadder but, hopefully, wiser man.

What made this lying stab in the back particularly gratuitous was that I had already resigned from Douglass College, so there was no need for them to be concerned about me at all, but only apparently a need for petty revenge—and perhaps envy. In my naive pleasure at having three new articles of mine accepted by scholarly journals during the academic year, I had shared the news with my colleagues—most of whom, I realize today, would never be published in any of those journals. I had also stated frankly that, if enrollments in economics courses no longer justified all the positions in the department, I understood that as the junior member I would have to be the one to go. What I did not understand at that point was that the department would be far more concerned about losing the position than about losing me. But to have a new young instructor express such independence probably did not sit well.

Despite all the negative feelings generated by what had happened, there was nevertheless a great sense of relief after I left my letter of resignation in the department chairman's mail box. Among the signs of this easing of tensions were my bowling scores, which had declined into the low 100s, but which now shot up and peaked at 279, my highest score ever.

My classes that spring were a sheer delight, now that the students with negative attitudes had transferred out. We not only got a lot of work done in class, we enjoyed doing it. There were so many outbursts of laughter that one student said that the teacher next door must wonder what was going on in here. The test score difference between my two introductory economics classes disappeared, lending weight to my suspicion that the negative attitudes of some students in the lower-performing class had affected others. I cannot recall any term in my whole career when I enjoyed teaching more than in my second—

and last—semester at Douglass College. For years afterwards, I kept getting Christmas cards and letters from students I had taught there.

To another friend I wrote about one of the 1960s sensations among the intelligentsia.

March 19, 1963

Dear Anne,

Have been reading James Baldwin recently, and frankly I cannot see what all the shouting is about. It reminds me of a kid I knew in junior high school, who said a few bright things and was black, and therefore was a genius. Baldwin can write with skill and certain poetic insights, but his talents do not include sustained, analytical reasoning. He is, in short, well endowed in those areas where there is an oversupply already, and is badly lacking in the things that are needed to make a dent in the race problem. Baldwin gives emotional release to those who feel as he does, but it is hard to imagine that he will change anybody's mind.

In the fall of 1963 I was teaching at Howard University and received what may have been the first of the many communications from my former students at Douglass College. I sent the first of many replies I would write over the years.

October 6, 1963

Dear Mrs. Mann,

It was a delightful surprise hearing from you. Of course you may use me as a reference. Your letter reminded me to write Dr. Talarico to tell my other former students the same.

Once I was told never to congratulate a girl on getting married, but best wishes to you and to the fortunate young man....

Your mention of the possibility of becoming a "do-gooder" strikes a responsive chord. I certainly do not think there is anything naive about wanting to improve a world that is full of crying problems. My interest in Howard University is certainly not unconnected with the fact that it is a Negro school, and that I know its inadequacies first-hand from spending my freshman year here before transferring to Harvard. Yet there are dangerous traps for the unwary in this field, and they in turn can do enormous harm to people who are already in a bad way.

It is so easy to play fairy godmother and so heart-breakingly difficult to get people to make the painful adjustments in themselves which are necessary for any permanent improvement. Let us face it—most people are pretty damned satisfied with themselves the way they are, though they would like to see lots of improvements in the world around them. There is probably no more thankless task than trying to get people to shed their illusions and realize that there are certain objective standards

> which they simply must meet, that they cannot go on whining their way through the world looking for favors (and reacting like wounded animals when they do not get them).

A similar view led me to react against an article in the *New York Times Magazine* by Whitney Young, head of the Urban League, urging preferential hiring of blacks. A year before the Civil Rights Act of 1964 decreed equal opportunity, there were already efforts to get "affirmative action." My first public statement against the idea was in a letter to the editor.

October 6, 1963

TO THE EDITOR:

As a Negro, I feel that the Urban League's Whitney M. Young ("Should There Be Compensation for Negroes?" Oct. 6) is tragically wrong in his scheme for special treatment for Negroes—wrong not only tactically and morally, but wrong in terms of its probable effect on Negroes themselves. How can anyone seriously expect to develop initiative, respect for work and responsibility among people who are "sought" for good jobs, who receive "conscious preferment" and other semantic evasions meaning special privileges?

The difference between all the other special aids to particular groups which Mr. Young cites—G.I. Bill, etc.—and the program which he is advocating for Negroes is very simple: they were all efforts to enable a particular group to meet a certain standard, not efforts to lower the standard for them.

While Mr. Young rejects the out-and-out job quota idea, he

accepts the basic reasoning behind the job quota system, that numerical under-representation of Negroes in certain jobs is evidence of discrimination. Has Mr. Young ever checked the numerical representation of Negroes in free evening high schools and colleges, in public libraries and at free public concerts?

People who have been trying for years to tell others that Negroes are basically no different from anybody else should not themselves lose sight of the fact that Negroes are just like everyone else in wanting something for nothing. The worst thing that could happen would be to hold out hopes of getting it.

I had taught a class at Howard University at night during the summer and was so pleasantly surprised by the students' performances that I thought that perhaps this would not be a bad place to spend my career, after all. However, the kinds of students who took summer school classes at night were by no means typical of the students I later encountered during the regular academic year. Moreover, these latter students found a sympathetic ear in the college dean, who interfered even more crudely than the department chairman at Douglass College. I submitted my resignation during the first month of the academic year—effective, by custom, at the end of the academic year but expressed a willingness to negotiate my leaving at the end of the fall semester by mutual agreement. My original impulse was simply to quit immediately and go take a job that had been offered me in private industry. However, in a phone conversation with Professors George Stigler and Milton Friedman of the University of Chicago, I was reluctantly persuaded to stick it out for the academic year, rather than damage my prospects of an academic career elsewhere by leaving without notice. I took this advice but, in retrospect, I wish that I had just walked out and let the chips fall where they may. Unfortunately, Mrs. G was away, probably overseas, so I could not get her advice.

In the midst of all this, another Douglass College student wrote me to ask for a letter of reference.

November 17, 1963

Dear Miss Tota,

It was a pleasant surprise hearing from you. Send the reference form along and I shall be happy to recommend you.

You should be very good as a teacher since you seem so outgoing and easygoing. Patience is a must, and I could probably use a lot more of it. At Douglass I had to correct exams in my apartment, because some of my exclamations would not have been appropriate on campus among young ladies.

The American Economic Association held its annual convention in Boston in 1963—ironically, taking me closer to Audrey, rather than away from her as in 1960, since she was still studying at the Harvard Law School. While I was in Boston, I phoned her to see if I could take her out. She said that the load of work at the law school would not let her go out but that I was welcome to come visit her there. However, she also mentioned that her room-mate was a woman who remembered me from the past, even though at first her name did not ring a bell with me. I decided that three would definitely be a crowd in this case and passed. When I got back home, I was surprised to see that Audrey had sent me a card.

When 1964 began, there was little to indicate that it would be a turning point in my life.

My deepening skepticism about the direction of the civil rights movement was expressed in a letter to a young lady named Mary, a black graduate student who had graduated from Barnard a few years earlier and to whom I was introduced vicariously through Gloria, though Mary and I had not met in person. As our paths took us to different places, we had a sporadic correspondence. It became a running joke that our attempts to get together in person somewhere in our travels were always thwarted by either her commitments or mine. So we just exchanged ideas on paper.

January 4, 1964

Dear Mary,

It was very good hearing from you again, though in Boston we were once more like ships that pass in the night. A friend to whom I mentioned this episode found it unbelievable that I should have been unable to see you in person in five years. However, I have made it my New Year's resolution to see you in 1964, even if it kills us both, which it probably will.

You mentioned that you planned to finish up your dissertation by the end of the summer. This is pretty fast moving. Have you been at it steadily since graduating from Barnard?

Your dissertation topic is in an area where any new light should be very valuable. To me the psychology of the Negro is the biggest single obstacle to racial progress. It isn't fashionable to say this, and it certainly isn't pleasant, but truth does not depend on these considerations. With all due respect to the courage and dedication of the various civil rights groups, I think that when all the laws have been passed and all the gates flung open, the net result will be one tremendous anticlimax unless there is a drastic change of attitude among Negroes. The current

> pleas for preferential treatment are a symptom of the attitude that needs changing and such treatment would be a big obstacle to the necessary change.

Then there was a brief note to Audrey.

> January 22, 1964
>
> Dear Audrey,
>
> Your card was a pleasant surprise. As you can see, I am no longer at Rutgers, but I will probably be moving to New York at the end of the academic year to work in private industry.
>
> I am currently teaching at Howard University—an act of madness which may mark the end of youthful idealism and the onset of a safe and sane middle age.
>
> Best wishes in everything. Hope to see you in New York.

Audrey and I re-established contact, but in a small, low-key and tentative kind of way.

> February 16, 1964
>
> Dear Audrey,
>
> Since the lady who answered the phone Saturday seemed apprehensive over receiving a long-distance call, this is just to say that it was I, and that it was nothing dire. A tempting job offer has arrived from Dartmouth and I wanted to see if you might know anything about Hanover and vicinity that might

make it seem more livable than it appeared to me.

Job for job, teaching at Dartmouth is preferable to working in private industry, but living in an isolated New England town is something else. A brief visit to Hanover and inquiries here and there have done little to alter my original feelings. However, a drowning man clutches at a straw, and I thought it would be worthwhile to see if you might know something about the area that would make a difference. If you do, of course, please call collect (526-4111), but at the moment I am reconciled to a non-academic interlude after June.

Good luck coming down the home stretch in law school.

Audrey did call back and we talked about Dartmouth and about racial issues, and she ended up seeking to interest me in some movement that she was going to be involved in when she went to New York after finishing law school in June. At first it sounded innocuous enough but then I had second thoughts.

February 22, 1964

Dear Audrey,

It was very enjoyable talking with you the other evening. Your confirming information about Dartmouth was especially welcome as there would have been an implied commitment for more than one year had I gone there.

Almost as soon as we had finished talking I began having sober second thoughts about contacting Strickland. Though I am concerned about racial problems, it hardly seems sensible to proffer help to a man and a movement whose specific ideas and methods are unknown to me. Painful as it is to back out of what I said I would do, it should be less painful right now and with you than later with someone I scarcely know.

I would like to discuss some of these things with you and/or your friend when I get to New York. As you probably realize already, I think some individuals and groups have greatly misconceived the problem. Perhaps if the omnibus civil rights bill goes through Congress undiluted, the bitter anticlimax that is sure to follow may provoke some real thought in quarters where slogans and labels hold sway at the moment. I doubt if it is an accident that the leadership of the various civil rights movements show such disproportionate representation of groups which deal in rarefied abstractions—clergymen, lawyers and inexperienced "intellectuals."

In terms of economic advancement, a bitter anticlimax did follow in the years after passage of the Civil Rights Act of 1964[1] but the re-thinking that I

---

1. Trends in economic improvements which had existed years before the Civil Rights Act of 1964 continued, such as reductions in black poverty and growing numbers of blacks in higher-level occupations, but the rate at which poverty was being reduced and the rate at which blacks were rising into higher-level occupations were both greater in the years *preceding* passage of the Civil Rights Act. By ignoring these pre-existing trends, black "leaders" and others have been able to make it appear that this legislation was the beginning and the cause of these trends. Even so, the economic advancement of blacks fell far short of what was expected by those who saw racial discrimination as the overwhelming cause of racial disparities in income and occupations. Other trends, such as crime rates and rates of unemployment and rates of unwed motherhood, worsened after the 1960s.

had hoped for did not occur. Instead, there were more demands for preferential treatment.

I decided to share my experience teaching at Howard with my elusive pen pal Mary, since she too was working on a doctorate and might well want to teach at a black college.

March 13, 1964

Dear Mary,

I have been awfully busy lately for someone who is not accomplishing anything. However, I decided that I would use the time during an exam Tuesday night to write you, and the setting suggested the bright idea of establishing a typical day at Howard University. Well, I did that but got no further before I was back on the treadmill. Tonight they [my students] are taking a quiz, so I can now add today as another sample:

March 10, 1964: My first class is at 10 A.M., but I was in my office at nine to keep an appointment with a failing student—who did not show up. This no longer surprises me. After I returned to my office at noon, a student from my 11 o'clock class who had lost 20 points on his exam (for looking at his notebook during the exam) came to my office to "explain" despite my note to him [saying] not to bother. A colleague with whom I share the office told me of suspicious goings-on in the Departmental office, and suggested I reproduce my own exams rather than leave them with the office staff. Around one o'clock I had to phone the library to inquire about books which were supposed to have been put on reserve in January, but were not (I had originally submitted my request last October). On my way to the Department office I encountered a girl student in one of my classes who asked to be excused from an upcoming exam on Friday in order to attend some university function. When I said "no" she shot back indignantly, "Why not?!"

March 12, 1964: Classes went very well this morning. The students had done the reading for a change, and even given it a little thought. Back at the office, my colleague informed me of an exchange between himself and the chairman. In a heated discussion he had remarked that "anything involving education seems to have a low priority in this department," to which the chairman replied: "Now I have said some nice things about you in letters of reference, and you might keep in mind that there will be other letters for me to write about you in future years." My colleague was shocked and incensed, but it struck me as one of the chairman's milder sins. I also learned that another instructor was "in trouble." Seems he had a quiz and locked out some students who were late. They went to see one of the deans (a popular activity around here) who put pressure on the instructor (ditto) who gave in (ditto) and held a re-test. I have only had direct pressure put on me once, and I made it sufficiently unpleasant that it would not be habit-forming. However, I occasionally get indirect pressure from people who give me a friendly warning that "the dean is furious" about something or other that I have done.

Since I had a job waiting for me in private industry at roughly double my academic salary, the dean's fury had a low priority among my concerns. One of the things that may have riled him was that, after he had sent out a directive on the conduct of final exams, outlining some ridiculous procedure, I announced to my class: "Contrary to what you may have heard from any other source, final exams in this course will be conducted as follows."

One of my other occasional correspondents was a left-wing professor at one of New York's colleges, whom I will call Hal. I had met him when I was teaching at Douglass College. Despite our ideological differences, we hit it off and remained friends for some years. He was giving me advice on the housing situation in New York and I was filling him in on the situation at Howard—and particularly why my summer school teaching left me more optimistic about the students than I should have been.

March 14, 1964

Dear Hal,

During the summer I wasn't able to see some of the truly ugly aspects of Howard (as distinguished from the merely ridiculous). The students in an evening summer school course are likely to be a little more motivated than most, and chairmen and deans are not such an obtrusive feature of the landscape as they are during the academic year. The common run of students at Howard are almost unbelievably lazy, dishonest, rude and irresponsible. All too frequently the school panders to their worst habits by giving deadline extensions, make-up exams, Incompletes, WP's ["withdrew passing" grades], etc. to the point where these things are regarded almost as Constitutional rights. The less pliable instructors are likely to have their students constantly running to chairmen and deans, and the crudest sort of pressure and intervention is commonplace here. . . .

A complicating factor at Howard is the maudlin sort of liberal, frequently a white instructor with what I call "the Albert Schweitzer syndrome." From these and others one hears a lot of give-the-poor-kids-a-break arguments and you-can't-expect-too-much warnings. Actually these kids are infinitely further advanced in the ability department than they are in the attitude department. Whenever you can get them to do the reading—no mean feat around here—they usually show themselves quite capable of handling it. But why should they do the work, when the university makes it so much easier for them to alibi, cheat, whine or intrigue?

Audrey was trying to decide which opportunities to pursue after finishing law school, including writing poetry, and was sharing some of this with me by mail. Her left-wing view of the world was quite a contrast with her views when I first met her, when she was very critical of the behavior of blacks who rented from her father. She was now like the convert who was more Catholic than the Pope.

March 26, 1964

Dear Audrey,

You seem to be weighing some pretty interesting alternatives for next year. There should be stimulating experiences either way, though of course more exotic in Africa.

As regards writing, the picture is not too clear. I am no judge of poetry, and particularly not of the kind of poetry you enclosed. I do know that writing in general requires a great deal of self-discipline, including the ability to ruthlessly edit your own work, cutting out phrases (or pages) that may represent considerable intellectual and emotional investment. This sort of discipline is seldom developed overnight and its importance seems to be consistently under-estimated by aspiring writers.

The only way to find out if your stuff is good enough as of a given moment is simply to try to get it published in places with worthwhile standards. Hard-boiled editors who have seen thousands of manuscripts over the years are a good, free source of judgment, though they are usually too busy to explain the basis of their judgments. Since you seem to be way over on the political left now, there will always be a tempting excuse available that socio-political bias, rather than professional judgment, caused adverse editorial decisions. Passing up this excuse is an additional piece of self-discipline required of a left-wing writer, if he is to remain in touch with reality and develop his own potential.

During the spring semester at Howard University, there was something of a replay of my last semester at Douglass College. In my introductory economics course, those students who didn't like my teaching—essentially the bottom half of the class—did not enrol in the second half of the course. But other students who had heard about me, and who wanted what they had heard, took their places. The enthusiasm in the class made it a joy to teach, one of the few bright spots of my year at Howard University. On one occasion, I had introduced a new topic that the class was fascinated with, just before a university holiday. Various good-natured grumblings arose that we would have to leave the subject dangling over the holiday. After more and more students echoed this sentiment, I told them that if they were really anxious to continue on this topic, I would be willing to come in and teach the class despite the holiday, if they were willing to attend. My offer was immediately accepted and we had a good time. Then a note arrived from the dean, chiding me for violating university rules by holding class on a holiday.

During the previous semester, a delegation of students had gone to the dean, demanding that I be fired. Now I was surprised to see a delegation of students coming to my office to ask—some to demand—that I rescind my resignation and stay on. This second delegation included people who had been in the first delegation that wanted me fired.

"Nothing I do seems to please you people," I said light-heartedly. But one of the students made a very serious comment that I could not answer: "How are we ever going to advance, if people like you come here for one year and then leave?"

His question went to the heart of what was wrong with Howard University. It was not that they could not get good people to teach there but that they could not keep them. Just during my one year at Howard, in the economics department alone there were three of us who later went on to teach at Ivy League universities and another man who returned to private industry where he was an economist for one of the big corporations. The usual excuses—too readily accepted by blacks and whites alike—such as lack of money or lack of research opportunities were not the problem. People came to Howard University knowing such things in advance. What they—and I—learned about the hard way after arriving was the anti-intellectual and even corrupt atmosphere that created a sense of futility.

My old mentor and idol from my undergraduate days at Howard University, Professor Sterling Brown, was still there and I learned more about Howard when I revisited him in his office after returning as a faculty member. He told me about a former colleague, Professor Abram L. Harris, who was the first black economist of any prominence, and whom I had encountered at the University of Chicago when I was a graduate student there.

Decades earlier, when Professor Harris was teaching at Howard, he wrote an article in a leading scholarly journal and this brought an invitation for him to give a paper at the University of Chicago. They had no idea that he was black before he arrived but, after hearing his presentation, they made him an offer of a faculty appointment, something very unusual at white institutions in those days. Recalling this episode to me, Sterling Brown said that Professor Harris had told him that, if the Howard University administration had said to him, "Abe, we're proud that you got this offer from a leading white university—but we need you here," he would have stayed. Unfortunately, it would never have occurred to the philistines who ran Howard to appeal to an idealism that was foreign to their own nature.

When the academic year ended, I went to work in New York as an economic analyst at the American Telephone & Telegraph Company, which was then the largest corporation in the world. I rented an apartment in Greenwich Village, within walking distance of the office where I worked. On my first night, as I entered the apartment, I could hear somewhere a song playing: "Hello Dolly, it's so nice to have you back where you belong." In the upbeat mood of the song, I thought of Audrey, who was also in New York now, and how wonderful it would be if we could get together again and be as we had once been during the magic summer of 1960. But I knew it was a long shot.

I heard from a former classmate at Harvard with whom I had been in sporadic contact by mail after graduating. He and I were both leftists back in our undergraduate days, so my letter to him brought him up to date on my ideological changes as well as events in my life.

July 13, 1964

Dear Bob,

I am a little chagrined to tell you of my experiences in Washington. I taught at Howard University, a Negro university where I spent my freshman year. I suppose my conscience would never have been 100% free had I not tried to do something to help what is a wretched situation there. But contrary to popular belief, the basic problem is not one of educational deficiencies but of a thorough corruption of values and spirit which makes everything else futile. . . .

The whole episode at Howard seemed to be part of the unofficial education that has changed my outlook drastically over the past decade. The same problems and the same people are still important to me, but the old solutions have crumbled on contact with reality. Recently, in unpacking my belongings after moving to New York, I came across some old scrapbooks in which I had a few letters to the editor from an earlier period. I was pleasantly surprised to find that I still agreed with most of the particular points I had made, but since then other points not originally seen or not sufficiently appreciated had shifted the over-all balance.

I am currently working as an economist at A.T.&T. When some people hear this they picture me sitting in the councils of the mighty, etc. Actually, I share a little cubby-hole office with another economist and we are in fact part of a vast faceless sea of humanity shifting papers at our desks. My reactions after a month on the job are mixed. One amusing feature is the conformity. A while back a group of new employees were invited to lunch with a couple of high company officials. As we sat around the table I was struck by the similarity of our gray suits. It was as if there were one vast gray garment with heads poking out here and there. All but two of us had striped ties. The head of our division ordered first and the next three guys ordered what he had ordered. I then ordered something else and a higher official sitting next to me decided he would have what I had ordered—and the rest of the group ordered the same.

Sometimes I liked to say that it was the bland leading the bland. But it was a pleasant place to work and the pay was the best I had yet, so I had the rare experience of being free of financial worries.

———————

I took Audrey out to dinner. It was a pleasant, low-key evening, spiced up a bit with banter about our ideological differences. She was working for the NAACP Legal Defense Fund and thought it was an unfair question when I asked her where the NAACP lawyers sent their own children to school. But, when I persisted and asked what was the answer to this "unfair" question, she admitted that most of these lawyers sent their children to private schools—even though they condemned whites as "racists" for doing the same thing after the racial desegregation of the public schools.

Audrey and I still enjoyed each other's company, though there was also a certain walking lightly, as was perhaps inevitable with two people who had both been hurt in their previous relationship with one another. After dinner, I took her home uptown on the west side in a taxi and, when we reached her apartment building, I told her that I would wait in the cab until she reached the door of the building and was safely inside, and then head home. But she asked me to come inside with her. Although it was late and her roommates who shared the apartment were probably asleep, we could talk some more. This was a little surprising to me because Audrey had played things even more close to the vest than usual this evening but it was fine with me. I got out of the cab and offered my hand to help her out but she got out without touching me and perhaps that indicated her ambivalence about the whole situation. We went upstairs and talked for a while. Before we parted, Audrey said that she was bogged down studying for the all-important bar examinations that she would have to take, so it would be a while before we could go out again, but that she would call me.

I did not know what to make of all this. However, I was involved with another woman in Washington. I went back to visit her there and she came up to visit me in New York. By the time Audrey phoned to tell me that she had passed the bar exam, I had just gotten married. Audrey laughed and said that it was hard to imagine me married. Yet she and I had once planned to get married.

In December 1964, A.T.&T. sent me to the American Economic Association's annual convention, held in Chicago that year. While there, I received a job offer from the chairman of the economics department at Cornell University. It was a pleasant surprise but I told him that, in view of my previous experiences, I would accept only if there would not be any interference with my teaching by administrators. He said there would be none and I sent him my acceptance in the first week of January, 1965. The new job would not pay as much as I was making at A.T.&T. but it would allow me to resume teaching, which was my primary reason—rather than research—for wanting an academic career. Moreover, an academic appointment would allow me more time to work on completion of my doctoral dissertation, without which a permanent teaching career was virtually impossible. My appointment would be for three years, which would at least provide some stability to replace my annual changes of jobs and cities.

Letters from former students at Douglass College and Howard University continued to arrive from time to time. To one of my students from Douglass College days I wrote:

April 20, 1965

Dear Miss Rosenthal,

I enjoyed your letter of February 23rd very much, but was delayed in answering by a number of things, including the premature birth of my son. Mother and child came through it fine, but it was pretty hectic for me for a while trying to suddenly round up all the things we didn't have (bottles, crib, diapers, etc.)

You should like Washington if you go there. The recruiter's statement that you would be married in 18 months sounds pretty reasonable. I somehow doubt that you will end up a spinster wherever you live, but there should be wider opportunities to socialize with young college people in the Management Intern program than in most other places. . . .

A while back I attended a party where two Douglass graduates were present. At the end of the evening, they told me that I wasn't nearly such an ogre as they had been told by other students. One learns to accept strange compliments in the academic world.

While my wife and I were shopping at a supermarket, with our infant son in my arms, we happened to run into Audrey. "This must be the little Sowell," she said, with a little laugh.

1966

One of the reasons for my returning to the academic world was to have time to write my doctoral dissertation so as to finally get my Ph.D., which seemed to be ever receding before me, like the horizon.

By now, Professor Stigler and I had abandoned the idea of my writing a dissertation on Say's Law under his direction, since we had irreconcilable differences in interpretation, and I was exploring the possibility of writing instead on the effects of minimum wage laws in Puerto Rico. I had gotten interested in that subject as a result of my research as a summer intern in the Labor Department back in 1960 and thought that the Puerto Rican situation provided an especially good test of these effects. However, after having spent more than a year trying to get the kind of data I wanted and that my new dissertation committee chairman, Professor H. Gregg Lewis, considered a prerequisite, in 1966 I was finally forced to admit that the data available simply did not meet either his standards or mine.

I wrote about the situation to a former colleague who had been with me at Howard University, who had also moved on, and who had written me about his own travails in trying to complete his doctorate.

April 24, 1966

Dear Ike,

Your wrestling with the Ph.D. octopus strikes a responsive chord. After more than a year of struggling with a budding thesis topic and the agony of re-learning statistics, it now appears that the whole thing will have to be scrapped for lack of certain data which the thesis adviser now regards as crucial. However, it is something of a relief to put it aside for a while and turn to other things until a new topic crystallizes. My objection to the Ph.D. grind is not its difficulty as such but that it is more of a test of endurance than of ability, and that so much depends on the individual caprice of thesis advisers. Unfortunately, many of the people who are attacking the present system seem to be favoring a move away from intellectual achievement to help those with "teaching" ability—by which I strongly suspect they really mean classroom entertainment talent.

The usual sequence of events in completing the requirements for the Ph.D. was to pass the language examinations, which were still common then, and afterwards proceed to write the dissertation. In my case, I sought to write the dissertation first while I was still back in Washington where I had hopes of collecting the statistical data needed from government sources. However, now that the dissertation on minimum wages had been abandoned, I turned my attention to studying for the language examinations. Little did I realize what this would lead to.

In addition to reading textbooks on the French language, I also began to read a book on economics in French, written by an obscure 19th century economist named Sismondi. What I discovered was that Sismondi's analysis strongly supported my interpretation of Malthus which Stigler had dismissed. The net result was that I returned to my original dissertation on Say's Law. Dealing with Stigler was by no means smooth sailing but it was sailing. Moreover, the fact that Milton Friedman was also on the dissertation committee proved to be crucial, for he was one of the few people with the stature to cause Stigler to reconsider some of his objections.

I brought my former room mate Ralph up to date on the situation at Cornell.

May 31, 1966

Dear Ralph,

Cornell seems to be a pleasant place to spend three years, and perhaps staying in one place that long will help me to fathom the academic maze. One thing I can't complain about here (in contrast to A.T.&T.) is conformity. We have a motley crew in the department, both personally and in terms of schools of economic thought. Standards seem to be applied with an eye on all sorts of quasi-political considerations, with a certain demoralizing effect on the more conscientious members of the department. When some people tried to apply pressure to me last fall,[2] I seized the opportunity to make a reputation as an unbending S.O.B., and I have been coasting on it undisturbed ever since.

A married couple who had been students of mine at Howard University sought my advice on where to go for graduate study. I had gotten the husband a job at A.T.&T. while I was there and now they were trying to decide where to apply to graduate school. I mentioned a number of places, including Cornell.

2.　See *A Personal Odyssey*, pp. 172-177.

August 11, 1966

Dear Rey and Frances,

If you come to Ithaca next year, as I hope you will, you will probably find it a very pleasant change. The graduate student apartments I mentioned before are two-bedroom and apparently the rent does not exceed $100 a month. There are baby-sitting pools, and I suspect you will make friends very easily. Indeed the problem is apt to be trying to manage a little privacy. This is partly because of the thin walls and partly because of Ithaca's small town psychology. People you have just met think nothing of asking your age, and then going on to personal questions. My wife is considered prudish because she doesn't join in the girls' talks about contraceptive devices. For the past several months we have been kept advised (whether we wanted to know or not) of any signs of progress by a neighbor who has been trying to get pregnant. A little while back, she burst into our apartment one day to tell her the good news that this time it wasn't a false alarm! She added: "I know my husband is happy I made it; I have been wearing the poor guy out."

Rey and Frances were still wrestling with their graduate school choices some months later and indicated that they were not hung up on finding a high-prestige institution. Since they were both excellent students who would qualify anywhere, I thought it necessary to let them know that their choice of graduate school was not just a matter of prestige but would affect the kind of teaching post they were likely to find when they finished graduate school—and that the difference between teaching at a top-notch college and a lower-ranked institution had serious implications, including a heavier teaching load at the lower-ranked school.

December 3, 1966

Dear Rey and Frances,

The number of courses that one must teach at a lesser school (and the fact that some will be in areas in which you have little or no preparation) means that you will be confronted with only two choices: (1) to drive yourself frantically, in order to do a decent job, leaving scarcely any time for yourself or your family and none for any intellectual activity on a scholarly level; or (2) to become a classroom fraud. Once you have had to grapple with this impossible situation, you will understand, though you may not condone, so many people who have taken the second alternative. I cannot believe that either of you would be satisfied to remain in such a situation; A.T.&T. or some other non-academic job would probably be easier to live with.

Because it is nearly impossible to do worthwhile scholarly work at a poor college. . . you will also lose a major attraction of academic life: academic freedom. With your family's livelihood and future prospects in the hands of the college administration (chiefly the department chairman), you are in no position to cross him if he wants you, for example, to water down your course in order to compete for enrollments (to which departmental appropriations are linked) or even to pass a failing football player. Academic freedom is not a matter of rules and regulations but of muscle and courage, in that order. Two things give the individual faculty member independent strength—initially, the prestige of the graduate department from which he came and later his own scholarly work, both of which give him a value in the market independent of what his chairman may think of him. Without this, he controls not only your present pay and advancement but your future elsewhere through letters of reference. I hope neither of you has any illusions about the sweet and genteel life behind the ivied walls; it can be a jungle. I could rattle off pages of incidents from each university at which I have taught, including Cornell. The differences in academic freedom are largely reflections of the relative muscle of the faculty and the administration, and as you go down the scale the balance of power is increasingly with the administration.

1967

While my doctoral dissertation seemed to be on track, I still had a year left on my contract at Cornell University, and I was by no means prepared to continue indefinitely pursuing the Ph.D. or remaining a junior faculty member at Cornell. I knew of too many people who poured too many years of their lives down a bottomless pit in a vain effort to complete a Ph.D. In fact, my impatience with both the Ph.D. process and with Cornell was expressed in a letter to my radical friend Hal in New York.

January 10, 1967

Dear Hal,

It looks as if I may finally be seeing a dissertation taking shape, though it is a little early for optimism, since I have not completed the first draft yet. I can hardly wait for the next year to go by, and end my career as an assistant professor. Win, lose or draw in the dissertation and tenure departments, I have had it with trying to support a family in this bracket. A.T.&T. is supposedly keeping a candle in the window for me. Incidentally, I recently received a letter from some talent-hunting outfit which says mysteriously that they have a job for which "you may be exceptionally well suited both by background and inclination." I am very curious as to what people think my background and inclinations are.

To another friend I was even more explicit.

March 10, 1967

Dear Ike,

Believe it or not, I am still wrestling with the Ph.D. thesis. I am now typing up footnotes—there are a million of them—for the first draft. It is almost impossible to believe that the ordeal is nearing the end. However, I will either make it this time or head back to the phone company.

An article titled "The American Negro College" by Christopher Jencks

and David Riesman appeared in the *Harvard Educational Review* and may well
have been the last honest account of black institutions of higher learning,
especially since the authors were widely vilified. However, I recognized the
ring of truth in what they said and wrote to David Riesman.

March 31, 1967

Dear Professor Riesman:

As a Negro and a teacher I found it heartening to finally see
in print a candid and knowledgeable appraisal of Negro colleges
as they are, instead of the polite nonsense that does no one any
good.

On one point your article seems ambiguous, however, and I
wonder if you know of any research that might shed additional
light. You and Mr. Jencks seem to assume (p. 31) that the Negro
schools fail almost entirely because of circumstances beyond
their control—the poor raw material with which they must
work—though elsewhere you suggest that they may particularly
repel the better students (p. 26). My impression—based on a year
studying and a year teaching at Howard University—is that
students with good preparation and capacity are a major casualty
of the system. While such students are a small fraction of the
total, they are a large number absolutely—perhaps two or three
hundred at Howard—who are capable of doing good work at the
top colleges in the country—far better than many of the Negro
students brought into such schools under "disadvantaged
students" programs.

> While these are strongly felt impressions, I should nevertheless like to see any empirical study which you may know of dealing with the fate of well-prepared students at Negro colleges. Even if no such study has been published, there is no reason to accept the all-purpose alibi of Negro college administrators that they are doing the best they can with what they have.

My marriage had been a rocky one from the beginning, with clashes and crises of varying severity, followed by reconciliations of varying lengths of time. But there was no sign of a permanent improvement. Still, I tried to stick it out for the sake of my little son. Nor was I the only one who saw the problems.

The most remarkable phone call I ever received was from a much older woman, who was the wife of my wife's physician. I barely knew this lady, having encountered her and her husband at some social gathering once or twice. But she spoke to me with great frankness and earnestness, as a mother would to a son—and she urged me to divorce my wife "before she destroys your life."

She told me nothing about what her conclusion was based on and I knew better than to ask if it came from what had been said between doctor and patient. This lady was taking a very great chance just by talking to me as she did. It may have been because she and her husband were black and saw me as a promising young black man with a wife who could only be a negative factor in his attempt to realize his promise or even to find personal peace.

I expressed my appreciation for her thoughts and words, and promised to carefully consider what she had said.

My son was a special concern because, although he was now two years old, he was still not talking.

There was even some progress on my doctoral dissertation at the University of Chicago and—to my great relief—my little son finally began to say a few words. I reported all of this in a letter to my friend Hal.

> December 9, 1967
>
> Dear Hal,
>
> I am now in the midst of revising my doctoral dissertation.... I first submitted it last March and expected it to be over before now, but it has gone through more adventures than Alice in Wonderland—and of about the same kind. It even went abroad for the summer, which is more than I can do. . . .
>
> Little John Stuart has finally begun to talk. You cannot imagine what it is like for parents waiting for a long overdue first word. We were somewhat reassured at a family gathering last summer when we learned that late talking was common among boys in my family. Still there is nothing like having the problem behind us. He first said "oo-way," sometimes pronounced "raisin" [by other people], and has since added "wayo" (radio), "Hawaii" (water), "ah-oh" (apple) and "ejeck" for Ajax—which he finds tasty for some reason.

1968

At the beginning of the year I brought my old room-mate Norton up to date on my situation at Cornell and my thoughts about teaching in a different environment. Despite the things I had published, I still thought of myself primarily as a teacher. Although teaching at Cornell was certainly better than teaching at Howard, what I would really have liked for the long run would have been the small-college atmosphere of Douglass College, without the negative aspects I encountered there.

January 13, 1968

Dear Nort,

The small college has always had certain appeal to me, but the big question mark has always been whether the closer student-faculty relationship which is possible there is utilized for intellectual purposes or for essentially public relations purposes, many of which are dysfunctional by artificially extending the students' adolescence—e.g., the drop-in-any-time philosophy of office hours, the mutual participation in "activities" for mutual participation's sake, etc. . . .

My contract has been renewed for three years, but I am a little restless for a number of reasons, and it is understood that I may not stay three years.

The renewal itself was something of a surprise because (1) they have usually been pretty hard-nosed about renewing anyone who doesn't have the Ph.D. in hand by the third year, (2) others have been let go who had powerful friends in strategic places, and (3) I had tangled with some of those powerful people. . . .

The idea of emphasizing teaching appeals to me, but too often "teaching" means student public relations, and is judged by how happy you keep them rather than how much they learn.

My sense of being on the sidelines on the racial developments of the times was suddenly ended when the Rockefeller Foundation decided to create a summer program to prepare students from black colleges to do postgraduate work in economics—and decided that I was the one to create such a program during the summers of 1968 and 1969 at Cornell. I agreed immediately, without even waiting to find out what the salary would be. As it turned out, they paid me well, thereby easing the financial strain which I had been under since leaving A.T.& T.

Despite this easing of financial pressures, my wife, who had not been working since we were married, now decided that she wanted to take a job as a lab technician at Cornell, and to put our son in a nursery school. Although little John had begun saying a few isolated and poorly articulated words now and then, he was still not really talking, even though he was three years old. I took his mother's decision as a sign that she had given up on John and wanted something else to do. She told me that I was "just being stubborn" by not "facing the facts" about John. After being put in nursery school, John became an unhappy little boy and he stopped saying most of the few words that he had been saying before.

Cornell was active on the racial front in another and very different program, suddenly bringing in large numbers of black students under lower admissions standards than they used for other students. By and large, these students scored above the national average on standardized tests—but well below the average of other students at Cornell—and many of the black students ended up on academic probation when they could not keep up with the pace of work geared to students with top-level academic qualifications. In other words, the black students at Cornell had all the qualifications to be successful at most of the colleges in the country but they were artificially turned into failures by being over-matched by the students and standards at Cornell. As of 1968, none of these black students enrolled in any of my courses.

The idea of lowering admissions standards for black students was not peculiar to Cornell but was in fact sweeping the academic world, from coast to coast. Even Martin Bronfenbrenner, a distinguished economist at Carnegie Mellon University, tried to justify lower admissions standards for black students but I was not buying that argument, as I explained in a letter to him.

June 8, 1968

Dear Professor Bronfenbrenner:

White liberals are busy supplying the black community with corrupted individuals carrying false credentials—the kind of thing you do to your enemy in wartime. Just as no one is surprised when college athletes are over-represented in cheating scandals, because their very recruitment and maintenance are fundamentally dishonest and certainly non-intellectual, no one should be surprised when Negro students who are corruptly maneuvered through college turn out to be corrupt college administrators and a major disaster to the interests of their students.

As it turned out, the consequences of the corruption started even before the students graduated. Failing and frustrated black students were ripe for demagogues blaming all their troubles on "racism" and urging militant action. They had already had a sit-in at the economics department office and more disruptions elsewhere on campus were to follow. This too was not peculiar to Cornell.

One day I found that a telephone message had been left for me by a secretary at the University of Chicago. When I called back to see what it was about, she simply asked when I would be prepared to go there and defend my dissertation. I hadn't even been notified that the committee had agreed to have it defended.

I flew out to the University Chicago and, after all the years of seemingly interminable delays, the defense of the dissertation was over in record time and Stigler and other members of the economics department took me to a posh restaurant in downtown Chicago to celebrate.

Because I fulfilled the Ph.D. requirements out of sequence, completion of the dissertation left me with a need to pass two language examinations before the degree would be officially conferred. But the main hurdle was now behind me. The remaining language requirement turned out to be a godsend. In order to save the cost of flying back to Chicago to be tested, I drove down to Binghamton, New York, where Professor Earl Hamilton of the University of Chicago was a visiting professor at the state university. He agreed to test me in both French and German. After I passed the French exam, we had a long and wide-ranging conversation, in the course of which he asked how things were going in my life. When I mentioned that my biggest concern was with my three-year-old son, who was still not talking, he asked:

"Have you taken him to doctors?"

"All kinds of doctors, all kinds of tests. They can find nothing wrong."

"Is he alert, active? Does he seem bright?"

"Yes. That's what makes it so puzzling."

"Have you and your wife been able to give him a lot of attention?"

"Not in the past several months. I have been tied up in my work and my wife took a job for a while, so he hasn't been getting the attention he needs. Now I have had some time lately, and I have been trying to teach him to talk, but it just doesn't work."

"Mr. Sowell," he said in a kind and gentle way, "Don't try to teach him to talk—not right now. You just give him lots of love and attention. Take him with you wherever you can. Let him know that you think he is the most wonderful little boy in the whole world. And when he feels confident and secure—he'll talk."

I followed his advice and John became a visibly happier little boy—and, months later, he began to talk.

The black militancy and white liberal indulgence that were sweeping the country did not spare my summer program. A disruptive student whom I wanted removed, and whom the economics department chairman agreed to remove, was kept on after intervention from higher up in the Cornell administration, with painful consequences to the program and for me. For the sake of those students who were trying to learn, I endured the deterioration. But I would not endure the betrayal. At the end of the program, I resigned both from the program, which had another summer scheduled for 1969, and from Cornell University, effective at the end of the academic year in June 1969. In contrast to my long letter of resignation from Howard University four years earlier, my resignation from Cornell was just one sentence. I had learned the futility of trying to talk sense to people who don't want to listen.

I mentioned some of this in a letter to the chairman of the economics department at the University of Chicago.

August 13, 1968

Dear Professor Harberger:

The program as a whole was not nearly as much of a success as I had hoped, or as it could have been. About halfway through, people with a very different philosophy (or susceptibility to pressure) began to make their influence felt, and the results were disastrous for the students. I do not plan to be associated with it in future. However, when the GRE scores are received (probably this week), I will have some idea whether I accomplished anything worthwhile.

Unlike many programs which judge themselves—and almost invariably find themselves successful—I had the performance of my program judged by having the students take the Graduate Record Examination in economics before beginning the program and then again afterwards, both tests being sent back to the Educational Testing Service in Princeton for grading. The GRE scores of the students in this program rose an average of 70 points, which to me was the only vindication that mattered. It also set a standard that would make the usual excuses elsewhere ring hollow.

I also wrote to Professor Stigler, with whom I was now on a first name basis.

September 21, 1968

Dear George,

I resigned from Cornell in the wake of the summer's events, which might seem foolhardy before having another job lined up, but a resignation serves to make one's availability known, if nothing else. Preliminary indications are that getting a job with

> equal or better pay should not be a great problem, though finding something that I will want to stay with for some years may be more difficult.
>
> It is still a little hard to believe that the dissertation is finally behind me, much less that we finished it on good terms.

I also wrote to Professor Martin Bronfenbrenner at Carnegie-Mellon University, whom I had also gotten to know better.

> October 1, 1968
>
> Dear Martin:
>
> You mentioned some time back that you would be interested in seeing a copy of my dissertation. I hope your reaction will not be that of the department secretary at the University of Chicago: "Is that all?"

Milton Friedman had insisted that he would not stand for a "long-winded" dissertation, so I turned in only about 50 or 60 pages, even though I had done enough work to write a book on the subject, as in fact I did in later years. But the dissertation itself was only about half the size of my undergraduate senior honors thesis at Harvard a decade earlier.

During the Christmas holidays, I received a card from Martin Bronfenbrenner. The printed part said:

Merry Christmas

Happy Hanukah

Take Your Choice

A handwritten note, however, was more serious.

> To Tom-
>
> I've been following your trail, it seems, trying to convince suspicious chairmen that you're not Eldridge Cleaver II. Somewhere along the line somebody gave you a bad press, or else misread a letter of recommendation.
>
> Martin B.

Perhaps I was less charitable than Martin because I thought it highly unlikely that anyone had so misread a letter of reference as to think I was like the Black Panthers. The misinformation sent to department chairmen while I was in the job market struck me as the usual knife in the back, with the usual disregard for truth. It reminded me of the story put out about me a few years earlier, that I was neglecting my students at Douglass College in order to spend my time on research, even though I did no research at all while at Douglass College.

———————

Up to this point I had not published a single article or book on racial issues and had no plans to do so. My only professional training was in economics and being black did not seem to me to be enough to qualify me to write on the subject. The very idea of a book on the economics of race had not occurred to me until I heard of a Professor Benjamin Rogge of Wabash College who had embarked on such a project and who gave a speech at Cornell while I was away, leading me to write to him.

> December 27, 1968
>
> Dear Professor Rogge:
>
> I was out of town when you lectured here on "The Welfare State Against the Negro." May I have a copy of your speech, if

one is still available? The announcement said that you are working on a book of the same title. I will be looking forward to seeing it when it appears, but in the meantime do you have any articles along the same lines? Although your theme is very original, it is surprising that someone else has not thought of it before—with such a wealth of material available!

Ben Rogge never finished that book. He had too many irons in the fire. He was an avid golfer, an essayist and a talented and popular speaker on the lecture circuit, as well as being an outstanding teacher and at one time a dean. I got to know him over the years and even sat in on one of his classes at Wabash College—which was superbly taught, by the way, probably better than most students would get at Harvard. Eventually Ben realized that he was never going to finish the projected book and, to my great surprise, he generously turned the manuscript over to me, to do with as I wished. I don't believe I took anything directly from his manuscript in my later writings on race but I took the more fundamental idea that a book on the economics of race could make a valuable contribution to much needed understanding in this area. For that I am grateful to Ben. Many years later, after his death, I had the honor of giving the Ben Rogge Lecture at Wabash College, where I was proud to acknowledge my debt to him.

Campus disruptions and violence reached a crescendo in 1969 and nowhere more so than at Cornell University. Moreover, coming events were casting their shadows before them all around the country. I wrote to my nephew about the students committing the disruptions and violence and the adults—including many faculty members—cheering them on.

January 30, 1969

Dear Cliff,

The generation gap being what it is, I didn't realize that young people were also looking back on "the good old days" before the present mess. I thought they were all busy celebrating the awakening of committed youth and other such drivel. Actually I am not so much put out with the young people as with their adult hangers-on who get their batteries re-charged or their pockets lined from them. Many of the mistakes that college students make are perfectly natural at their age—and most of them centuries old, despite the emphasis on "newness" (which is also centuries old)—but the intolerance, emotionalism, and violence which surround these ideas are the real problem. Many of their adult hangers-on romanticize or condone these things as excusable in the great struggle against The System. In thirty eight years, I have never encountered a single person who believed in everything about the existing society, but the idea that the agonies that have plagued man for thousands of years, in every part of the globe, under all kinds of different arrangements, are going to be gotten around by changing something called The System or by being obnoxious to something called The Establishment seems optimistic beyond words. I guess it is the naive optimism of the revolutionaries that is so hard to take, including their naive optimism about themselves in failing to see how much of what they do is part of the general cussedness of man and has no real connection with the ideals they espouse.

My own personal situation was still not clarified, as I explained in a letter to my sister, Mary Frances.

February 13, 1969

Dear Mary,

It has been a long time since I have had time to sit down and write a letter that was not in response to an emergency, or a job offer, or a student reference. A great deal of time has gone into exploring job possibilities. There are plenty of offers, but most of them would put me in an impossible situation. Universities are anxious to have black faces on the faculty now, and this could easily mean being caught in the middle of various student-administration confrontations going on around the country. Some would like me to be a sort of Guru in residence for black students, with my time being spent at their meetings, affairs, etc.; if the administration doesn't think this way, the students themselves are likely to in some places, and to be nasty if I don't. After all the years I spent preparing myself for serious work, it makes no sense to fritter my time away in bits and dabs on public relations. Most of the noise and hell-raising on campus is about things that won't amount to a hill of beans in the long run, whether the students win or lose.

I also wrote about the situation to my former college room-mate Norton.

February 23, 1969

Dear Nort,

These are certainly times that are trying Sowell. I finally got my Ph.D. in December, just when it has become virtually worthless, with the academic scene being what it is. There are plenty of job offers, but almost all of them would put me right in the middle of confrontations in a period when rationality has gone out the window and, in one case, the department chairman's office [at UCLA] has been bombed after he had a difference of opinion with the local black student leaders. My best offer came from the University of Wisconsin, which hasn't reached that stage yet, but is obviously on its way. I am reliably informed that the militants have already made up their list of "Uncle Toms" among the black faculty there, and that it takes very little to qualify. The people who really sicken me are the white liberals who promote and romanticize this sort of thing. . . .

Little John's vocabulary, which contracted to almost nothing when I was working on the program and Jean took a part-time job at the university, has begun expanding again. Without wanting to jinx things, I think he is on his way.

A brief note to a bookstore in New York also throws light on my situation.

> March 22, 1969
>
> Dear Sirs:
>
> Please send me a copy of *Divorce and Custody for Men* by Charles Metz. Payment is enclosed. Thank you.

I had not yet taken the doctor's wife's advice but I was thinking about it.

Of all the campus disruptions of the 1960s, that at Cornell in 1969 was the worst. Heavily armed black students seized control of a campus building and from a commanding position in a tower issued demands on the university, while some professors received death threats on the phone. The academic administrators not only caved, they and much of the faculty rationalized their abject surrender as being a result of "understanding" the situation of blacks. I lost whatever residual respect I had for Cornell and for the academic world in general.

It looked to me like time to leave academia and take one of the jobs available in private industry. I had a long talk on the phone with an old friend and colleague, Bernard Anderson, who was teaching at the Wharton School. During that conversation he urged me to stay in the academic world, saying that I had much to contribute there. The decisive factor, however, was an offer from Brandeis University, which I had not only visited before but where I had also made contact with black student organizations on campus and found them more amenable to reason than the corresponding black student organizations at Cornell. I went back to Brandeis, where a meeting was arranged between me and the black students and where we both spoke frankly and bluntly. I told them that, if I came there, it would not be to be Guru in residence to black students or to take part in campus politics, but to do what I had spent years preparing to do, be an economist. As I left, some of the black students held out their hands to shake mine and some expressed a hope that they would see me in the fall.

The dean at Brandeis was also a very blunt man, wholly unlike the mealy-mouth administrators at Cornell. When I returned to Ithaca and told my colleagues some of the things he said, they found it hard to believe. I accepted the offer from Brandeis and wrote to the chairman of the economics department, a distinguished authority on the Soviet economy, Professor Joseph S. Berliner.

I also wrote to both Milton Friedman and George Stigler about my current situation and that of the academic world.

May 28, 1969

Dear Mr. Friedman:

After a great deal of soul-searching, I have decided to continue in an academic career, although this is not a good time for a man to be rational and black and on a university campus. I have turned down a number of offers that would have been gratifying a few years ago, and was just about to go to work for the National Bureau [of Economic Research] when I heard from Brandeis, where I thought there was at least a chance of doing something worthwhile. Reversing current trends, I asked for a confrontation with the local black students' organization and, after a lively two-hour discussion, decided that there was at least a basis for cautious optimism there, which is more than can be said of other places, and a great deal more than can be said of Cornell.

May 28, 1969

Dear George:

If you think the well-publicized events here at Cornell were weird, you should hear the reasoning about those events by faculty and students. Apparently the general consensus is that the only salvation for the university is the further pursuit of the kinds of policies which led up to the present disaster. When I point out that Chicago has avoided much of the turmoil of other places without being "responsive" and "re-structuring," this is dismissed as biased testimony or—even worse—not intellectually chic. The great untold story here is the victimization and terrorization of those Negro students who want to get an education; one such student lived with us for ten days during the crisis, and I escorted her to class on most of those days.

My first public comment on the situation at Cornell was in a letter to the *New York Times*.

June 1, 1969

To the Editor:

Mere stupidity may cause some problems, but a certain kind of cleverness is necessary to produce the kind of profound disaster which has occurred at Cornell. In cleverness the Perkins administration has been beyond compare—and beneath contempt. It is fashionable to say that a responsive administration is needed to prevent campus disorders. The Perkins administration has been a veritable weathervane following the shifting cross-currents of campus politics.

Before I could mail that letter, a reporter from the *New York Times* stopped by my office and I gave it to him. My comment in the last sentence appeared on the front page of the *New York Times* and was quoted by others in the media. As a result, my sudden notoriety caused the university trustees to invite me to testify at hearings on the campus crisis, where the subtext was whether the university president should go. He went, though there were a lot more people testifying against him besides me. In fact, I was surprised at how many blacks testified against him. One of the administration's trump cards was to claim that its critics were people whose real animus was against the blacks brought on campus by Perkins et al. After a series of black witnesses had testified against Perkins, one of the white critics later told me in amazement that the trustees for the first time seemed to listen and to take him and his colleagues seriously. The race card had finally been trumped. Perkins was through at Cornell. I described the situation to my old room-mate Norton.

June 16, 1969

Dear Nort,

I would love to believe that I had some influence on the decision to ditch Perkins, but I probably just drove a few extra nails into the coffin.

The trustees and I were alternately intense and collapsing in laughter. The really revealing testimony was by a member of the special committee for admitting black students. One committee member described her uphill struggle, against determined opposition, to gain admission for two black students with College Board scores in the 700s! The doctrinaires who dominate the committee were against the students because they were felt to be "middle class," ideologically if not financially. One had a father who was an alcoholic and a mother who was a maid.

Cornell has been a model disaster and as such may serve as a useful object lesson for higher education generally. It has been thoroughly "politicized," not only in the conventional sense, but also in the more fundamental sense that many people who should know better evaluate every statement, position or action in terms of its presumed effect on students or other interest groups rather than of its intrinsic merits. One colleague whose judgment I previously respected signed an almost maudlin eulogy to Perkins, asking him to stay on as President—even though I had never heard him speak of Perkins in any terms but those of revulsion and contempt.

Once again, my plans to stop teaching summer school were put aside, this time because of an offer to teach at UCLA, which I wanted to see. The UCLA economics department had tried to recruit me for a regular appointment but I had declined because, coming there in the wake of a bomb placed at the department office after the chairman had rebuffed attempts to get him to hire a black professor would have put me in an impossible position. I was told that in fact he had gotten my name for an opening they had without knowing what my race was. But, whatever the facts, I would have come branded as a token black, given the circumstances.

It was a very pleasant summer and a much needed respite from the pressures of the previous months. The UCLA economics department, like the department at the University of Virginia, was an outpost of University of Chicago economists, so there were colleagues who were like-minded both as regards economics and the current campus scene. Fortunately, my dear friend Gloria and her husband were now living in Los Angeles and she found us a very nice little house to rent before we got there. We drove across country, seeing many parts of the United States for the first time, including the Grand Canyon and Los Angeles itself. It was a much needed period of decompression and our whole little family benefitted. It was one of the more pleasant interludes in the marriage and little John was now not only talking but had learned to read the signs on the highways while we were driving across the country.

The 1970s

The country changed directions in the 1960s and my personal life changed directions in the 1970s. As the decade unfolded, I began to do work that I had not done before, live where I had not lived before, write on things I had not written about before, and formed relationships that I had not had before. When the decade ended, my life had changed dramatically.

1970

Being at Brandeis was a much better experience than being at Cornell and relations among the people in the smaller economics department there were much more congenial than in Cornell's large and polarized department.

Efforts by some other universities to recruit me did not seriously tempt me until I was invited to give a paper at UCLA in January and was immediately struck by the balmy weather in Los Angeles, which was such a contrast to frozen Massachusetts. More than climate was involved, however. With its phalanx of University of Chicago economists, UCLA had more kindred souls, including Bill Allen, who specialized in my own specialty, the history of economic thought. Moreover, my old friends Gloria and Rodney lived in Los Angeles and I made new friends with Walter Williams and his wife.

I had met Walter at UCLA the previous summer when I was a visiting professor and he had looked me up because someone told him that there was another black economist who shared his views on racial issues. Walter was teaching at a local college while completing his Ph.D. at UCLA. During this 1970 visit, he and his wife hosted a lively social gathering for me at their apartment after I gave my talk at UCLA and that was the beginning of an enduring friendship.

Also present at my talk, and later at the gathering at Walter's apartment, was a black woman from the UCLA administration who was shocked by the rough-and-tumble style of debate among Chicago economists. I was told later that she had expressed her shock to the chairman of the UCLA economics department, saying that if the department didn't want to hire me, that was their business but that she had never seen such "hostility." The chairman's reply, I was told, was: "What are you talking about? These guys love Tom. Of course we are going to hire him." And they did. I was appointed as an associate professor with tenure, which I was later told was unusual. When I resigned from Brandeis, it was the first time I left an academic institution with good feelings toward my colleagues and regret at parting company with them.

Moving to California was the first of the changes in my life during the 1970s but by no means the last or the biggest.

———————————

Walter Williams had been invited to be on a panel discussing racial issues at the annual meeting of the American Economic Association and wondered whether the offer was a bona fide one that he should accept or whether he was just being used as a token black and being put in the middle of a messy situation.

June 12, 1970

Dear Walter,

My apologies for the delay in replying. Things have been hectic: a new baby girl, a manuscript deadline, preparation to move to Los Angeles, etc.

Your appearance on the A.E.A. panel does have some potential for an awkward situation—especially since last year's disruption was so blandly accepted—but against this must be weighed the opportunity to put some much-needed sanity into discussions of important issues which are often dominated by rhetoric and fashion or lost in a fog of confused emotions. In addition to whatever particular insights you contribute to the particular subject, the very fact that you sit there and talk sense should have a sobering effect on some of the guilty white liberals, who need every example of rationality they can get. Last fall I had similar apprehensions to yours about addressing a symposium on violence, and my talk was not made any easier by some black militant types sitting down front who slouched in their seats with looks of scorn and disdain, but I did the job in the most straightforward and candid way I know, and by the end of the question-and-answer period they joined in the applause.

My new colleagues at UCLA encouraged me to write something about my experiences at Cornell, perhaps just as a way to get me to stop talking about the subject. I wrote an article about academic racial policies in general and it was published in the December 13, 1970 issue of the *New York Times Magazine*. It was my first article on a racial issue and the response was gratifying, as I explained to a former Cornell colleague, Jack Wolfowitz, who was now teaching at the University of Illinois, as part of a widespread faculty exodus after the guns-on-campus crisis of 1969.

December 21, 1970

Dear Jack:

The general response to the article has been as wonderful as the most vain man could desire. Especially gratifying is the fact that the bulk of the earliest and most enthusiastic response was from black educators. The first thing Monday morning (12/14) I received a long distance phone call from a black psychologist at Princeton, followed by a telegram from a Negro schoolteacher in New York, followed later by a five-page letter from an African graduate student, a letter and a post-card from school teachers in Harlem, a letter from a black undergraduate who is getting his degree after seven years of night school, etc. The story

> everywhere is the same: "I have been trying to tell people the same things you said, but they wouldn't listen."

My article included a prophecy which, unfortunately, came true in the years that followed:

> When the failures of many programs become too great to disguise, or to hide under euphemisms and apologetics, the conclusion that will be drawn in many quarters will not be that these were half-baked schemes, but that black people just don't have it.

In the early months of 1971, letters continued to arrive in response to my December article in the *New York Times*. Out of more than a hundred letters that came in, from blacks and whites alike, the overwhelming majority were favorable. However, there were a few negative or even nasty reactions. The most ludicrous reactions were at Cornell, where there were heated denials in the local campus newspaper that some events mentioned in my article had happened at Cornell. What made this ludicrous and a dead giveaway was that the article never said where these particular events happened, as I explained in a letter to the *Cornell Daily Sun*.

> January 1, 1971
>
> To the Editor:
>
> The vehement reactions at Cornell to my article in the *Times* are reminiscent of the woman who protested too much. The article was not about Cornell, but about attitudes and conditions as I found them from visits to and contacts at dozens of leading

colleges and universities from coast to coast. Some of the *anonymous* episodes mentioned were in fact from Cornell, but the denials that they happened at Cornell—which was not charged in the article—are more damaging than my original statements. One of the oldest clues in mystery stories is the suspect who denies having stabbed the victim—before anyone has revealed how the murder occurred. . . .

Among the other responses to my article was a semi-literate letter to the *Cornell Daily Sun*, written by one of the people in Cornell's black studies program, assuring everyone that academic quality was being maintained. You had to laugh or cry—or perhaps both.

I experienced my first California earthquake, a big one on February 9, 1971, and mentioned it in a letter to another former Cornell colleague, Heywood Fleisig.

February 24, 1971

Dear Woody,

After the earthquake of a couple of weeks ago, we have been having so-called "after shocks"—some of which are respectable earthquakes in their own right. I have, however, slept through the strongest of these as measured on the Richter scale—much to the annoyance of Jean, who claims it is another example of my insensitivity. Some of my colleagues at UCLA have gotten equally blasé about them. At one gathering, the speaker had just

> finished making some point when the building trembled, and a colleague observed drily, "That didn't seem like an earth-shaking statement to me."

Californians are able to live with earthquakes because so many structures are built to absorb the stresses created by these earthquakes. But of course this is expensive and people in other parts of the world are often unable to afford such expenses. A powerful earthquake that may kill a handful of people in California will kill hundreds in some less affluent country and thousands in some Third World nation. Many on the left have never understood that the creation of wealth has proven to be one of the most effective ways of promoting safety, much more so than safety advocates or safety laws, many of which inhibit the creation of wealth.

A white former colleague informed me of what other white professors were saying about blacks behind the scene.

> March 29, 1971
>
> Dear Jack,
>
> Thanks for your comments on my article and your account of your colleague's arguments. It supports what I have long suspected: scratch an ultra-liberal and you'll find a bigot underneath. I often wonder if some of the so-called "militants" have not also written off black people's potential and set about providing substitutes for achievement—"our unifying myths," as one of them loftily told me. That particular individual has since fallen victim to the very irrationality he was trying to harness for his own purposes, and others may meet the same fate before it is

over. The tragedy is that many innocents will be sacrificed with them and much desperately needed talent will go down the drain.

I am currently planning a book on black education, so please send me any information or references that you think I ought to have. Was Turner's quote in any printed source? I suspect he is not making an idle boast when he says that different criteria are applied in the hiring of black faculty. Chandler Morse advocated that some time ago, and there have been specific instances, at Cornell and elsewhere, of black studies people vetoing appointments of black faculty to *other* departments—those vetoed of course being people with strong academic credentials. A long letter to the *Times* by one of my students at Cornell said that he had been told that [black militants] at Cornell had said that "Sowell must go," and were apparently planning to include that among their other demands to the administration. [My resignation the preceding August made this moot].

One of the things I am reading in preparation for my book is a doctoral dissertation on gifted black students. The first striking thing I came across was that such students listed their childhood as "very unhappy" about five times as often as black students with average IQs. I suddenly thought of a friend of mine who talks about the harassments and beatings he was subjected to because he tried to be a good student. . . . It then occurred to me that I escaped some of that only because I happened to be a

> friend of two guys who were among the toughest in the class when I was in Harlem, and after elementary school attended integrated, middle class schools. When one begins to add up all the negatives on attitudes to which black kids are subjected, it is amazing that any manage to run the gauntlet and emerge with enough left to do a decent job.

The harassment of higher IQ or more conscientious black students by other black students was a foretaste of what would become a more widespread hostility in later years toward those who would be accused of "acting white."

———————

A professor at the University of Oregon wrote to me about an instructor there whom the black students had decided to boycott. He was blacklisted by them or—as they preferred to say—"whitelisted."

> April 19, 1971
>
> Dear Professor Porter,
>
> The attempt to "whitelist" instructors is all too painfully reminiscent of my own experience some years ago. When I taught at Howard University, a predominantly Negro institution with a sizeable and pampered foreign student contingent, I once observed in class that *all* students were the same to me and all would be held to the same standards. In the atmosphere which had developed, this was regarded as being "anti-foreign student," and an organized boycott of my course by foreign students took place in the following semester.

Former students continued to write me to ask for letters of reference, some of them being apologetic, so that it was necessary to put them at ease.

March 14, 1971

Dear Frances,

Writing letters of recommendation is one of the normal academic duties—more interesting than sharpening pencils and less trouble than removing chalk dust from clothes—so do not feel any hesitancy about asking for more when needed. Your reference, which has already been sent, was very easy to write— with none of the usual anguish of being torn between honesty and compassion.

Frances had been a top student in two of my classes at Howard University, seven years earlier.

My radical friend Hal and I occasionally jousted over our ideological differences.

September 14, 1971

Dear Hal,

Regarding our political differences, I am afraid that there is a breath-taking disproportion between the hasty, naive, and crude way in which most leftists analyze capitalism and the effort and attention which they then devote to trying to destroy it. To you it may seem obvious or reasonable that people should not make a profit on the basic necessities of life, but to me the more essential something is the more important it is that the structure of incentives be such as to cause it to be produced in large volume at low cost. Nothing would please me more than to see a situation created in which "exorbitant" profits could be made by educating ghetto kids. There would be more geniuses coming out of the Harlem school system than we would know what to do with.

1972

I was surprised to receive an inquiry from Congressman Augustus Hawkins, a black liberal Democrat, soliciting my views on issues revolving around "full employment." But I replied.

January 4, 1972

Dear Congressman Hawkins:

While I have been very much disturbed by the upward drift in the average unemployment rate over the past few years, it seems to me that the real problem is not that the "average" man has a significantly harder time finding a job—a condition that

> might be remedied by more aggregate demand—but that particular segments of the population are finding it *extremely* hard to find a job, and it is their astronomical rate of unemployment which is causing the average to rise. Even with respect to the black population, it is not the "average" black man who is having a hard time finding a job, but particular sub-groups who are finding it nearly impossible to get work. The unemployment figures which I have at hand for 1967, 1968, 1969 and 1970 show the unemployment rate for black males, aged 35-44, to be less than 4% for all of these years, and less than 3% for a couple of years. By contrast, the unemployment rate for black males, aged 16-17, has averaged about 25% to more than 30% over the past decade. This kind of phenomenon does not look like an aggregate demand problem or "full employment" problem.

This apparently was not what the Congressman wanted to hear for I never heard from him again. Politicians like Hawkins like to see issues as national problems for which a huge government program is the answer, when in fact often these are problems peculiar to particular segments of society—and are often brought on by existing government programs with especially negative impacts on those segments. In this case, minimum wage laws price inexperienced and unskilled workers out of jobs. In other words, government was not the solution but the cause of the problem.

Over the years since the end of my summer program for black students at Cornell, I had spent considerable time writing letters and engaging in discussions with a variety of academics across the country, in hopes of setting up some kind of high-quality institution for blacks. These time-consuming efforts were finally brought to an end when Professor John Hope Franklin of the University of Chicago declined to support the idea. It had already become increasingly clear that the idea was a long shot, so that only strong support from someone of his prominence could have saved it. The fact that the idea now went into limbo—never to return—also had its good side, as I recognized then and still more so now in retrospect.

March 7, 1972

Dear Professor Franklin:

Although I had hoped to see an early launching of an institute of the sort described in my proposal, it would have been a very heavy burden on me at this stage of my own development. I know that for it to succeed, it had to get a very high level of commitment from a very high percentage of the recognized black scholars in the country. In all frankness, my initial disappointment on reading your letter was followed immediately by a sense of personal relief at not having to pursue the matter further at this time. One index of my relief was that I went directly to a bowling alley and bowled my highest score in years (268)!

My highest bowling score (279) came right after I resigned from Douglass College, producing a similar feeling of relief and relaxation.

I received a rather attractive offer of a two-year visiting professorship at Stanford University, which would have allowed me to teach half-time and get paid full-time, so as to have ample time left for research or study. My only concern was about the campus atmosphere as regards student disruptions and violence over either racial issues or any of the other issues which had been setting off such disruptions and violence since the 1960s. I had witnessed one such disruption while eating lunch at the Stanford faculty club during a visit— and, more important, had witnessed the meek acceptance of it by the faculty present. I also phoned around to various people at Stanford—black and white —to find out if I as a black faculty member would be expected to either toe the line on issues defined by black militants on campus or at least maintain a discreet silence. The answers did not satisfy me, so I turned down the offer. Afterwards I wrote to a black friend in the Stanford administration to explain my decision.

March 19, 1972

Dear Hank:

Despite a very attractive offer from Stanford and a rather pleasant impression of Palo Alto, I decided that it was not worth being in the middle of a "situation." None of the people whom I talked with at some length by phone suggested that there would be any real danger, and indeed it was their reassurances more than anything else which disturbed me, for they seemed to assume that *of course* I would have sufficient circumspection not to let myself appear as an antagonist to self-righteous messiahs (at least one of those I spoke with would fall in the latter category himself). All seemed to assume that it was the same "everywhere" for a black faculty member. It never seemed to occur to them that I might have been a few places myself, and might be in touch with a few others. As one who spoke and voted against continuing one program for black students at Brandeis, and who denounced the president of Cornell in the mass media while an assistant professor there, it is a little late in the day for

> me to start learning circumspection. Moreover, when I put this
> together with the faculty club disruptions and the supineness with
> which they were accepted by those present, as well as some other
> comments tending to confirm the same atmosphere, it just did not
> look like something I wanted to be part of.

Stanford had already mastered the approach that would bring "peace" to campuses across the country after the turmoil of the 1960s—pre-emptive surrender.

———————————

This was a time of my life—at age 42—when I was ready to do something different but I hadn't decided what. Teaching UCLA students was getting tiresome and, after more than a decade of writing almost exclusively, at least in my academic work, on the history of economic thought, I wanted to move on to something else, at least for a while.

Among the career prospects I explored were think tanks, including the Rand Corporation in California and the Urban Institute in Washington, where Walter Williams now worked. Since I had tenure at UCLA, I could take leave to go work in either place and still have the safety net of being able to return to UCLA. Among the alternative fields of work, I became interested in the history and economics of American ethnic groups. In early July, I declined an offer from the Rand Corporation and accepted an offer from the Urban Institute to set up my own research project there on American ethnic groups.

> July 13, 1972
>
> Dear Woody,
>
> I have taken leave from UCLA to go head up a research
> project on American ethnic minorities at the Urban Institute in
> Washington. At one time I used to boast that I was one of the few
> people left in this country who was *not* an expert on race, but

now that I have seen what the experts have said and done, it seems like time for us amateurs to get into the act and try to introduce some elements of sanity.

A letter arrived from the chairman of the economics department at Swarthmore that seemed to me one more sad sign of the times and it provoked a lengthy reply.

September 18, 1972

Dear Professor Pierson:

This morning I was pleased to receive a letter from Swarthmore college, an institution for which I have long had respect, and reports from which have added to my admiration. Then I opened the letter and learned that "Swarthmore College is actively looking for a black economist. . . " and the phrase that came immediately to my mind was one from a bygone era, when a very different kind of emotionalism was abroad, and a witness facing Senator Joseph McCarthy said, "Sir, have you no shame?"

What *purpose* is to be served by this sort of thing? Surely a labor economist of your reputation must know that unemployment among black Ph.D.s is one of the least of our social problems, and has been for many years—long before "affirmative action." In general, even the salary is no higher at a top college than at less prestigious institutions for a given individual. So you are doing very little for black faculty members with broadcast recruiting campaigns like this (I note the letter is mimeographed). Maybe you think you are doing something for race relations. If you are going to find Swarthmore-quality black faculty members, that is one thing. But Swarthmore-quality faculty members are found through Swarthmore-quality channels and not through mimeographed letters of this sort. Many a self-respecting black scholar would never accept an offer like this, even if he would enjoy teaching at Swarthmore otherwise. When Bill Allen was chairman at U.C.L.A. he violently refused to hire anyone on the basis of ethnic representation—and thereby made it possible for me to come there a year later with my head held up. Your approach tends to make the job unattractive to anyone who regards himself as a scholar or a man, and thereby throws it open to opportunists.

Despite all the brave talk in academia about "affirmative action" without lowering quality standards, you and I both know that it takes many years to create a qualified faculty member of any color, and no increased demand is going to immediately increase the supply *unless* you lower quality. Now what good is going to come from lower standards that will make "black" equivalent to "substandard" in the eyes of black and white students alike? Can you imagine that this is going to *reduce* racism? On the contrary, more and more thoughtful people are beginning to worry that the next generation will see an increasing amount of bigotry among those whites educated at some of the most liberal institutions, where this is the picture that is presented to them, however noble the rhetoric that accompanies it.

You and I both know that many of these "special" recruiting efforts are not aimed at helping black faculty members or black or white students, but rather at hanging on to the school's federal money. Now, I have nothing against money. I have not been so familiar with it as to breed contempt. But there are limits to what should be done to get it, and particularly so for an institution with a proud tradition, at a time when the government itself is wavering and having second thoughts about this policy, and when just a little courage from a few men in "responsible" positions might make a difference.

Word of this letter spread and caused it to be published in a couple of places. The deterioration in race relations on college campuses became so common that eventually a new term was coined: the "new racism"—that is, more racial polarization than had existed on those same campuses decades earlier.

1973

Although my research project at the Urban Institute began in the middle of the summer of 1972, it began with a modest budget, just enough to maintain a skeleton staff while proposals were written and grants applied for to carry out these proposals. By the beginning of 1973, I was already a battle-scarred veteran of bureaucratic in-fighting and back-stabbing, and was by no means certain that I would remain for the two years that my project was scheduled to run, even if we got all the money we needed from various outside sources that we were approaching. Some idea of my feelings toward the administrative staff of the Urban Institute may be indicated by a letter to one of our outside consultants who had not gotten paid.

January 18, 1973

Dear Ivan:

First of all, let me apologize for our stupid bureaucrats. Given the stringent laws on murder, it is not feasible to shoot them, and anything else is only partially effective.

Milton Friedman was recovering from heart surgery. He was also among those who asked to reprint my letter to the economics department chairman at Swarthmore the previous September.

January 18, 1973

Dear Milton:

It was very good to learn that you are getting better and will be back in action soon.

I am of course delighted that you want to republish my letter to Swarthmore and have no objection whatever. It has, however, been published in the January issue of *Commentary*. I enclose another letter on the subject, which you may do with as you see fit.

One of the interesting and heartening developments of the

past few years has been the tendency of a small but growing number of black students to reject black mysticism and white paternalism alike and try to do solid work—even when their previous education has been inadequate to the task. A black faculty member at Harvard recently told me that black students had gone to some white faculty members with double standards and explained that they needed *accurate* grades in order to plan their lives on any rational basis. What a commentary on our times when underprivileged kids have to explain the facts of life to Harvard professors.

While attending a Ford Foundation conference on race and ethnicity, I wrote to someone at Stanford about the current situation among black intellectuals.

February 13, 1973

Dear Mr. Gragg,

The pathetic intellectual level of a speech by Kenneth Clark last night made me realize more than ever that our hopes as a race must depend on the younger generation. I do not idolize youth—which is often both pretentious and ridiculous—but it does seem to me that the mental caliber of many blacks in the intellectual pipeline is far superior to the mental caliber of our finished products.

Kenneth Clark had the airs of an intellectual—but only the airs. He was one of that generation of blacks who happened to be on the scene when some white elites suddenly decided that they needed some blacks to be thrust into prominence, so that mediocrities like Professor Clark, columnist Carl Rowan, and Judge Leon Higginbotham were given an inflated status and acquired inflated egos that made them resent a new generation of more competent blacks that came after them.

During the conference, when Kenneth Clark learned that my project was doing research on race and IQ, he tried privately to dissuade me from doing such research, ostensibly on grounds that to do so would "dignify" the theories of Arthur Jensen, but I suspected that it was because he was afraid of what that research would find. In any event, stifling research was hardly the sign of someone with intellectual integrity. I did not share Kenneth Clark's fears but, even in the unlikely event that the research ended up confirming Jensen's theory of a racial basis for differences in average IQ, was I supposed to suppress the results? Wherever black people were going, and wherever we wished to go, we had to get there from where we were—which meant that we had to know where we were, not where we wished we were or where we wished others to think we were. The same principle applied well beyond the subject of IQs. Too many people were preoccupied with protecting the image of blacks in the eyes of whites, rather than with knowing what the facts were, as a basis for whatever was to be done to make things better.

I also wrote to an official of the Ford Foundation, not only about that conference but more broadly about its policies in the racial area in general.

February 20, 1973

Dear ******:

The conference on race and ethnicity—enlightening in some respects and trying in others. One of the enclosed papers gives my summary remarks, and the other the write-up of my project here at the Urban Institute.

When I questioned how serious the Ford Foundation was about race and ethnicity, I was not simply indulging in overstatement for effect. There is all the difference in the world between wanting to be "with it" and wanting to advance a cause in the most effective way possible. Quite frankly, I have been shocked, appalled, and baffled by the policies of the Ford Foundation in this whole area over the past several years. When I arrived home, it so happens that the first person I talked with outside my family was a man who brought fresh painful news about a major Ford-sponsored operation for blacks which he had just visited. He confessed that when he left, it was all he could do to fight back the tears (you would have to know what a tough customer he is to appreciate the full import of these words). This well-financed operation was headed by a man whom the Ford Foundation had backed to the hilt, but whose professional competence can only be called laughable—or cryable. He is only one of the many such cultural *gauleiters* whom Ford has set up in business.

It may appear ungracious to censure an organization which is donating money for black people merely because it is not all being done in the best possible manner. The heart of the matter is that this money is often used to drain off some of our best young people into counterproductive activities run by incompetents and charlatans. Dangling $5,000 a year fellowships for fraudulent programs in front of poor black students is destroying the race's major capital assets—its promising young people—in exchange for idiocy and rhetoric. This is what my friend found so shattering. Another bitter black scholar suggested to me some time ago that black intellectuals sign an open letter to the Ford Foundation saying "keep your money." I have no time to organize such a thing, but if he decides to do it, I will certainly sign it.

My first appearance on a television talk show was a very positive experience. The hostess was a young black woman who expressed to me her desire to pass on her knowledge of television broadcasting to students at a black college.

May 30, 1973

Dear Phyllis:

Let me say again what a pleasure it was to be on "Straight Talk." My only previous appearance on television was as a contestant on "Jeopardy," and this clearly beats that by miles. I haven't seen the program I was on, but my relatives in New York saw it and liked it, so I accept that as unbiased evidence.

Your interest in teaching television skills in a black college prompted me to write the enclosed letter to an old friend who is very knowledgeable about these schools. Frankly, my fear is that you could interrupt a promising career and end up with only disillusionment to show for it. The tragedy is that you are needed and yet your skills and abilities may not be usable in the institutional setting in which you would find yourself. During the one year I taught at Howard University, I witnessed the departure of economists who went to teach at three Ivy League universities, to work for corporations that are household words, and one who set up his own consulting firm. There is little doubt that each of these men would have been willing to spend their lives building up that department if they thought there was any real hope of doing so. Institutional forces are enormously powerful, and the isolated individual wins only a few scattered, partial and temporary victories against them. The attitudes of the students are also a great discouragement that can wear you down in the long run, and this is not unrelated to the institutional leadership, for many students would respond to leadership that had some sense of purpose itself—where purpose is defined in some terms other than political or short-run self-interest.

Among white institutions, the "high risk" black student was still in vogue in many special minority student programs. A form letter received by a black student who had applied to a Harvard summer program to help prepare black students for medical school informed him: "It is the feeling of the Admissions Committee that your current qualifications are outstanding and should be strong enough to make you a viable candidate for admission to medical or dental school, without the help of this program." In other words, high-risk students were preferred. I wrote to one of the officials of this program.

June 4, 1973

Dear Mr. * * * * * *:

An old colleague of mine at another institution recently sent me the enclosed letter which one of his black students had received. The student in question had come from an educationally deficient background but had, by very hard work, overcome some of those deficiencies and wanted to do still more along the same line, to beef himself up intellectually for a career in medical science. I can well understand that the sheer arithmetic of your situation will not permit you to take every promising student who applies. What shocks me as an educator in general, and as a black educator in particular, is that this letter indicates that he was rejected precisely because he was *too* promising. Moreover, the fact that this is a *form* letter suggests that this is not simply an unfortunate decision for one student but a general policy of favoring the less promising over the more promising student.

This situation was appalling enough in itself. It is doubly tragic in view of the difficulties faced in medical school by many black students brought in under "special" programs. Moreover, people in a position to know have been candid enough with me to say that all these difficulties have not been resolved either by heroic efforts by the students or by dedicated teaching by the faculty, but in many cases simply by lowering standards. The

> people concerned were not at obscure medical schools.
>
> What sort of grotesque situation have we talked ourselves into when promising pre-med students are passed over in favor of "high risk" students? The term "high risk" has particularly grim overtones in a field where today's student will tomorrow have lives in his hands. Would you want *your* children to be operated on by the people you are accepting or the people you are rejecting for having outstanding qualifications?

My statement that I was not referring to "obscure medical schools" only hinted at the fact that the Harvard Medical School was what I specifically had in mind, having been privately informed of the policies brewing there a few years earlier by a high official of that medical school. A few years after this letter was written, a professor at the Harvard Medical School went public with the revelation that black students there were being allowed to go through without meeting the usual standards. He pointed out that "trusting patients" will "pay for our irresponsibility." He was, predictably, labeled a "racist." Nor were such policies confined to Harvard. Out in California, a black student admitted to medical school under affirmative action was in later years often pointed out as a vindication of that policy, since he went back to practice medicine in the black community. In the midst of such praise, however, the death of one of his patients led to a suspension of his license and—after a fuller investigation—a permanent revocation of his license, after findings of his incompetence.

The people at the Harvard Medical School were not only oblivious to my objections, they were apparently also oblivious to similar criticisms by the much better known Harvard Professor David Riesman, famous for his book *The Lonely Crowd*. Professor Riesman mentioned his own experience with people at the Harvard Medical School in a letter to me.

> August 27, 1973
>
> Dear Dr. Sowell:
>
> Did I write you—I know I meant to—about the letter you sent along to me, the form letter from Harvard's Career Summer

Program?   For I wanted to tell you of a somewhat similar experience I had when the program was being organized a few years ago and I was consulted by two white, idealistic doctors at the Harvard Medical School about it. . . . I remember these doctors saying that it would be pointless to recruit for Harvard Medical School a young woman from Spelman College, since, of course, she was already advantaged; the program would only make sense if one could recruit students from less-adequate Negro colleges. Since there were, at that time, hardly any women, and hardly any blacks at Harvard Medical School, a young, black science educator at the Harvard Graduate School of Education and I argued vehemently that this was a crazy policy: it would be marvelous to have a Spelman College student as a model to white and black students alike, men and women alike, at Harvard Medical School; moreover, given a certain coziness at Spelman, the jump for such a young woman would not be easy. But I don't think we made much headway against the pattern that your letter describes and against which you have fought. . . .

If your work should bring you this way, I should love to meet and talk with you.

With good wishes,

Sincerely,

David Riesman

Eventually I did visit David Riesman in his home in Cambridge and we subsequently exchanged letters sporadically over the years.

––––––––––––––––

After experiencing many misadventures and delays at the Urban Institute,[1] I finally received enough grant money to bring my project up to full strength and launch an all-out research effort in the middle of the year. I wrote to a colleague at another institution.

July 18, 1973

Dear Mike:

We now have money! Filthy lucre. I feel corrupted already....

Incidentally, one of the grants for this project stipulates that the money is to be used "during the incumbency of Thomas Sowell" as director of the research. I am slowly learning the facts of life in the research racket.

Fortunately for me, the people who put that proviso in my grant already knew the facts of life—that nothing would be easier for the Urban Institute than to use me as a front to get the money and then replace me with someone more pliable who would run the project the way the Urban Institute administration wanted it run, rather than the way I insisted on running it. There was a lot of dirty work going on behind my back at the Urban Institute but, fortunately, I had a source inside the administration who kept me informed, so that I could minimize the damage.

Now that I had money, I tried to recruit my old pen pal from graduate school days but she was unavailable.

––––––––––––––––

1. See my *A Personal Odyssey*, pp. 233–243.

July 20, 1973

Dear Mary:

You'll be sorry you did not join us on our IQ study. It is turning out to be very exciting stuff. Jensen and company are vulnerable empirically, while the usual philosophical-political objections seem as ineffective as water off a duck's back.

Had I listened to Kenneth Clark's objections to research on race and IQ, I would never have discovered that a number of white groups, here and overseas, had IQs very similar to those of blacks or that there were particular black schools where IQs equaled or exceeded the national average—or that black women greatly outnumbered black men at higher IQ levels. Whatever the particular reasons for these things, they clearly suggested that race could not explain such disparities.

A note from Martin Bronfenbrenner was one of the signs of the times.

October 3, 1973

Dear Tom,

Thanks for you letter of October 1 and your material on Arthur Jensen. Congratulations for resisting the temptation to call him a Fascist or a reactionary and let it go at that. . . .

Despite the pressures and hassles at the Urban Institute, there were some lighter moments, including a memo from the young lady in charge of IQ collections.

October 12, 1973

TO: Mr. Sowell

Re: Progress Report

Your happy, intelligent, well-informed crew would like to meet with you on Monday afternoon for 45 min. to give you a report on our present situation, and to give you a detailed plan for the next 8 weeks in terms of our data collecting goals.

J.M.

The Urban Institute management encouraged people to run to them with any problems they had with me, much as students were encouraged to run to deans at Howard University. Here as well, this had the inevitable effect of undermining my authority. It also polarized the project's staff between those who were loyal to me and those who were not. Fortunately, as it turned out, the project was running out of money and the Ford Foundation postponed acting on my request for additional funds. That enabled me to fire all the troublemakers for lack of money, leaving them no administrative or legal recourse—after which the Ford Foundation granted me all the money I had asked for before. This might have been a happy coincidence but my own suspicion is that, since I had made no secret of the fact that I was considering quitting—and losing me would have meant losing the money granted in my name—those who had encouraged the troublemakers now found them expendable. The Urban Institute's close ties with the Ford Foundation might help explain the odd—and convenient—sequence of events.

Now that my project consisted only of those loyal to me, there was a dramatic change in the whole atmosphere. Not only did the work get done better and with fewer distractions, everyone seemed more relaxed and we had much good humor. Before, there were members of the project who would literally not speak to each other. As the year went on and various studies within the project came to an end, those people working on those particular studies who had been loyal to me were simply let go by the Urban Institute, in contrast to their finding work elsewhere in the Institute for some of the biggest troublemakers. I tried to help those who were leaving to find jobs elsewhere but succeeded in only one case that I am aware of. Even a secretary who had been working for the Urban Institute before I got there, and who joined my project and was loyal to me, was let go when the project ended. Fortunately, I received another grant on my own to conduct some research for a few months after leaving the Urban Institute, and was able to hire her and another secretary to do research.

I summarized my experiences to a former colleague at Cornell.

April 16, 1974

Dear George:

This stint at the Urban Institute has given me new experiences—most of which I could have done without—but I have learned something about fund-raising . . . about administration and—God help us—about human nature. Even after Cornell, I was not prepared for the level of Byzantine intrigue and amorality around here. To see people for whom I risked something, to get them more money or other benefits, turn around and knife me in the back for some petty advantage requires more fortitude than I can muster. It is said that I have become a difficult person to deal with.

While there was now a modus vivendi of sorts on the job, that was not true at home. I was in the tenth year of a marriage growing increasingly sour, and being kept together only for the sake of the children. One of the puzzling ironies of the situation was that there were really no major problems between my wife and me, such as drunkenness, infidelity or fundamental differences in values. It was just that every little problem became insoluble and my wife always seemed to be trying to prove something. Though the situation was deteriorating, there was nothing really new. It was just that the discord became more frequent and the reconciliations more transient. I began to read more about divorce and consulted a lawyer. But still I hesitated to take the irrevocable step that would tear the family apart.

Returning to California produced very mixed feelings. My ambivalence about resuming teaching at UCLA and my apprehensions about my marriage were all burdens. But California itself was a welcome sight because it felt like I was home again and the people in the economics department showed me much appreciated little considerations to ease my return. Perhaps the biggest plus was that I was simply no longer at the Urban Institute. I wrote back to my project secretary who was still at work there, taking care of chores that continued after my departure.

August 22, 1974

Dear Margo:

It is good to be back in California. It is good not to be supervising anybody. It is good not to be concerned about what the administration is doing *this* time. My consumption of alcohol has dropped sharply.

Even at its peak, my consumption of alcohol was what most people would have considered moderate drinking—perhaps a bottle of wine or two per week. But it was high for me.

By now I had re-established contact with the family in which I had grown up in Harlem. This included Birdie, my sister in that family. She was someone especially dear to me.

> August 25, 1974
>
> Dear Birdie,
>
> We have now found a place to live in California. Jean and the children like it, so I took it, even though it means a long drive to work for me. If the marriage is to survive, this is where it should have the best chance.
>
> I am sorry Jean burdened you with our troubles. One of the many differences between Jean and me is that I would never have gone to her family with my version of the story. It is all right that you know, and it makes me feel good that you care, but it was my place to discuss it with you, as I expected to do the last time I was in New York—and as I probably will when I am back east this fall.
>
> California is still as pleasant as ever.
>
> Love to all,
>
> Tommy

In order to give my marriage whatever chance it might still have, I had agreed to rent a house that Jean wanted which cost more than I could really afford and, because of California's skyrocketing housing costs, I had to rent far out in the San Fernando Valley, giving me a long and exhausting commute to and from UCLA. If I thought this sacrifice might be appreciated, much less reciprocated, I was sadly mistaken. After an ugly and sometimes stormy two months, I finally walked out.

I moved into a little studio apartment in Venice, a Los Angeles neighborhood that could charitably be called modest, and began to consult divorce lawyers.

Somehow I learned that Audrey was also divorced and, though I had not seen or communicated with her in nine years, I phoned her in New York. Someone who spoke to me on the phone later that day said that I sounded so much more upbeat than I had in quite a while. Nothing had changed—except that I had spoken with Audrey. Now I wrote to her.

October 27, 1974

Dear Audrey,

It was good to hear your voice again, and good to learn that you have found a professional niche that satisfies you. I have found a lot of satisfaction in my work, but not Satisfaction with a capital "s," in the sense of one particular post in which I could settle permanently for the long haul. . . .

You performed a service by reminding me that I was drinking a lot while at A.T. & T. because I had forgotten that. Apparently non-academic jobs do that to me. My consumption of alcohol has dropped off sharply since returning to UCLA, despite my domestic problems. . . .

You suggested that therapy had helped you through the emotional stress of a divorce. My judgment may be premature—I have been physically separated only a week—but I have neither experienced nor anticipate emotional trauma from the separation. The marriage was a trauma and the legalistic maneuvers will probably be a real pain, but ending the marital relationship has been just one big relief—aside from the children, where the possibility of trauma (for them and me) remains. Sometimes I feel like an idiot for having taken so long to see the obvious need to end it, but perhaps the many times in years past when I agonized over the prospect of splitting up the family have had some value in freeing me of guilt and emotional wrenching when I finally faced up to the decision as inescapable. . . .

My next trip to the east will be to Cambridge on November 7th. Very likely I will be in New York on November 8th and/or 9th. Would you be available for dinner either of those evenings?

Audrey's reply was a brief note.

Nov. 4, 1974

Dear Tom—

Would love to see you for dinner sometime but will be tied up Nov. 8th + 9th.

Try me again.

Audrey

We never got together for dinner, though I am not sure why. Maybe by the time I was back east again Audrey had someone else in her life. It is conceivable, though less likely, that I changed my mind. After the first warm glow of that phone conversation with her wore off, I began to become uneasy as I recalled Audrey's reaction to my saying that I was agonizing over whether to have a custody battle for my children. She immediately urged me not to do it— on grounds that trying to raise children would ruin my career. If she thought I would leave my children in the lurch for the sake of my career, she really did not understand me very well.

In any event, I moved on. Within a relatively short time, a woman I knew in Venice and I went from being friends to being more than friends. However, we had been friends so long that at first it seemed almost as if I were committing incest. Still it was a good relationship as we went biking together along the beaches and driving up and down the coast. I was content, though she was not Audrey.

1975

Although the ugly business of a divorce was still going on as the new year began, I was hopeful that this would be the year when it would end. Between Gloria and her family and my friend in Venice, I had people who had known me a long time to help me through this rough period. Phone calls and a visit from my sister Mary Frances also helped, along with letters from my sisters in my adopted family, Birdie and Ruth.

A great amount of work kept me busy, which may have been a good thing, since it left me less time to brood. There was much work to finish up in absentia from my Urban Institute project and I had gotten a couple of small grants to study academically successful black schools and to write a monograph on affirmative action. Being close to the Venice bicycle path also gave me opportunities to bike regularly and relax. I became more exercise conscious and liked to walk up the eight flights of stairs to my office at UCLA, sometimes trailing behind me some puffing students.

I was so busy with so many things that my personal letters often got written when I was on planes, as with this letter to Birdie and her husband Lacy, on a trip back from Washington.

February 22, 1975

Dear Birdie and Lacy,

One of the few advantages of making business trips is that it gives you a few free moments to write family and friends.

Things are still going along about as before as regards the divorce and custody action. The hearing scheduled for next week will have to be postponed about two months, and it will probably be longer than that before the divorce is final. The chances of a man getting custody of children are very small, unless the wife is so bad that she is in an asylum or in jail. Still I am going to try and will be prepared to go back to court later if I am not satisfied with the way Jean is raising the children. . . .

I'll bet you will never guess what this trip was for. I was invited to have lunch with the President in the White House! There were about eight of us, and we talked about various things for about an hour and a half. It so happened that I was seated next to the President and found him a very relaxed and likable person. The enclosed card with the Presidential seal was used to show me where I was to sit. I thought you or the children might like it for a souvenir.

The little group having lunch at the White House included intellectuals like Edward Banfield and Gertrude Himmelfarb. It was the first public recognition of my work and came at a good time for me personally.

A letter from Walter Williams was like a bulletin from a war front.

March 3, 1975

Dear Tom:

Sometimes it is a very lonely struggle trying to help our people, particularly the ones who do not realize that help is needed. Incidentally, I heard from a very reliable source that ****** Hospital here has an all but written policy of prohibiting the flunking of black medical students.

Walter does not publicize his efforts to help blacks or others. However, despite his attacks on politicians who promote the welfare state, in his private life Walter has for years been generous with both his time and his money on behalf of less fortunate people. He sees no contradiction between his public stance and his private actions, since he feels free to do whatever he likes with his own money but does not consider politicians free to do whatever they like with the taxpayers' money.

I continued to keep in touch with Birdie.

> April 30, 1975
>
> Dear Birdie,
>
> Last Sunday, while I was loading Lorraine's bicycle onto the car, she ran and picked a flower for me. She handed it to me and said, "This is for you, daddy. You can have it and keep it as long as you want." I have been feeling good ever since.

Various letters I received brought examples of the signs of the times but at least one letter from the University of Oregon suggested that there was some improvement.

> 9 June 1975
>
> Dear Professor Sowell:
>
> The enclosed clipping is a welcome suggestion that "black education" may have changed for the better even at the University of Oregon since 1969, when I was informed by a "project director" that it was my own fault if the functionally

illiterate black students in one of my classes didn't do satisfactory work—I should "inspire" them to do so! Those were the days, too, when some white instructors informed black students not to pay attention to English instructors who insisted on correct spelling and grammar: "You talk good ghetto English and that is just as 'valid' as any other form of language." Also, if you "gave"—and gave was usually the word—a black student a grade lower than B- you were just a racist pig.

Dr. DuBois would have turned over in his grave—even as far away as Ghana!

I am confident that your book was an important factor in bringing about a change—a slow change and one by no means yet completed—in the direction of a more rational approach.

Sincerely,

Kenneth Wiggins Porter

Professor Emeritus

My work, as well as my personal life, began to take a new direction. Just as I had turned away from writing almost exclusively about the history of economic thought after the first dozen years of my career, now I wanted to turn away from writing almost exclusively about race and ethnicity. For more than a year, an ambitious new project had been taking shape in my mind—a book about the ways that knowledge is used in different kinds of institutions and organizations, and what that implies about decisions made by individuals, families, businesses and government.

In May I applied to the Center for Advanced Study in the Behavioral

Sciences in northern California for a fellowship to spend a year researching and writing on this subject. A couple of months later I heard back from Lloyd Cutler, Director of the Center, and responded.

July 2, 1975

Dear Mr. Cutler:

My belated but warm thanks for your recent letter offering me an opportunity to become a Fellow at the Center for Advanced Study in 1976-77. I accept your offer and look forward to it as a chance of a lifetime to do the kind of work in the kind of company that one dreams of.

The book that would emerge from this, years later, would be called *Knowledge and Decisions*.

This was not the only good news that summer. The long nightmare of the divorce finally came to an end. The judge awarded my ex-wife less alimony and child support than I had offered at the outset. She turned angrily on her lawyer in the courtroom. He had acted throughout as if he were Sir Galahad rescuing the damsel in distress from the monster, so now that he was getting an instant dose of reality I had to laugh. Among the people to whom I wrote with the news was Mrs. Gadsden.

September 4, 1975

Dear Mrs. G,

It's over! I am a free man—though "free" may be a strange word for a legal process that has cost me thousands. Even an uncontested divorce in a no-fault state with terminal alimony is still an ugly, embittering experience. At least it was carried out in a way that made it so. My former wife (what a lovely phrase) made everything as exasperating and expensive as possible, while periodically attempting a reconciliation. Still, the children have come through it in better shape than I would have thought and I see them regularly and have warm moments along with a few painful ones. All in all, it has worked out better than I thought a year ago, and there has never been a moment when I considered turning back. It has been years since I have known such peace. My consumption of alcohol has dropped to practically nothing and the only time I have taken an aspirin was when my brother died. Recently I have moved into a new apartment, which I like very much. The old place was much too small, but I had formed an attachment to it as the place where I made a much needed transition in my life, not only as regards the marriage but as regards my outlook on life. As I left the old apartment for the last time, I kissed the door and sang a few bars of "That's all, that's all."

My interest in photography is reviving. At a recent showing of my slides, I was urged to turn professional. I expect to buy an enlarger that I have wanted for years. Only in the past year have I realized how much I had been subordinating my own needs and how little it was appreciated.

I am presently taking a few days' vacation traveling at a leisurely pace up the California coast—and of course it would be anti-social to travel alone. Life seems good, and my only regret is that I did not have the wisdom to make life better earlier.

Nothing so epitomized for me what was wrong with the court-ordered busing of black school children from their own neighborhoods to places where there were schools for white children than the situation in the Boston area, where black youngsters were bused from their own neighborhood schools with low academic standards to a white school with even lower standards. A friend in the Boston area informed me that the white school in south Boston "had sent only *three* of several hundred graduates to college the year before." This was one of the things I discussed in a letter to prominent education historian Diane Ravitch.

September 20, 1975

Dear Ms. Ravitch:

The assumptions behind the "integration" and "busing" crusades would not stand up under a half-hour of scrutiny in Logic I. The hard facts do not support the belief that sitting a black child next to a white child generally produces either educational or psychological benefits to either. . . . What an insult to black children and what an unconscionable exploitation of them to take them across town and through dangerous idiots, in the name of "quality integrated education"—in South Boston?!!

The new year began with me in my one-bedroom apartment in an upscale complex in Marina del Rey, not too far from where I had lived in Venice as far as distance was concerned, but a different world otherwise. I now also had an enlarger again, for the first time in nearly 20 years. The first picture I printed with it was one of me and my little nephew Jimmy—the son of Birdie and Lacy—taken in 1951. Jimmy had since died tragically in 1960.

January 24, 1976

Dear Birdie and Lacy,

The other evening I was looking through my negative file, and decided to print some negatives from the 1950s. Three of these pictures are enclosed, together with a picture of me taken last year. The picture of Jimmy and me together in 1951 was emotionally very difficult for me to print—I cried when I saw the picture emerging in the chemicals—but I thought you might want a copy, since Birdie mentioned that she is putting an album together. In addition to everything else, Jimmy was the first newborn baby I had ever known, and he melted my heart when I first saw him coming home from the hospital. Every December 7th, when they mention Pearl Harbor, I remember that I was sitting by Jimmy's crib when I heard the news.

For a long time after printing the picture of Jimmy, I thought of how much this family has suffered at each generation. I was lucky enough to come along just when things were beginning to open up for black people, and before the ghetto became unbearable. I often wonder what would have happened if the generation before me had had the same opportunities—especially Lacy, who has the personality as well as the ability to do remarkable things. I only hope the later generations can make the most of their broader opportunities. Sometimes I worry that much of what we learned the hard way will be lost and perhaps have to be re-learned through more bad experience. There are whole areas of my life that John and Lorraine cannot really imagine, and I am not sure that they will understand it much better when they are older. I only hope that they do not become simply spoiled or else vulnerable to a lot of fancy-sounding talk.

When I declined the nomination I told you about, I received phone calls from people I know who had been asked by the White House to try to get me to reconsider. I did think it over, and talked it over with some more people and, after a lot of soul-searching, decided that this is what I ought to do after all. Before anything official can be done, the FBI and the Internal Revenue Service will have to clear me. So if any government agents contact you, don't be afraid that I am in trouble. And don't be afraid of what you tell them. I have nothing to hide. It's good to be able to say that after 45 years.

My love to everyone.

The nomination referred to was President Ford's nomination of me to become a member of the Federal Trade Commission.

The UCLA administration sent around cards on which faculty members were supposed to state their racial or ethnic identity, as a means of facilitating affirmative action. I checked "Other" and, in the blank provided, wrote "Non-racist."

My colleagues, however, were either more ambivalent or were unwilling to challenge the campus powers that be. I sent a memo to the department chairman.

> February 21, 1976
>
> If the Dutch could wear a star of David during the Nazi occupation, I don't see why tenured faculty members have to cooperate with the racial-ethnic census under "affirmative action." The administration's threat to keep sending IBM cards to those who don't cooperate cannot mean much. We all have wastebaskets.

Those who think that tenure promotes independence have a hard time explaining how readily professors cave in to the slightest pressure.

Data from other studies confirmed what my own research on affirmative action in the academic world had found—that the differences in income between black and white faculty members *with the same qualifications* were trivial or non-existent, and in some cases black professors earned more than comparable white professors. In other words, the real differences were in qualifications, not race. I wrote to a scholar at another university whose study had turned up similar results.

April 13, 1976

Dear Professor Mommsen:

It so happens that I was at H.E.W. [Department of Health, Education and Welfare in Washington] some time after your study on black-white salary differentials was published. I twitted them about the $62 per year salary differential between black and white Ph.D.s and asked if this was what their program was all about! I suggested that they simply mail $62 to every black Ph.D., and offered to take mine immediately in cash, to save them the trouble of processing a check. My comments were not well received.

Believers in affirmative action were not about to give in to mere facts. Critics of my study in one publication were typical. I replied to the editor.

May 5, 1976

Dear Mr. Seltzer:

The very authors who said it was "grossly unfair" for me to leave the impression that "affirmative action has achieved little or no benefits for blacks" *themselves* note in the very same paragraph "the diminished gains for black employment during the past four to five years"—i.e., after "goals," "quotas" or "affirmative action." Indeed, black income as a percentage of white income has *declined* over that span, nationally, in academic and non-academic occupations alike. What this means is that blacks' own pre-quota achievements account for the relative rise of black incomes, occupations, and related advancement. Put bluntly, blacks have had the worst of both worlds—black progress has largely been the result of lifting oneself by the bootstraps but is then *seen* by whites as receiving something for nothing. A program which does little more than de-legitimate what people have achieved on their own is worse than useless.

My nomination to the Federal Trade Commission proved to be a curse in many ways. I had to turn down much-needed opportunities to make some money by giving talks or consulting, since these activities could raise questions about conflicts of interest with my impending duties as a member of the FTC. As time dragged on with neither confirmation hearings nor any indication of any movement in that direction, other people began to question me about what I was going to do with respect to them. The department chairman at UCLA wanted to know if I were going to teach my next scheduled courses or whether he would have to find someone else to teach them. The Center for Advanced Study in the Behavioral Sciences wanted to know whether I would be using the fellowship they had offered me or whether they should offer it to someone else. My friend in Venice wanted to know what my moving to Washington would mean for our relationship. Did I expect her to go with me? And, if so, as what? After a bitter divorce, I was not ready to get married again so soon, even though her question was one that she had a right to ask.

Inquiries to a White House staffer as to what the delay meant brought only soothing assurances, even though I had said from the outset that I would withdraw immediately if there were any opposition. Eventually I discovered that, contrary to the upbeat assurances I had been getting, the Senate committee charged with confirming nominations to the Federal Trade Commission had informed the White House months earlier that they were not going to hold hearings on my nomination, figuring that their party's candidate for President was likely to win that year's election and would then choose his own nominee. I went directly to the office of my White House contact, gave him a few choice words and walked out. A newspaper account said that I slammed the door on my way out of his office but I do not remember whether I did or not. I was certainly angry enough to have done it. Back at my hotel, I penned a brief note to him on hotel stationery.

May 21, 1976

Dear Mr. ******,

As a result of my discovery that I had been grossly misled about my nomination to the Federal Trade Commission, I am no longer willing to continue as a nominee.

The fact that my letters of resignation were getting shorter over the years reflected my growing conviction that it was a waste of time to explain or justify to people who couldn't care less about the truth.

At about this time, my study of successful black schools was published and I sent reprints to many people, including my old friend at the Wharton School.

May 21, 1976

Dear Bernard,

The enclosed paper is my latest attempt to direct some attention toward the ingredients of success rather than lamentations over failure. It was necessarily sketchy, given some of the non-objective factors involved, but whatever its scientific shortcomings, it was the most emotionally satisfying piece of research I have ever done. More than once I found myself on the verge of tears at the inspiring flesh-and-blood results before my eyes.

On a very different topic, I will paraphrase the late Adlai

Stevenson by saying, "A funny thing happened to me on my way to the Federal Trade Commission." Despite your good advice, I allowed the White House, Brimmer, *et.al.*, to get me to reconsider my initial decision to decline the nomination. Then followed months of shilly-shallying and soft soap, until I went to Washington on my own to confront staffers at the White House and on the hill. The net result is that I concluded that a White House staffer had been less than candid, and I was less than diplomatic in telling him so. I also sent them a note saying that I was no longer willing to continue to be a nominee.

I also brought Birdie and Lacy up to date on the situation.

June 1, 1976

Dear Birdie and Lacy,

I was a little surprised, but very pleased, when Ruth told me that you had had doubts about my taking the job in Washington. Most of the people who know me best have also had doubts from the beginning. When an FBI agent asked a former teacher of mine [Mrs. G] whether she thought I was a man of integrity, she said, "Tom has *too much* integrity to be in Washington." Still, I allowed people to talk me out of my original refusal of the nomination—and lived to regret it.

I later learned that the White House had also contacted Milton Friedman to ask him to persuade me to accept the FTC nomination but that he had declined to do so. I wish I had known this at the time, as it might have caused me to continue to decline the nomination and saved me a lot of grief.

Although there were many occasions to lament the sloppy work and immaturity of students at UCLA, there were many other students there who were quite good and who appreciated my teaching. One student who complained about me in a letter to the campus newspaper was immediately counter-attacked by other students who had taken my courses. This continued a pattern of my classes having the effect of polarizing students against one another, as at Douglass College and Howard University, in addition to the polarization within my project at the Urban Institute.

Some of the UCLA students were not merely good but gems. I commented to one of these on her term paper.

June 21, 1976

Dear Miss Knipps:

I do not recall ever reading a better student paper in more than a decade of teaching.

You will undoubtedly do well in whatever you do in life, and I would not be surprised in the years ahead to see your name in the scholarly journals, or the media, depending upon what course you choose. I hope that the road may be smooth and straight for you, but if it has rocky places and detours, have the courage and the confidence to know that these can be overcome and even become part of your human capital. Above all, never let yourself be caught in the intellectual cul-de-sac of a clique or a preconception, or be afraid to change your course, or to keep on changing it as you acquire more evidence or more insight. "Commitment" is a ringing word, but truth is a better guide.

With that, I took leave of UCLA and headed north to become a Fellow at the Center for Advanced Study in the Behavioral Sciences, across the street from Stanford University. I wrote to Mrs. Gadsden, using my new address in Palo Alto.

June 29, 1976

Dear Mrs. G,

The new address above is somewhat in anticipation. Next week I move up to Palo Alto, where I will be a Fellow at the Center for Advanced Study in the Behavioral Sciences. It is something I had been looking forward to for the past few years. It could not have come at a better time. My personal and professional lives are both at crossroads, and a year away from the pressures will be good for me. I need, among other things, to decide if I ever want to teach again . . . . I am also winding up a relationship with a woman who is both "liberated" and clinging—the world's worst combination—but is otherwise a fine person. We will both need time to recover.

Unpredictable madness continues to add a light touch to life. Recently the *New York Times* asked me to do an article titled "On Being a Black 'Conservative'" (I appreciated the quotes around "conservative"), and a situation comedy scheduled to air this fall called me in as a consultant on one of the characters who is a black conservative!

Keep the faith. I am happy just to keep my sanity.

Mrs. G was home in Washington, instead of on one of her many international trips, so I heard back from her soon.

> July 2, 1976
>
> Tom, My Dear,
>
> Your decision to withdraw came as no surprise to me. I had no conviction that you would be well served as a Republican appointee in this climate of controversy and irrationality that we call federal government. The Center will be a far more congenial home for you than the Federal Trade Commission here. . . .
>
> Your two comments about "conservative" impel me to react! I find the label ludicrous for *you*. . . . Whether in or out of quotes, the label does not fit you. . . .
>
> Affectionately and
>
> gratefully,
>
> Mrs. 'G.'

Although the Center for Advanced Study was located near Stanford University, it was in a separate, fenced area up on a hill, leading to some speculation on campus as to what we were doing at this think tank.

> Dear Nort,
>
> The people at Stanford think that all we do is play volleyball at the Center, but I tell them it is "gruelling" work: "Nothing but profound thoughts all day long."

Actually, I seldom showed up at the Center but did most of my work at home in my apartment. Collective creativity never struck me as a promising way to get intellectual work done.

I was invited to give a talk on the east coast and used the trip to go see people in Atlanta, Washington, and New York. Atlanta showed the most dramatic change since I first saw it in 1952.

Back then, I was among a group of young Marines on our way by train from Camp Lejeune to the Pensacola Naval Air Station, where we would be studying photography. We changed trains in Atlanta and the man in charge, who knew nothing about the South, marched us all into a restaurant in the train station for lunch. The police were called and removed the three of us who were black.

This time I went to an upscale restaurant in Atlanta, taking my friend from Venice, who was now living in Atlanta. Since she was a blonde, there was a time when I could have been lynched just for being involved with her. But no one at the restaurant paid any special attention to us. It was a very popular place and jammed with people. The hostess said that there was no table for two available but, just as we turned to leave, she had an idea and told us to wait. There was a table for four occupied by a white couple. She said she would go ask them if it was OK if we joined them. They agreed and the four of us spent a very enjoyable evening together. I often think of this episode when demagogues try to say that there has been no real change in racial matters over the years. The South has changed more than any other region.

After my visit to New York, where I saw family members, I wrote to Ruth Ellen, Birdie's and Lacy's daughter, who was now grown and had children of her own. I always ran her names together when I wrote to her.

> July 21, 1976
>
> Dear Ruthellen,
>
> I have thought some more about our conversation on raising children. I was really very lucky in my early life. I had four adults all to myself, and three of them were young people in the

prime of their lives, with lots of energy, and with no children of their own. I was eleven years old before Jimmy was born, and of course my development pattern was already set by then. Your mother taught me to read long before I went to school, and your father had me following the news before I reached the teen years. When Birdie was reading to me regularly and teaching me to read, she was a young woman who had no household to look after and she was not yet married. Compare the amount of time and attention I received at that stage with what most children get. . . .

Just in quantitative terms, I must have had five times the adult input of most black children. In qualitative terms, it was even more. Birdie and Lacy were a carefree young couple during my formative years. But by the time you were a little child, Lacy was working long hours to support his growing family, and Birdie had her hands full with two small children, and was still trying to help me through my teen years. Even at that time, I realized what a change had taken place in their lives, and I was sorry not to see Lacy as much as I had been used to. But I didn't realize that I had already had the benefit of their best, and was perhaps more fortunate than their own children in that respect. I realize it now and am grateful for it.

My own children have more material things than I had, but now—after the divorce—they will never have the kind of time and attention I received.

I wrote to President Ford on a very different matter.

July 25, 1976

Dear Mr. President:

I am told that a Presidential nominee who no longer wishes to continue as a nominee should address his request for withdrawal to the President himself. Would you please consider this as my request for withdrawal of my nomination to the Federal Trade Commission?

Let me also take this opportunity to thank you for inviting me to attend the White House luncheon where the problem of busing was discussed.

This was one of three visits to the White House during the Ford administration. It was pleasant each time but there is no evidence that anything I said or did had the slightest influence on policy in this or later administrations that invited me to the White House. Most of my appearances before Congressional committees and government agencies over the years likewise had no visible effect. Yet some people became unhinged at the thought of my sinister influence in Washington. When Kenneth Clark went ballistic over that in a debate with me during my trip to the east coast, I told him that, if this was all he had to worry about, he was a very fortunate man. By this time, I had lost whatever residual respect for him I once had, and made no effort to conceal that fact.

Over the years, I began routinely declining invitations from Washington officials, including invitations to White House state dinners, though I would agree to meet with officials if I happened to be in Washington for other reasons. But invitations for me to fly across the country from California to D.C. usually caused me to recall the old slogan from the days of travel restrictions during World War II: "Is this trip necessary?"

A long letter from David Riesman arrived unexpectedly.

August 10, 1976

Dear Dr. Sowell:

Although you wrote me in the summer of 1973 about your work on IQ growing out of your earlier book, *Black Education: Myths and Tragedies*, I have only now had a chance to read that book and to make myself a one-person Gideon Society for it. In the autobiographical sections it is simply magnificent; I had no idea from our exchanges that you had this sort of a struggle for an education, against enemies within the families and among the peer group, and everywhere else. . . . When James Perkins [former president of Cornell University] with whom I sat on the Carnegie Commission on Higher Education told me at the beginning of the COSEP program that all the blacks recruited in this program were successful at Cornell, I said to him that either his admissions people or the officials of the program or somebody was lying to him. . . . Your comment on page 273, that "Jensen is less convinced of the racial intelligence theory than many of those who are denouncing him" is something that was told me a few years ago by a black friend whom I have known for a great many years, and who spoke about "creeping Jensenism" among blacks. It was his judgment that, since

Affirmative Action and similar efforts had removed so many of the alibis blacks once had for not succeeding in American terms, or "succeeding" only in a hustler way, there really must be something to Jensen. Lacking your extraordinary courage, physical and moral, he would never be quoted on this. . . .

                    Sincerely,

                    David Riesman

                                        September 2, 1976

Dear Professor Riesman:

It was very gratifying to receive your recent letter, and I read your reprint in one sitting, in the wee hours of the morning. The intellectual insights received were to some extent offset by a personal sense of the bleakness of the academic scene, at a time when I am pondering whether to return to teaching after my year at the Center. My own academic career has coincided almost exactly with the general decline in intellectual standards and in standards of decency. Last summer, after attending a conference at Princeton, I decided to stop by Douglass College, where I first began teaching. As I walked around the deserted campus, many warm memories and emotions came flooding in, but the contrast with the present was enough to make it a traumatic experience. I left vowing never to return there again. . . .

Your comments on "creeping Jensenism" among blacks

prodded my conscience to get moving on publishing the findings of a research project I directed in Washington a couple of years ago. We collected 70,000 IQ records, from a dozen ethnic groups, going back several decades. The pattern that emerged was that those ethnic groups which were in a similar situation to blacks, half a century ago, had very similar (and sometimes lower) IQs, and as their socioeconomic status rose over the decades, so did their IQs—by about 30 points in the case of Polish-Americans, despite the Polish "joke" fad. In a sense, my conclusions go counter to both Jensen and his critics. Both try to find an explanation for a unique black experience, whereas it seems to me that there is little that needs explaining. . . .

My warm thanks for mentioning my book; would that my publisher would do as much!

I wrote to Birdie and Lacy about a little incident that would assume growing importance in the years ahead.

September 20, 1976

Dear Birdie and Lacy,

The first time I went to Yosemite, it rained both days I was there with the kids. I went back a month later and it rained again for two days—the first rain since I had been there before. I was beginning to think I was jinxed, especially since I was supposed to be back in Palo Alto on the third day for a date with a very interesting woman I had met. However, I decided to stay over in Yosemite the morning of the third day, in case the weather changed, so I could get a few morning pictures anyway. Well, it turned out to be gorgeous weather, and the upshot of it was that I postponed the date for a day, so I could spend the afternoon in Yosemite. Ordinarily I would have been very reluctant to do that, but the woman herself sensed the situation when I phoned her from Yosemite and she made the suggestion. It certainly got our relationship off to a good start. I can really appreciate a considerate woman, especially after having had the opposite experience.

Her name was Mary and it was a name that I would be speaking for many years ahead.

1977

The IQ research from my project at the Urban Institute finally saw the light of day when it was published as a feature article in the *New York Times Magazine* of March 27, 1977. It made an impression on a number of people, including Professor Arthur Jensen, who said that it was the strongest case against his conclusions that he had seen. Someone in Britain—I believe it was the BBC—wanted to arrange a debate between Professor Jensen and me but neither of us liked the idea.

A number of readers wrote to me in response to my *New York Times Magazine* article about race and IQ and I replied to some of them.

April 14, 1977

Dear Mr. * * * * * *:

You are quite right about the disgraceful early history of intelligence testing. Among other things, it shows what can happen when scholars become eager to be "relevant" to policy issues of the day. Even in our own times, grossly exaggerated claims have almost become the norm on both sides of the IQ controversy. Just before Jensen's work, people were saying that science had "proved" the equality of the races, when in fact science had barely formulated the question, much less answered it, one way or another. More recently, Herrnstein, Shockley, *et.al.*, have attempted to make sweeping policy prescriptions for millions of human beings on the basis of evidence and reasoning that would get a student flunked in Logic I.

Ruth, my sister in the family in which I grew up, died. I talked with Birdie on the phone but she did not think I should make a trip across the country for the funeral.

June 27, 1977

Dear Birdie and Lacy,

Just a quick note on the run. The enclosed money order is to help with the phone bills in connection with Ruth's funeral. . . .

In about three weeks I will be heading for Amherst. . . . It has been a good year here in Palo Alto, largely because of a very good woman I met. She has been very understanding since our first date, which I postponed to stay an extra day in Yosemite. It has been a very relaxed relationship, and I don't believe we had a single real argument.

I was going to be a visiting professor for the fall semester at Amherst College. Just before leaving, I acquired custody of my son and we went together. We also visited Birdie and Lacy and I wrote them shortly before Thanksgiving.

November 24, 1977

Dear Birdie and Lacy,

I have a lot to be thankful for this year. It was so good seeing you all, and especially to see you in good health and good spirits. Having John with me has made me happier and apparently he is happier too. I think one of the reasons he felt so at home with you was that I told him beforehand that you were among the dearest people in the world to me.

John and I are invited over to join a friend's family for Thanksgiving dinner. Hardly a week goes by without at least one invitation to something. I am being spoiled in the east. I don't get that kind of attention in Los Angeles.

For reasons unknown, Professor Henry Manne of the University of Miami law school decided that I was the man to give an academic paper there on the legal concept of "state action" and its implications—for a conference that would be attended by leading constitutional law professors across the United States and from other countries. Although I confessed to him that I didn't even know what the concept meant, he was full of confidence that I would master it in no time. Since he was offering a generous honorarium that was much needed, I agreed to do it.

What Henry Manne's confidence was based on, I had no idea. As I began to read the legal cases on "state action," I increasingly felt that I had no clue as to what principle was involved. Eventually, however, I realized that in fact there was *no* principle involved and only then did these cases make any sense as examples of disingenuous judicial policy-making.

Just as I had finally figured all this out and was about to start writing, I noticed the clock and remembered that I had a conference scheduled with John's teacher. From there he and I went to a laundromat to wash our clothes. From there we were off to the supermarket to buy groceries. After we got back home and I prepared dinner and spent some time afterwards with him until it was time for him to go to bed, I found myself too exhausted to do any writing. Although John was not a very demanding child, taking care of him nevertheless took time. My book on knowledge was taking longer to write than any other book I had written before. The paper for the University of Miami did not really add to the delay because much of it was scheduled to be incorporated into the book that was to be called *Knowledge and Decisions*.

I wrote to my friend and colleague Walter Williams about all this.

November 30, 1977

Dear Walter:

The enclosed paper is going to be delivered at the University of Miami Law School next month. Then it should be published somewhere, and finally it will be cannibalized to re-appear in my book on knowledge. And to think people claim we are a wasteful society who do not recycle things!

The Urban Institute study is finally in press. Who would have thought we would all live to see it? Or am I jinxing us? . . . .

John is doing better in many ways, not the least of which is chess. He is leading me 37 games to 34 this month.

The research for my book *Knowledge and Decisions* kindled an interest in the law, and the research that grew out of that made me increasingly skeptical and critical of much legal sophistry. This was expressed in a letter to the *New York Times* provoked by a book review written by well-known law professor Paul Brest.

December 11, 1977

Dear Sirs:

It must take a special kind of gall for Paul Brest to say that the Supreme Court's justification for ignoring the "original intent" of those who wrote the Constitution is "the consent of the living" and "values widely and deeply held by our society." Polls have repeatedly shown blacks as well as whites opposed to quotas—and to school busing. Add the court's disregard of both original intent and current opinion in such areas as capital punishment, and the declining prestige of the court itself, and the picture presented by Professor Brest ends up a complete farce.

1978

Issues of reparations for past injustices, including preferential treatment in the present, continued to arise from time to time and I responded to some of these issues in replies to some of the letters I received.

February 15, 1978

Dear Mr. *****:

Your letter was moving, as something that comes from the heart. In some ways I think we are more in agreement than you might think. Things have been done that are simply unforgivable. Nothing that is done to benefit me today will ever compensate for the murder or torture of another man. I would be ashamed to accept anything on any pretense that it does. Galling as it is, death has put millions of victims and victimizers beyond all human power to help or punish. We have a moral right to feel bitterness toward some and anguish for others, but our actual choices of what to do are limited to the living.

I have seen so-called "preferential admissions" destroy many fine young people here and at other colleges and universities. They need *money* to go to college; they do not need admissions policies that put them where they are likely to fail when they are perfectly capable of succeeding somewhere else. With the financial aid concentrated at the toughest schools, and with many of our young people forced to go where there is money, disasters are built in. Something like the old G.I. Bill would allow them to receive financial aid without going in over their heads academically. Finally, it is no favor to the black community to send them "doctors" who have been let through medical school without really learning what they need to know. I certainly don't want my children operated on by such "doctors," and I don't know anyone else who does.

From time to time, I exchanged letters with public officials over policy issues. A letter from Senator William Proxmire of Wisconsin, a prominent Democrat, raised a question in which I had long had an interest.

February 20, 1978

Dear Mr. Sowell:

Paul McCracken has told me of your work in studying the problem of black unemployment and the perplexing failure of black unemployment to improve in the past year anything like the way white unemployment improved.

In view of the enactment of a whole series of anti-discrimination laws in the 60's and in view of the substantial improvement in the education of young blacks, it is very difficult to understand why teenage unemployment, particularly, has been so persistently high and why, given the substantial increase in the black population, participation in the work force by blacks has not increased in the same proportion as white participation has increased.

Any views at all you may have on this subject would be very welcome indeed.

Sincerely,

Bill Proxmire

Since I seldom passed up an opportunity to explain a little economics to those who were making policy, I was happy to have an opportunity to discuss this with one of the more sensible members of Congress.

March 13, 1978

Dear Senator Proxmire:

The extremely high unemployment rates among black teenagers and young adults appear quite puzzling at first, in view of the anti-discrimination laws that you mentioned—and still more puzzling when looking back through time and seeing that those unemployment rates were nowhere near as high—nor significantly different from their white contemporaries—back in the late 1940s and early 1950s. However, this additional puzzle also provides a clue as to what is and is not a major influence on the current situation.

"Racism" has been an all too easy explanation, but surely no one would say that there was *less* racism in the 1940s and 1950s than today. The same point is reinforced when looking at the steep *decline* in unemployment rates among young blacks between their late teens and late twenties. They have not ceased being black, but they have somehow ceased being unemployable. You mentioned the difference in labor force participation rates between the black and white populations as a whole. Historically, that too is a relatively recent phenomenon. Every census from 1890 through 1930 showed blacks with a *higher* labor force participation rate than whites. In recent years it is just the reverse, and the gap is widening. Again, it is hard to believe that there was less racism in the earlier period.

What has been true of the post-1930 era in general, and the post-1950 era in particular is (1) a growing elimination of low-skilled, low-wage jobs, and (2) the creation of more alternatives such as unemployment benefits, welfare, etc. The rise of various forms of wage-fixing, through unions and government—but especially the Fair Labor Standards Act—has simply priced inexperienced black youngsters out of the market. The timing of the effects is about as conclusive as social data ever get. Although the minimum wage law was passed in 1938, its level and coverage remained virtually unchanged in money terms through a decade marked by inflation that virtually repealed the law as an economic reality. Beginning in the 1950s, the minimum wage was repeatedly raised—and perhaps equally or more important—its coverage broadened so that there was "no place to hide" for the low-skill worker whose labor could not command the wage the government made a prerequisite for his employment. Numerous studies by independent academic economists, using different techniques, have documented that this has had an especially devastating effect on black teenagers.

Some people argue that the answer to black youth unemployment is either a general "full employment" policy or specific job-creation programs targeted for that group. Neither seems promising to me. Black teenage unemployment has never been as low, during even the fullest employment years of the past quarter-century of rising minimum wages, as it was in the *recession* year of 1949. Full employment has simply never compensated for pricing these young people out of the market. Job-creating programs on top of full employment have not done it either.

The steep decline in unemployment rates among black youths between their late teens and mid-to-late twenties suggests an enormous value to early job experience, even in so-called "dead end" jobs. This seems far less likely to be due to "skills," as ordinarily conceived, than to acquiring the necessary work habits—the discipline of a schedule, the ability to work with others, and the general shedding of immaturity. As one who was once part of those black teenage unemployment statistics—thank God, in the 1940s when it wasn't so bad—I know how painful the adjustment can be for both young workers and for the employer. In retrospect, it is easy enough to see that it would never have paid an employer to hire me at a "reasonable" wage for an experienced adult. What worries me about job-creation is that the jobs created will be watered down in their on-the-job requirements and therefore unduly prolong the transition to maturity. Working for a "program" that has to hire you (legally or politically) may be counterproductive preparation for working for a private employer who doesn't. Much of the special problems of the black youngster is due precisely to his having been passed through schools without any real standards. To extend that same principle into the first stage of the job market may simply postpone his adjustment to the adult world of work.

Senator Proxmire's reply indicated that this may have been one of my few discussions with politicians that was worthwhile.

March 22, 1978

Dear Professor Sowell:

Thank you so much for your excellent letter of March 13 setting forth your thoughtful, persuasive analysis and reason for the perplexing performance of black unemployment in recent years.

Your analysis is unique in its historic perspective. By going back to 1890 when you were able to throw into relief the effect of the elimination of low-skilled, low-wage jobs and the creation of alternatives such as unemployment benefits and welfare plus the Fair Labor Standards Act and especially the broadening of the minimum wage law.

This is most helpful.

> Many thanks.
>
> Sincerely,
>
> Bill Proxmire

Among the educational issues I dealt with were remedial education—in this case, in a memo to Bill Allen, a colleague at UCLA.

> May 17, 1978
>
> TO: William R. Allen
>
> FROM: Thomas Sowell
>
> SUBJECT: Remedial Training at UCLA
>
> Your general economic approach to remedial education is one that is easy to agree with. However, the same question can be approached from the standpoint of the best interests of the students rather than the alternative use of resources by UCLA. The first question I would ask is: Why should a student with some given educational background be directed to an institution whose student body has a substantially different educational background when there are plenty of institutions whose students have educational backgrounds comparable to his? The fact that the first set of institutions—research universities, such as UCLA—stand higher in the academic pecking order is of pathetically little relevance to his education. If anything, it means

that the teaching may receive less emphasis and be pitched at a level that presupposed the kind of reading speed, math background, etc., found in the general student body at such a school. Plenty of intelligent, conscientious, and deserving students—especially from minority backgrounds—simply have not had the kinds of education that produce such reading speed, math facility, etc. . . .

There is no advantage to failing at UCLA over failing somewhere else, and there is certainly no advantage to having a student fail at UCLA who could have succeeded somewhere else. Nor is it educationally or psychologically beneficial to spend four years preoccupied with "survival"—avoiding courses that might push you over the edge—thereby distorting the whole educational experience and so constricting future opportunities.

Because so much depends on the sheer *speed* with which a student can assimilate verbal and mathematical materials, he may be able to absorb and understand *more* material where the pace is suitable for his level of reading and math than at a "better" institution with a faster pace adapted to students whose reading and math scores are higher. This is especially so in logically structured material, such as economics or mathematics, where a failure to understand the foundations can plague all subsequent efforts to understand material built on those foundations. A student who is perfectly capable of understanding economics taught at a certain pace can find it incomprehensible when taught at a much faster pace. To create "special" programs for such students at fast-paced institutions is to attempt to duplicate what already exists at institutions that proceed at a more "normal" pace.

Finally, it is questionable whether professors in a research institution, or their graduate assistants, are better able to teach remedial courses than professors at institutions that put a greater emphasis on teaching.

The College of the City of New York (CCNY), a quality institution once described as "the poor man's Harvard," faced demands for "open admissions"—no academic standards for getting in. I wrote to one of the faculty members there who had opposed the drive to fling the doors open to all comers—and who apparently had suffered denunciations for his efforts.

May 18, 1978

Dear Professor Gross:

Someone had to say what you said, and apparently no one else had the courage. The jackals will have their day, but the power of one man speaking the truth is indicated by their outcries.

It so happens that I grew up in Harlem near CCNY and one of my thwarted dreams was to go there when I reached college age. It was several years later when the G.I. Bill enabled me to

> go away to college. But while I can understand how other young
> people have the same ambition I had, what is the point of going
> to CCNY if it is no longer CCNY after you are admitted?

The educational situation among minority students continued to generate letters back and forth, often involving the question of whether "test bias" explained the low performance of black students.

June 9, 1978

Dear Mrs. Copeland:

I know all too well the educational handicaps that so many of our youngsters have to overcome, having been through it myself. At the age of eight, I moved from Charlotte, N.C., to New York City, and found the higher educational standards very difficult to cope with. From being the top student in my class down south I was suddenly the bottom student—and trailing the pack by a substantial margin, at that. Decades later, when I was conducting some research on IQs, I happened to come across the IQs of the school I went to in Harlem, as of the time I entered it. The kids I had trouble keeping up with had an average IQ of 84! I will not retell all the rest of the story, having done so already in *Black Education: Myths and Tragedies.*[2] Suffice it to say, within a few years I was able to hold my own in a class where the average IQ was over 120. This does not mean that IQs are irrelevant. I had in fact changed a lot in those years.

---

2. Also in my *A Personal Odyssey*, Chapter 2.

It so happens that one of my file drawers is full of various IQ tests, and I am appalled at some of the questions they ask to test "intelligence." Still, here as elsewhere in life, the real question is not how they stack up against what we might hope for, but how do they compare to the alternatives? All the other methods of mass assessment that I know of are even more biased against the poor and the disadvantaged. My personal experience is in accord with this: I was assigned to a class for backward students just a year before I was assigned to a class for advanced students. The first assignment was *not* based on test scores and the second assignment was.

In general, the tragic fact is that most of the poor test results among poor, disadvantaged, and minority youngsters reflect their actual level of achievement, not test bias. However, it is also true that similar scores were common among various European minorities as of about World War I, and their IQs have risen as their circumstances changed. I don't have the slightest doubt that the same thing will happen with blacks, and to some extent has already been happening in some places, as the enclosed study indicates.

When someone I knew received an appointment to the White House staff, I sent my congratulations.

January 9, 1979

Dear ******:

I am delighted that there will now be one more person in Washington with his head screwed on right. I hope there will be enough of you to have a game of bridge. I cannot imagine that there will be enough for a baseball game.

Trying to get some UCLA students to think could be a real struggle. A lengthy critique of one student's presentation in a seminar that I taught included the following.

April 25, 1979

More profoundly disturbing than the lack of analytic thinking in your presentation was an apparent unawareness of any distinction between analysis and cursory conclusions. Even after analytic points were spelled out to you, your response was "But didn't I just say the same things?" No. You did *not* say the same thing. Many people noted that apples fell off trees long before Newton, but they did not say "the same thing" as Newton.

It is precisely the systematic development of whys and wherefores that constitutes physics—or economics.

System, structure, logic, and definition are not mere traditions, like etiquette. They are the very guts of what reasoning is all about. They are what enable you to distinguish between some words that have a good ring to the ear and an idea that makes sense. That distinction is more than formalistic. It has been a matter of life and death in such places as Jonestown and Nazi Germany, and California abounds with little groups that prey on those who cannot make such distinctions.

With other students I sometimes used a different analogy, pointing out that a pile of building materials dumped onto an empty lot is not a house, even if these materials contain everything that a house contains. Whether any of this got through is something I have no way of knowing—and it is probably just as well.

The 1980s

The 1980s were another turning point in my life in many ways, personal and professional. The first, and one of the most important, of these changes was set in motion by the completion and publication of the book I had been working on since the mid-1970s, *Knowledge and Decisions*. I considered it the most important book I had written, and apparently so did others.

1980

One of the first indications of the impact that *Knowledge and Decisions* would have came in a letter from a leading economist, James Buchanan, who would later win a Nobel Prize in economics.

---

21 January 1980

Dear Tom:

Thanks for sending me a copy of your *Knowledge and Decisions*. (I can give to some colleague the copy I ordered from Basic Books.)

You have written a great book, and I do not recall ever having said that to anyone. I hope that the book has the success it surely deserves to have. It should be required reading for every social scientist, philosopher, intellectual and politician. I wish I had written it. . . .

Sincerely,

Jim Buchanan

Two economists who had already received Nobel Prizes—Milton Friedman and Friedrich Hayek—also publicly praised *Knowledge and Decisions* and Senator Daniel Patrick Moynihan added his congratulations.

January 28, 1980

Dear Tom:

I have been reading in *Knowledge and Decisions*, snatching quotes for various purposes. How on earth did you get time to think something through that complex! Will power, I suppose. And brainpower. I once had traces of the latter, anyway, and salute you!

> Best,
>
> Pat

The most important consequence of *Knowledge and Decisions*, however, was that Milton Friedman brought it to the attention of Glenn Campbell, Director of the Hoover Institution.

February 19, 1980

Dear Tom:

I am pleased to confirm our telephone conversation of February 14; namely, that the President of Stanford University has approved your appointment as a Senior Fellow on the staff of the Hoover Institution on War, Revolution, and Peace, effective at your earliest convenience, and hopefully, no later than September 1 of this year.

> Sincerely yours,
>
> Glenn

Becoming a Senior Fellow at the Hoover Institution meant becoming a permanent scholar in residence at this think tank on the Stanford campus—with no teaching or other duties and with freedom to write on whatever I wished to write on. It was the chance of a lifetime for an enjoyable and fulfilling career. Yet there was also a certain irony in this, since teaching is what first attracted me to the academic world, with research and publication being sidelines, and even to some extent ways of creating reading material for use in my classes.

———————

Among the questions that continued to arouse my interest were education and the role of intellectuals in affecting public policy.

June 23, 1980

Dear Professor Levine:

We are certainly more in accord on education than on some other subjects. Your idea for academically selective high schools, along the lines of those in New York, is one I have long believed in, and tried to promote, with an unbroken record of failure.

In this and other ways, I am coming more and more to believe that ideas are accepted or rejected because they fit in with some pre-existing over-all vision of the world, or because they enhance the prospects of some special interests. Our idea does neither.

Intellectuals affect policy indirectly, by shaping the general vision within which discussion takes place. They also turn out floods of "studies" which "prove" the kind of corollaries implied by the vision. Many of the most influential of these studies are shabby and pathetic as analysis. The two that come to mind most readily are Kenneth Clark's study cited in *Brown v. Board of*

> *Education* and the Thorstein Sellin study which provided the basis
> for the dogma that capital punishment does not deter. Most people
> in their own lives would not have changed their brand of socks on
> the basis of the kind of "evidence" presented in these studies. But
> both studies told people what they wanted to hear, and what was
> part of a larger vision of the social process.

In the wake of the landslide election of Ronald Reagan to be President of the United States, a number of black organizations launched bitter attacks on his administration—which did not yet exist. Some of us thought that the public should not be led to believe that these organizations represented the views of all blacks, on this or a whole range of other issues. The result was that a conference called "Black Alternatives" was hastily organized in a period of a couple of weeks and was held at the Fairmont Hotel in San Francisco in December 1980. I gave the keynote address. Since this conference was about exploring alternatives, people of varying views took part, leading to healthy debates rather than the kinds of bitter recriminations usually associated with differences of opinion on racial issues. The success of the Fairmont conference was reflected not only in the spirit of good will which prevailed there but also in more and better press coverage than we had anticipated. It also led to plans to create an on-going organization to sponsor more such conferences in the future and promote views different from those of the traditional black civil rights organizations. Among those who generously agreed to fly out to San Francisco on short notice was an old friend at the Wharton School in Philadelphia.

> December 16, 1980
>
> Dear Bernard:
>
> It would be hard to over-estimate the importance of your
> contribution to the success of the conference. The first session,
> and the tone it set, was important for the way the audience

perceived what we were about. It was also important for the way the conference was perceived by the press, and therefore by a still larger audience elsewhere. If we had had a party line and an Amen corner of discussants, we would have been discredited from the outset. The vigor of your disagreement with Walter [Williams], and the courtesy and friendship that went with it, were priceless (if a Chicago economist may use that word).

1981

The most important event of 1981 was that I remarried. I wed my dear friend Mary, whom I had first met during my year at the Center for Advanced Study in 1976. I waited longer than I should have, as a result of a terrible first marriage and bitter divorce. But better late than never.

Nineteen eighty one was also a financial turning point, as my increased visibility brought more invitations to give speeches across the country, the fees lifting me from a state of being almost completely broke after a costly divorce and its on-going financial obligations to being able, by the fall of the year, to put a down payment on a house, for the first time in my life. This increased visibility also caused me to get more mail from strangers. Some suggested that I run for public office.

January 5, 1981

Dear Mr. ******,

Thank you for your letter of encouragement. I happen to think that if the country is going to survive as a free and prosperous nation, it is going to be through the efforts of people like you who have risen through adversity, not those who were born with a silver spoon in their mouth—who sometimes think the answer is to have the government put silver spoons in *everybody's* mouth.

While I appreciate your suggestion that I could contribute by becoming part of the government, I am more inclined to the opinion (and the example) of Milton Friedman, that some individuals can contribute more by staying out of government. Certainly it is hard to imagine Reagan's election victory without the changed climate of opinion to which Milton Friedman contributed over the past 20 years.

A weekly column that I had been writing for the *Los Angeles Herald Examiner* when I was teaching at UCLA ended after I left Los Angeles, and I made no attempt to resume it elsewhere. However, in January 1981 *Washington Post* editor Meg Greenfield offered me an opportunity to have a bi-weekly column in that paper and also sent me some clippings about the Washington school system, leading to my reply.

January 15, 1981

Dear Meg:

Thank you for sending me the clippings about Vincent Read and the D.C. school system—though, frankly, they ruined my whole day. Still, I am grateful to learn of someone like Mr. Read, whom I may want to contact at some point.

The idea of writing a bi-weekly column for the *Post* seems more attractive the more I think of it, though I wouldn't be able to start until April. However, I did a couple of columns on a subject I think needs to be confronted clearly—and just once. I hope you find them suitable, but in any event I look forward to talking more about the idea of a column when you are out here in March for our conference.

Here are the two columns, which were published in the *Washington Post* in February 1981.

BLACKER THAN THOU

Most white people are unaware of the internal social history of blacks and what it means in the struggle for black leadership today. Throughout the Western Hemisphere, those blacks whose ancestors somehow became free during the era of slavery had a head start in economic and social development. So too did those who worked as house servants or in a few other special roles among slaves, for they absorbed more of the dominant culture than did field hands. The descendants of both special groups have historically been overrepresented among black leaders and among more prosperous blacks generally. Their descendants have also typically been lighter in complexion than other blacks, for their ancestors' closer association with whites took many forms. Why is this history important today? Because the traditional light-skinned elite have found themselves increasingly challenged by rising members of the black masses. Generations of snobbishness by the lighter-skinned elite have left a legacy of hostility within the black community, which makes current issues difficult to resolve—or even discuss rationally—on their merits. Moreover, some members of the old elite have in recent times become converts to blackness—and, like other converts, are often the most extreme. Just as religious converts sometimes become holier-than-thou, so these converts become blacker-than-thou.

Many of the giants of the black civil rights movement have been of this sort. W. E. B. DuBois, who helped found the NAACP, epitomized the militant black leader who was not only distant from but snobbish toward the people in whose name he spoke. DuBois grew up among educated whites in Massachusetts, and he and his white friends looked down on Irish working-class people. As a young man, DuBois had his first experience living among blacks, and he did not condescend to speak to the people in the barbershop where he had his hair cut. In his heyday as a civil rights leader, DuBois lived at 409 Edgecombe Avenue in New York—then a stately apartment building with uniformed doormen and a separate (and by no means equal) entrance for the servants and delivery people through the basement.

No small part of the historic clash between the followers of DuBois and those of Booker T. Washington was that DuBois' followers were elite descendants of "free persons of color" and Booker T. Washington was "up from slavery." Despite much caricaturing of their political positions in recent years, their substantive differences on the issues of their times were small and almost trivial. Their agendas were the same, even when their priorities were different. Many other leaders in other groups have cooperated despite much larger political differences.

In our own time, Andrew Young has thundered from the left on all sorts of issues, and always from a militant stance of being blacker-than-thou. He is a descendant of the privileged elite of New Orleans—historically, the most snobbish of the black elites. (Light-skinned jazz great Jelly Roll Morton was disowned by his Creole grandmother for associating with common Negroes.) Andrew Young's family has gone to college for generations, which is more than most white people can say.

Young's primary concern has been to defend the image of blacks—which is to say, to defend his own image in the white elite circles in which he moves. What happens to actual flesh-and-blood blacks seems never to have aroused the same fervor in Andrew Young. Though not a reticent man, he had relatively little to say when thousands of Africans were tortured and slaughtered by Idi Amin and other tyrants. He saved his outbursts for those who sullied the image of blacks.

Historically, the black elite has been preoccupied with symbolism rather than pragmatism. Like other human beings, they have been able to rationalize their special perspective and self-interest as the general good. Much of their demand for removing racial barriers was a demand that they be allowed to join the white elite and escape the black masses. It would be hard to understand the zeal and resources that went into the battle against restrictive covenants (at a period of history when most blacks were too poor to buy a house anywhere) without understanding that this was a way for the black elite to escape the black masses.

Whatever the crosscurrents of motivations that moved the civil rights establishment, there were areas of crying injustices— Jim Crow laws and lynchings—where they made historic contributions that should never be forgotten. The point here is that there is no reason to expect their agendas and priorities to permanently coincide with those of the black masses in whose name they speak. Public opinion polls make it painfully clear that the two sets of black opinions are often diametrically opposed.

Public opinion polls show that most blacks favor tougher treatment of criminals. The NAACP has gone in the opposite direction, following the lead of white middle-class liberals. Most blacks favor education vouchers that would give them a choice of where to send their children to school and some leverage in dealing with public school bureaucrats. The black "leadership" is totally opposed, for they have their own grand designs that could not be carried out if every black were free to make up his own mind. Central to the civil rights crusade is school busing—which has never had majority support among blacks and which has even been opposed by local NAACP chapters. Job quotas are another civil rights organization crusade, but rejected by most blacks.

Black "leadership" in general does not depend on expressing the opinions of blacks but on having access to whites—in the media, in politics and in philanthropy. Whites who have a limited time to give to the problems of blacks need a few familiar blacks they can turn to. The civil rights organizations provide that convenience. Confronted with the anomaly that black "spokesmen" regularly appear on television saying things directly opposite to black public opinion, a well-known newsman replied: "We can put Ben Hooks and Jesse Jackson on television, but we can't put the Gallup Poll on television."

For the moment, the conventional black leadership has a virtual monopoly on expressing what blacks are supposed to believe. But it is an insecure monopoly. It is vulnerable to exposure to the truth. And after years of being able to get by with a few cliches and charges of "racism" against its critics, the old conventional leadership is in no condition to conduct an intellectual battle over issues of substance. Smears and innuendoes are about all it has left. Some of those will be explored in a subsequent piece.

BLACKER   THAN   THOU (II)

One of my most memorable evenings was spent with two old friends with radically different political views. They were dinner guests, and the revealing exchange between them spoke volumes about internal black social differences.

One was Walter Williams, a black economist from a ghetto background. Walter's economic research convinced him that blacks had more to gain through the economic system than the political system. This conclusion caused the media to give him the misnomer "a black conservative," though I have never heard Walter express the slightest nostalgia for bygone days.

The other friend was a black sociologist whom I will call Hal, who was the latest of several generations of his family to go to college. Hal was the classic ultra-militant. He had a picture of Mao on his living room wall and a picture of Eldridge Cleaver in the kitchen (at that time). He had hung out with Malcolm X and had protested everything but the weather. He was at his most eloquent in denouncing "this fascist country" while looking out the window of his air-conditioned condominium in a white neighborhood.

Hal's eloquence was so great that many affluent white housewives enrolled in the college course he taught, just to hear this black man "tell it like it is." So many people tried to enroll in his course that the administration had to ask him to give priority to those students who needed it to graduate. Only after that should it be made available to white housewives looking for their jollies.

Hal seldom wasted his eloquence on me—for I was not above reminding him that I had to give him directions to Harlem, even after he had lived in New York for several years.

One of the things I had never known before this dinner was that Walter and Hal both grew up in Philadelphia, and at the same time. Once Walter learned this, he immediately began asking about various childhood friends from the ghetto.

"Do you know Bill—?"

"No."

"What about Joe—?"

"No."

It went on and on, with Hal looking more and more uneasy. Finally, a puzzled Walter asked him: "Well, where did you live?"

When Hal replied, Walter said: "I didn't know any black

people lived out there."

"We were the only ones."

Hal is by no means unique, which is why there is no point singling him out by giving his real name. He is only one of many members of the black elite who know little or nothing about the ghetto, but who lecture, write and consult on the subject. Many are blacker-than-thou.

One of the architects of the disastrous "open admissions" programs in New York's municipal colleges is a black man who attended otherwise all-white private schools throughout his childhood, then went on to Harvard from freshman to PhD and did post-doctoral work at the Sorbonne. He has accused me of not speaking for ghetto blacks. The first head of the EEOC was another member of the old black elite whose childhood was spent in private, predominantly white schools. He was a key figure in the process that turned "equal opportunity" into quotas (that didn't work), to the accompaniment of militant rhetoric that eventually propelled him upward into the job of Secretary of the Army.

Very often the media regard the most noisy blacks as the most typical blacks. Those of us who take a different economic or political view—people like Walter Williams or myself—are grilled about our backgrounds by reporters who suspect that we are middle-class, because we disagree with those whom the press has blindly accepted as the voice of blacks. The old elite is very good at playing on media misconceptions, especially when they have run out of substantive arguments. A recent smear campaign against Walter Williams, myself and other new voices among blacks has played the theme that we have either forgotten our roots or never had any.

One of those whose monopoly of blackness is being threatened is columnist Carl Rowan, who claims the new black voices are "Horatio Algers" who don't want other blacks to be helped to advance. Disagreeing with Carl Rowan about the best way to advance blacks is the same as being against the advancement of blacks, as far as he is concerned. He even puts outrageous attacks on blacks in quotation marks, as if he is actually quoting someone. He cannot quote what we actually said, because that would expose the falseness of his attacks.

Someone that Rowan does quote is Patricia Roberts Harris from the Carter Cabinet, who asserts that Williams and Sowell "don't know what poverty is." This would be funny if it were not such a pathetic sign of intellectual bankruptcy. Neither of us was ever as middle class as Patricia Roberts Harris. None of our parents was a schoolteacher, or even finished high school. I was almost 9 years old before I lived in a home with [hot] running water.

Ironically, Patricia Roberts Harris and I were students at the same college, but under entirely different conditions. I worked full time and went to school at night. Patricia Harris was a campus social leader in an "exclusive" sorority—meaning that it was for middle-class (light-skinned) women. That was before it became fashionable to be blacker-than-thou.

The great social and economic issues facing black Americans today need to be argued out in terms of substance, evidence and analysis. The problem is that blacker-than-thou arguments confuse the issues, and these seem to be the only kinds of arguments the old conventional black leadership has left. They are on as shaky ground there as they are on more substantive matters. But the false issues they raise must be confronted, precisely so that we can then turn our attention to matters of far greater importance for black people and for this country.

These two columns sparked the bitterest attacks on me before or since. An entire page of a later issue of the *Washington Post*—which is not a tabloid—was devoted exclusively to denunciations of me by Patricia Roberts Harris, columnist Carl Rowan and assorted others. This was due, I believe, not only to what I had said, or even that I had revealed the dirty little secret of internal color discrimination among blacks in a white newspaper, but that I did so in a Washington paper. Had I said the same things in Los Angeles or Denver, critics could have simply denied the facts and called me a liar. But too many blacks in Washington were all too well aware of the truth of the damaging charge of internal color discrimination for critics to do anything other than vent their anger and frustration.

A humorous note was struck by a former Cornell colleague, Bob Kilpatrick, in a brief letter which included the following:

> February 16, 1981
>
> Dear Tom,
>
> If your previous writings were not a strong enough signal that you weren't seeking a political job, I trust that your recent pair of articles on the op-ed page of the *Post* will do the trick.

The planned conference referred to in my letter to Meg Greenfield was to be a sequel to the highly successful "Black Alternatives" conference which had been held at the Fairmont Hotel in San Francisco a couple of months earlier. This second conference was planned to mark the establishment of a permanent organization to air alternative views to those of the traditional civil rights organizations on racial issues. But, despite many efforts by many people to organize this conference to be held at the Hoover Institution in March, and to create the beginnings of organizational chapters in various parts of the country, this second conference never took place nor did the projected organization materialize. Despite all my warnings to those who were organizing this effort, that an organization had to be in place before anything was announced in the media, so that the inevitable responses from the public and the media could be directed to whoever would head up this organization—rather than to me—one of those who knew about our plans could not keep his mouth shut and leaked news of the impending organization to a reporter for the *Washington Post*.

I couldn't get any research or writing done and my secretary could not type a letter without multiple interruptions by phone calls, all day long and day after day. We also had the task of proofreading the galleys of my new book, *Ethnic America*, so that it could be published that fall. All this, on top of trying to arrange innumerable details for the planned conference, had both of us working overtime, night after night, until exhaustion caught up with me and my rising blood pressure forced me to cancel everything and just stay home to recover. The cancellation led to a new round of sensationalized stories, depicting me as being hospitalized by hostile protest calls, when in fact I was not in a hospital and had not been in a hospital in more than a decade—and the vast majority of the calls were from enthusiastic supporters wanting to know how they could join the new organization or wanting more details about it, as well as innumerable media inquiries.

I thought that those in various parts of the country who had tried to help get this conference and this organization started deserved a better explanation of

what had happened than they were getting from the media, so I sent out a letter
to them all.

March 16, 1981

Dear Colleagues and Friends:

This letter is to bring you up to date in the wake of the
cancellation of the Black Alternatives Conference II.

Let me, first of all, express my appreciation to those who
were concerned about my health. Although I have been
temporarily sidelined with medical problems, I am neither
hospitalized nor bedridden. I am taking it easy for a couple of
weeks, and will probably never resume as frenetic a pace as I
have had for the past two months. Looking back at the incredible
amount and variety of work undertaken during that period, I can
see now that I was lucky to have lasted as long as I did, and to
have suffered nothing worse than a passing setback.

One of the ideas I was exploring was some way of enabling
black people who are receptive to alternative policy approaches
to be in touch with each other. Sensationalized and distorted
accounts of these preliminary explorations appeared in the press
as a result of leaks. The good side of this, however, was a
gratifying response from blacks around the country—from
students, community and professional people—wanting to be part
of a rethinking of our vision. . . .

All this response, without my having lifted a finger to recruit anyone, convinced me that (1) there was an important constituency out there, and that (2) the task of organizing them far exceeded what I could take on and still continue to research and write. . . .

My thanks to all those who have helped me in many ways—from my secretary who has borne the brunt of protecting my time from innumerable telephone interruptions, to colleagues around the country who have agreed to travel great distances at inconvenient times for no money, to help forward the cause of rational discussion of differences on the problems of our race and our country.

A week later I wrote to Meg Greenfield.

March 23, 1981

Dear Meg:

I am in the process of cutting back my activities in order to minimize medical problems. I shall not be writing a column for the *Post* as originally planned. The problem is not so much time as it is having other people expecting me to do things and carrying the weight of those expectations. Therefore, I am clearing my calendar. If and when I write anything suitable for the press, I shall at that time consider the question of a suitable outlet for it.

A year later, I submitted one column that was published in the

Washington Post but made no effort to write a regular column anywhere.

The failure of the second "Black Alternatives" conference to take place, and still more so the failure of the projected organization to materialize, were a continuing disappointment to me as I saw, again and again, that there was nothing like the rational atmosphere elsewhere when it came to discussing racial issues. This inability to have reasoned discussions of racial issues troubled me, even when I was not involved. Not only militant extremists but even "moderate" and "respectable" black intellectuals increasingly responded to unwelcome news with ad hominem attacks on whoever turned up the facts that they did not want to face. I wrote a letter to the *New York Times* in response to one such ad hominem attack on the distinguished scholar James Coleman.

April 20, 1981

To the Editor:

The degeneration of reasoned discourse on serious issues is nowhere better illustrated than in the current controversy over James Coleman's recent report on private schools. Questions of *fact* are turned into questions of *motive*. It is especially sad to see Yale Professor James Comer use *The New York Times* for a lengthy attack on Coleman in which not one fact was contradicted nor a single countervailing fact asserted. Instead, he regales us with other people's bad motives—to restore "separate and unequal schools," to "write off the poor and limit their opportunities," to pander to "the grumbling of middle income parents."

Even more important than the issues involved in this particular controversy is the fundamental question whether we shall expect—and demand—facts and reasons, or whether we shall continue to accept presumptions of moral superiority as a justification of intellectual garbage.

———————

Amid all the odd things that were going on, a letter arrived in the mail at the Hoover Institution from Audrey, whom I had last spoken with back in 1974—and it was nine years before that when I last saw her. She was now living in California. As in the past, it was not always easy to figure out what Audrey meant. In fact I handed the letter to my secretary and said:

"Women are too subtle for me, Beverly. What is she saying?"

Beverly read it and replied: "She's saying, 'Come up and see me sometime.'"

May 13, 1981

Dear Audrey:

Your letter was of course a pleasant surprise. To say that much has happened over the years is an understatement. The baby I was holding in my arms the last time I saw you is now 16 years old, wears the same size shoe as I do, has a higher chess rating than I do, and operates his own computer (which I can't). The last time I talked with you on the phone—1974—I was at one of my lowest ebbs, but now I am in one of the happiest periods of my life. Back in 1974, I was wrestling with the question of whether to start a custody battle for my children. My lawyer—thank God—talked me out of it at the eleventh hour. Three years later I received custody of my son anyway, and his development and happiness have improved a lot since then. My daughter visits me, and will in fact be here this coming weekend. I have also met a wonderful woman and we were married in January.

Incidentally, it would be a decade later before I would finally begin to use a computer. Before then, a colleague at Stanford who was more up to date on the computer revolution called me "the last of the Luddites."

Among the recurring problems with much that is said in the media and in academia are unsubstantiated assertions that become "well-known facts" by sheer repetition. My concern over this was expressed in various ways to various academics and others. Among the academics were Glenn Loury and Robert Klitgaard, at the time professors respectively at the University of Michigan and at Harvard.

May 27, 1981

Dear Ms. ******:

I would be fascinated to see the "clear proof" that "exploitation" (meaning what?) both exists and is responsible for the poverty of the Third World. For years I have looked in vain for this evidence, reading reams of Marxist rhetoric and liberal moralizing in hopes of finding some factual needle in the verbal haystack. You can save an old man a lot of needless work if you will send me the "clear proof" you have found.

June 15, 1981

Dear Professor Loury:

You assert as something that "should be clear" something that is not clear at all: "Racial minorities are undoubtedly worse off today by virtue of the historical use of procedures which did not respect their liberty." It is indeed obvious that Kunta Kinte was worse off because of slavery, but it is not equally clear that Alex Haley is. When Haley visited his ancestral village, he did not find the people living better than he did, even before receiving the royalties from *Roots*. Certainly blacks would be better off if—once in America—we were treated like other Americans. But that is another issue and independent of the proposition expressed. If Kunta Kinte's liberty had been respected, it by no means follows that Alex Haley would be better off. Kunta Kinte's liberty should have been respected on entirely different grounds.

August 18, 1981

Dear Professor Klitgaard:

What I find somewhat disconcerting are your offhand assertions—without a speck of evidence—that Malay-Chinese differences are "myths and stereotypes" or "caricatures." It is hard to make any sense of the history of the Chinese in southeast Asia without acknowledging that they are indeed very different from most of the indigenous peoples of that region. If these differences are popularly expressed in imprecise language, that seems secondary to the reality. At the very least, the question whether or to what degree there are performance differences behind the income differences is absolutely crucial. It is not enough to glide from differences to inequalities to inequities to "solutions," however fashionable this series of non-sequiturs has become.

As the media became more aware of me, I became more aware of the media—and of media irresponsibility. Many in the media needed no facts whatever to make a story. One such story involved a supposed controversy between me and Urban League president Vernon Jordan.

July 8, 1981

Dear Vernon:

You may or may not have noticed some press statements suggesting that there is some bitter controversy between us. The first one I saw was a column in the *Washington Post* denouncing me for having "castigated" Vernon Jordan. I looked in vain through my articles in question for any mention of Vernon Jordan or the Urban League. Indeed, I looked through the indexes of my books and could not find your name anywhere! Nevertheless, I have seen the same theme picked up by other journalists.

Vernon Jordan's reply included the following paragraph:

> July 30, 1981
>
> Dear Tom:
>
> Yes, I have seen those reports in the papers—pay them no mind. It is difficult for some people to understand that political or ideological differences need be no bar to friendship and mutual respect. And anyway, the press loves a good fight so if one does not exist, it will try to create one.

For months I declined all attempts to get me to give media interviews. However, the publication of *Ethnic America* made it necessary for me to publicize the book by going on talk shows and giving interviews during a September book tour. *Ethnic America* received more media attention than any other book of mine, before or since. It was reviewed on the front page of the *New York Times* book review section and in the *Washington Post* book review section, as well as in *Time*, *Newsweek*, the *Wall Street Journal*, and other publications. I was interviewed on *Meet the Press* and William F. Buckley's *Firing Line*, as well as on *Donahue*, which was a big show at that time, and on other programs. My talk at the Harvard Club in New York and a dinner in my honor at the Manhattan Institute attracted such media heavyweights as Mike Wallace, Bill Buckley, and the editor of *Time* magazine.

Although my purpose during this book tour was to publicize *Ethnic America* and my ideas on race and ethnicity in general, much of the media seemed determined to link me to the Reagan administration, with which I had once had only the most tenuous connection as a member of an outside advisory panel on economics—a post from which I resigned after one meeting, when a check of my blood pressure showed that the stress of the travel and the meeting was too much. By the time of my September book tour, there was no connection at all, and all the rumors that I would become part of the Reagan cabinet had long since been disproved by my declining the offer. Yet, the *New York Times'* review of *Ethnic America* depicted it as a book "to be feared—as a signpost pointing to the probable future direction of the current national administration"—even though this was a history book, without a single policy recommendation, and was written more than a year before Ronald Reagan became President. Such media hype and spin probably increased the book's sales but I was still appalled at the gross inaccuracy. I was similarly appalled when I was interviewed on *Meet the Press*, where one of the first questions asked for my views "as a spokesman for the Reagan administration," to which my reply was: "I am not now, nor have I ever been, a spokesman for the Reagan administration."

Back in those days, *Meet the Press* had a panel of reporters who asked questions, as did its moderator, who was Bill Monroe at the time. Never before was I as fully aware of how ignorant and misinformed some media reporters were, as I proceeded to demonstrate to them and to the viewing audience during the program. Apparently my demonstration was effective, judging by many comments that arrived in the mail afterwards, including a letter from the U.S. Attorney General, William French Smith.

September 28, 1981

Dear Tom:

I want to wholeheartedly congratulate you for your excellent performance on *Meet the Press*. Your handling of the questions was simply superb. As a veteran of that program, I was pleased to see a guest turn the tables on the grand inquisitors so skillfully!

My warmest wishes for continued success in your fine work.

Kindest regards.

Sincerely,

Bill

The distinguished scholar W. Allen Wallis, then chancellor of the University of Rochester, had also seen the program.

---

28 September 1981

Dear Tom:

You gave by far the best performance I have ever seen on *Meet the Press* or any similar program. You were quick, informative, concise, and devastating, but in a nice way. Congratulations!

For the first time ever, I have sent off for a transcript.

Sincerely,

Allen

There was even a letter from *Meet the Press* moderator Bill Monroe.

September 30, 1981

Dear Tom:

I enjoyed the program we did with you.

It almost certainly could have been better. The panelists, including myself, seemed a little flat-footed. . . .

But even if it wasn't as good as it could have been, it had plenty of electricity. Our letters made that clear. About 60 percent of them expressed enthusiastic receptivity to you and what you had to say. (That is a much larger-than-normal favorable proportion.) About 20 percent were outraged by your attitude that blacks don't need government help. And about 20 percent felt the panel of reporters, Marvin in particular but all of us in general, were outmatched intellectually. . . .

Sincerely,

Bill

The "Marvin" referred to was Marvin Kalb, who was unbelievably narrow and shallow—and who went on in later years to become dean of Columbia University's school of journalism.

In case I had any remaining doubts about the utter irresponsibility of the media, CBS reporter Lem Tucker said in a broadcast on October 13, 1981 that my views "seem to place him in the school that believes that maybe most blacks are genetically inferior to white people." An attorney whom I did not know, but who knew of me through my writings and knew what a crock Tucker's statement was, wrote to me, offering to represent me in suing CBS for slander. However, knowing how iffy the law of libel and slander can be, I decided not to invest the huge amount of time that a lawsuit would require and instead wrote to a number of people at CBS, including Mike Wallace and the president of the network, William Paley.

December 17, 1981

Dear Mr. Paley:

One of your reporters is quoted as having represented me as a supporter of the doctrine of racial inferiority, even though this is a doctrine I have *attacked* in four books,[1] two newspapers,[2] a magazine,[3] and in miscellaneous speeches.[4] Before a charge that serious and that damaging is broadcast coast-to-coast, it is reasonable to expect some minimal attempt to check for accuracy.

Sincerely,

Thomas Sowell

Senior Fellow

1. *Black Education: Myths and Tragedies*, pp. 265-288; *Essays and Data on American Ethnic Groups*, pp. 203-238; *Race and Economics*, pp. 213-219; *Ethnic America*, pp. 281-282.
2. *New York Times Magazine*, March 27, 1977, p. 57 ff; *Los Angeles Herald-Examiner*, October 3, 1979, reprinted in the *Washington Post*.

3. *Change*, May 1973.
4. For example, at the Educational Testing Service in Princeton in 1977.

The irony was that I had collected more IQ data—70,000 IQs from my Urban Institute project—in opposition to the theory of genetic inferiority than any other black writer or perhaps any writer of any color.

1982

What the media said about me was a passing distraction that could be put aside when there was work to do but what they did, including harassing my secretary Beverly, was not so easily ignored. When I saw her in obvious distress and apparently on the verge of tears after receiving some boorish phone calls from media people, I got an answering machine, despite her attempts to tell me that she could handle the pressure. I also began turning down, or ignoring, interview requests and began to work at home more and more. This took pressure off me but may have made Beverly's job harder, as she often had to cope with problems at work alone.

Beverly was a good secretary in many ways but she took a lot on herself that she did not have to and we had different conceptions of what her role should be. Nevertheless, I was surprised when she suddenly quit.

January 28, 1982

Dear Beverly:

I am of course very sorry to lose a very good secretary. But I have also gotten to know you somewhat over the past year or so, and if I may consider myself a friend, then as a friend I think you may have made the best decision. Just this past weekend I expressed my concern to my wife that you seemed to be making the job far harder on yourself than it needed to be, partly by trying to shape my decisions instead of simply getting me the information that I needed to make my own decisions. She suggested that I take you to lunch and air our different conceptions of the work. But, by the time I reached the office on Monday, you had made your decision.

Best of luck in whatever you do. I hope it is unnecessary to assure you that I will write recommendations for you, whenever you need them in the years ahead. You are a good person as well as a good secretary, and more than once I have been pained to see how much you were hurt by people who had only the most transient and marginal relationship to you. The world needs sensitive people, but sometimes they pay a high price for their sensitivity. My way of working and my situation in general was not the best suited for your temperament. I hope that my loss will prove to be your gain.

It was months later before I found a satisfactory replacement, and for much of that time I simply did without a secretary entirely, rather than put up with an unsatisfactory one.[1] Eventually, however, a secretary who had worked

---

1. One secretary hired during this period, a young graduate of a well-known and expensive eastern college, typed a draft of my book on Marxism from transcribed dictation. Where I said, "Engels had to flee to Britain," she wrote "Engels had to flea to Brittain." Nor was this the only example of her lack of familiarity with spelling ordinary words. Another secretary violated my strict rule against either answering the phone or telling anyone where my office was. All it took was someone claiming to be "an old friend" of mine to get her to pick up the phone, instead of letting the message be recorded. She told him where the office was and then, when

with me years earlier, at the Center for Advanced Study, applied for the job and I hired her immediately. I was told that some people at the Hoover Institution found it hard to believe that anyone who had worked for me before would work for me again. But my new secretary, Agnes, was both very good and very dedicated, and she stayed on until her retirement nine years later. Many people who dealt with her, whether by phone or in person inside the Hoover Institution, commented on how well she handled herself and congratulated me on having such an outstanding secretary.[2] Far from suffering from being in the office alone almost all the time, Agnes relished it. She brought her radio, so that she could listen to classical music, and decorated the office with various plants. In my annual evaluation of her work for the personnel department, I said "On a scale from one to ten, she is an eleven."

After turning away from my research and writing on the history of ideas a decade earlier, and exploring racial and other themes, I now returned to the history of ideas, doing research and writing for a book that would be titled *Marxism: Philosophy and Economics.* I mentioned this in a letter to one of the participants in the 1980 Fairmont conference with whom I had remained sporadically in contact.

> March 13, 1982
>
> Dear Maria,
>
> Someone who was at the Fairmont conference recently sent me a group of photos of some of the participants, so here are yours. That now seems like another era ago in some very distant place. Tony Brown told me that I was a damn fool even to

---

he got there, she was frightened of him. It turned out after investigation that he was someone with a history of mental problems. I fired that secretary immediately.

2. Agnes, incidentally, had only a high school education, but from an earlier time with higher standards, and her spelling was flawless.

consider being part of a political movement, and it turned out that he was right. One of the signs of the times was a recent visit here by a woman who had been in the Reagan administration. Her parting words to me were an apology to me for having urged me to join the cabinet. . . .

Currently I am writing a book on the economic theories of Karl Marx. It is such a relief to be returning to my field after writing about race. While much of the response to my writings on race and ethnicity has been gratifying, some of it has been so ignorant, so loud-and-wrong, that I felt embarrassed for people who did not have enough sense to feel embarrassed for themselves. . . .

I began my career writing about Marx, more than twenty years ago, and it has long been my ambition to find time to write a book on the subject. Milton Friedman says that anything you have wanted to do for twenty years is bound to be a disappointment. However, I am pleased with what I have done so far, and I'm getting near the end. Usually when I get to the last chapter, I just want it over with—and don't care whether the reviewers like it, the people buy it, or anything else. This time I am not so impatient. Could I be mellowing?

———————

Another sporadic correspondent was a former colleague from Cornell days, Bob Kilpatrick, who informed me of the death of another former Cornell colleague.

March 14, 1982

Dear Bob:

I was very sorry about the passing of Jack Wolfowitz—and sorrier still that I had never been able to find an occasion to tell him of my esteem for him and the values he represented. One of the reasons I have come to cherish Christmas and the publication of my books is that these provide settings in which you can tell your friends how much they mean to you, without embarrassment.

In April 1982, Mary and I went overseas for the first time for either of us. We flew first to London, then Paris, Rome, and Zurich. In Switzerland I gave a talk at St. Gallen.

I like to make sure everything is left in order before I go on a long trip, in case I don't live to make it back. Before leaving on this first trip overseas, I thought it especially important that I leave a letter to my children behind, to be opened by them in the event that I did not return.

April 19, 1982

My dear children,

Although we all know that life does not last forever, still we are shocked when it ends for someone close to us. That is only human.

I am writing to say some things we do not say very often in the ordinary routine of life. My love for you and the happiness you have brought into my life are more than you can know. From the moment I first saw you as newborn babies I loved you. Many a time I have seen you asleep and my heart has filled with warmth and fulfillment and a sense of peace. There have been times when coming home to be greeted by your smiling upturned faces was all that I had that made life worth living. It has meant more to me than all the applause I have heard or praise I have read or honors I have received. Caesar entering Rome in triumph could not have known more happiness.

The role of parent and child has many frictions built in, that neither can escape, and the emotional attachments are so strong that every disagreement or disappointment is magnified many times. Yet the very pain and anger we feel reveals the love underneath. My hope has been to live to see the time when all the surface turmoil of growing up is over and behind us, when the love that is there is no longer covered over by the weeds and tangles of everyday parent-child relations—the criticisms, the warnings, the punishments and resentments that are the price we pay for passing on a complex civilization from one generation to the next. In this process, we all make mistakes, say and do things we later regret or overlook things we wish we had done to make each other happy. Above all, do not in later years judge yourself harshly for what you did or did not do as children. I knew you were children and the joy you brought as children outweighed all else.

I love you. I wish I could be with you always but I have always known that I could not. My hope and my task was to bring you to the point where you could continue without me. We have meant too much to each other to part without grief. My grief will be over when you read this but I have shed my tears in writing it. Grief must run its course, and then life will continue for you and you will develop into wiser and deeper people with new relations, including—if you are lucky—children of your own to love as I have loved you.

When I can return to you only in memory, I hope that the memory will be a real part of your life—not an idealized picture, but with the three-dimensional and contradictory features that make up human beings and human relations—the laughter we shared, the tears that you and I have both shed over each other, the arguments, the tender moments and the quiet times we sat together with the warm glow of our love for each other.

Daddy

Since I returned home safely, this letter was never sent to the children but instead remained in my files over the years.

As in the past, I continued my sporadic correspondence with my erstwhile mentor and dear friend, Mrs. Gadsden.

October 4, 1982

Dear Mrs. G,

I have been traveling and without a secretary for some time, so I am only belatedly catching up on my backlog of messages and correspondence.

I don't know who "they" are who told your friend that I don't have time for "these Africans." I very seldom meet with any of the various visitors—domestic or foreign—who pass through campus, and have had my office number removed from directories. The only visitor I can recall agreeing to see at Stanford was in fact an African whom you recommended. To say that I don't meet with Africans is like saying that I don't go sky-diving with blacks—true in itself, but somewhat misleading.

I was planning to write a book of sketches of blacks with various viewpoints to be titled *New Black Voices*. Among the people I interviewed for that book (which I ended up not publishing) was black journalist Chuck Stone. He had a fascinating career, which included being an aide to legendary black Congressman Adam Clayton Powell. Chuck had written a couple of books and was now spending a year in residence at Harvard's Kennedy School, where I stopped by to see him and tape an interview during a trip to Massachusetts.

October 4, 1982

Dear Chuck:

It was good to see you again, and especially to have you share so openly your life and your thoughts. I will be happy if I can convey this well enough that the readers will enjoy it half as much as I did.

Hope you have a good time at the Kennedy School and get what you want out of it. Quite frankly, I have to disagree almost 100 percent with the advice that was handed out at dinner. There is nothing magic about chit-chatting with famous professors. Nor is much to be gained by auditing their lectures without having done the reading—and having taken the time to wrestle with the ideas in it. What the Kennedy School honchos are advocating is like trying to get into shape by watching sports on TV or arguing about sports at the local bar.

When someone at the dinner expressed happiness at how "balanced" the group was, I was reminded of a story about a government request to an employer for "a list of your employees broken down by sex." The reply was: "We don't have any employees broken down by sex, but we do have some that are debilitated by alcohol."

The preciousness of Harvard is no more enchanting after a quarter of a century than it was when it turned me off as an undergraduate. I can still recall the sigh of relief with which I settled back in the cab that sped me away from Kirkland House before graduation. I left a forwarding address so that they could mail me the diploma. Having mellowed somewhat over the years, I was planning to finally attend a class reunion (the 25th)

> next year. Now, after having encountered the Harvard mystique once more at the Kennedy School, it is 6-to-5 and pick 'em. It might be nice to see a few old classmates again, but if I ever have any money to leave behind to an institution, it will be to the University of Chicago.

I did not go back to Harvard for the 25th reunion. Nor have I gone back to any other reunions, not even when I taught at Brandeis University, a 20 minute drive away.

It was not just irresponsible journalists who completely distorted things I had said. Even a serious scholar like Christopher Jencks did the same thing in a long set of book reviews that ran in two consecutive issues of the *New York Review of Books* in March 1983. He reviewed jointly *Ethnic America* and a lesser known little book of mine, *Markets and Minorities*. My long reply, published in a later issue of the *New York Review of Books*, began by itemizing Jencks' straw men.

> If imitation is the sincerest form of flattery, straw men must be a close second. No critic would have to invent a position to attack if he could deal with the real arguments.
>
> Christopher Jencks' voluminous review of *Ethnic America* and *Markets and Minorities* repeatedly creates straw men, with which he is repeatedly "astonished."
>
> STRAW MAN: According to Jencks, my position is that

"discrimination tends to disappear once markets become competitive." MARKETS AND MINORITIES: "The competitiveness of the market puts a price on discrimination, thereby reducing but not necessarily eliminating it." (pp. 39-40)

STRAW MAN: "Discrimination . . . tends to disappear once government stops enforcing it." ETHNIC AMERICA: "Translating subjective prejudice into overt economic discrimination is costly for profit-seeking competitive firms, although less so for government, public utilities, regulated industries like banking, or nonprofit organizations such as universities or hospitals." (p. 292)

STRAW MAN: ". . . current discrimination in the labor market has no effect on black earnings." ETHNIC AMERICA: "The point here is not to definitively solve the question as to how much of the intergroup differences in income, social acceptance, etc., have been due to the behavior and attitudes of particular ethnic groups and how much to the behavior of the larger society. The point is that this is a complex question, not a simple axiom." (p. 294)

STRAW MAN: ". . .if the median black, Indian, or Hispanic were as old as the median European, he would be almost as affluent." MARKETS AND MINORITIES: "Differences in median age are only part of the statistical picture." (p. 11)

STRAW MAN: "Sowell argues for patience." Since I don't

even discuss any such thing in either book, there is nothing to quote. But in the first book I wrote on the subject, I said at the outset: "History . . . gives little support to the view that time automatically erodes racial aversions, fears, and animosities, or even tames the overt behavior based on such feelings." (*Race and Economics*, p. vi). All my subsequent books on ethnicity make it a point to show retrogressions in intergroup relations over time, as well as examples of progress. *Markets and Minorities* mentions these retrogressions (pp. 72-73) and *Ethnic America* discusses them repeatedly (pp. 71, 82, 161-162, 192, 201-202, 203, 204, 206, 210-211, 254). I shall leave it to Jencks to supply the pages where I argue for "patience."

There was much more in my reply but this is enough to show the level of Jencks' criticisms. As someone once said, you don't need to eat a whole egg to know that it is rotten.

———————————

Although I was now working on another book on the history of ideas—*A Conflict of Visions*—I could not completely escape the subject of race and ethnicity. Critics of *Ethnic America* objected to its thesis that the differing internal cultures that various groups brought to American society had more influence over their fate in that society than did the way the other members of that society treated them. In order to deal with these critics, I wrote *The Economics and Politics of Race: An International Perspective*, which compared various groups in different countries, showing how their own internal cultural patterns could be seen again and again in very different societies, producing similar results in those disparate societies.

Among the people to whom I sent a copy of *The Economics and Politics of Race* was the distinguished scholar David Riesman, with whom I exchanged letters sporadically. He commented on that book and on my projected *A*

Conflict of Visions.

October 18, 1983

Dear Tom:

Thank you so very much for *The Economics and Politics of Race*, and for your good letter of October 12. . . .

As I read and reflect on your pages, I am reminded, as I so often am, of how powerful a motive envy is when organized into nation-states or subcultural nationalism. The Malays, as you know, harm themselves by resenting Chinese accomplishment, keeping them out of the universities and out of the government. I am happy for the division of labor among peoples, cultures, nation-states. If you and I can write books and exchange ideas, why should we be resentful if the Japanese, better at spatial configurations, make the machines by which we communicate? But then, you and I are not defensive about our limitations; we know that all of us, and all peoples, have limitations. . . .

I love your prospect for a book to be called *A Conflict of Visions*. Ever so much in contemporary ideology seems to me to go back to Rousseau, a complex figure, as you know; I am thinking here of the Rouseauistic belief that social order is the villain, that human protoplasm is innately benign—a verdict which paradoxically leads to the subtle totalistic implications of the concept of the general will.

> Sincerely,
>
> David

1984

As 1984 began, I was engrossed in research for two books on the history of ideas—*A Conflict of Visions* and *Marxism: Philosophy and Economics*. However, I knew that 1984 was bound to produce much literature on the 20th anniversary of the Civil Rights Act of 1964 and the 30th anniversary of the landmark Supreme Court desegregation decision, *Brown v. Board of Education*. I also knew what the party line on these events would be, and how misleading it would be. So I had to stop and write a little book titled *Civil Rights: Rhetoric or Reality?* It was one of a number of books I have written over the years, not because I wanted to, but because it was a book that needed to be written and because I knew that no one else was likely to write it. It shot down a lot of myths about civil rights laws and policies and their consequences for minorities and women.

Another project sort of crept up on me. The Scripps-Howard News Service asked me and three other economists to write for a weekly column on economic issues. Since there were four of us, I would be writing only about once a month, and that seemed quite do-able, so I became a regular columnist once again, though with less frequency than when I was writing a weekly column for the *Los Angeles Herald-Examiner* back in the late 1970s. However, before the year was out, this little experiment came to an end and the rotating column was discontinued. Scripps-Howard then asked me to become a regular columnist, writing about subjects in general once a week, and I accepted. My column went out to Scripps-Howard newspapers across the country.

The turning of all sorts of specialized institutions and publications into propaganda outlets for all sorts of politically correct causes was one of the bothersome developments of our times. I responded to one such effort in *Modern Photography* magazine with a letter to the editors.

January 3, 1984

Dear Editors:

Julia Scully's column in the January issue is as self-congratulatory as it is tangential to photography. She urges us to stop thinking politically in terms of "good guys" and "bad guys"—while herself discussing all sorts of political issues as if there were only one "good" side. From environmentalism to nuclear policy, she is on the side of the angels. Her only question is how effectively photography can be mobilized for that side.

Someone is always discovering the one and only truth—which has, of course, varied enormously from person to person.

What is even more amazing than the unending supply of zealots, each with a monopoly on truth and virtue, is that institutions and publications set up for entirely different purposes allow them to intrude their zealotry. I am sure Ms. Scully would see the point if I were to urge that photography be slanted to promote a return to religion or the build-up of our military forces.

If a small part of human life, such as photography, has enough complexities to merit its own specialized publications, organizations, and scientific research, then we can rest assured that the survival of humanity, the preservation of freedom, and the promotion of justice also merit specialized attention from those prepared to weigh its complexities and difficult trade-offs.

> We all have something to contribute to the world, provided we remember what it is—and where it is appropriate.

A story in the press about a black mayor in Alabama who advocated relaxing the minimum wage law for teenagers caused me to write to him. Originally a believer in minimum wage laws, I had over the years become convinced by a growing body of evidence that these laws caused inexperienced and low-skilled people to be unemployed, even when they were perfectly capable of working, when their productivity had not yet reached the point where it was worth what the minimum wage laws specified.

March 27, 1984

Dear Mr. Ford:

One of the most heartening actions by black leaders in many years was your support for a relaxation of the minimum wage laws for teenagers. It was not clear from the story in *Business Week* whether this was also the official position of the National Conference of Black Mayors. As a black economist, I certainly hope so.

Not only do many young blacks need to be bringing in some money to low-income households; they need the work experience even more than they need the money. There is no way to move up the ladder without first getting on the ladder—and for almost everybody, that usually means getting on at the bottom. My own work experience as a teenager was enormously valuable to me, not only then but now. At the time I thought my boss was terribly harsh in his criticism of my work and work habits. Now, decades later, I wonder how the man found the patience to put up with my incompetence. There is no way he could have paid me the minimum wage and broken even on the deal.

Most black youngsters do not have parents who can hire them in the family business or use influence to get them jobs in a friend's business. Their only hope is to get a start somewhere out in the harsh competition of the marketplace—or the even harsher competition of crime. After they get some experience under their belts, they will be worth more than the minimum wage. But to prevent them from getting the experience in the first place, by insisting that they receive the minimum wage from day one, is a great disservice to them.

We also do them a disservice by looking down on "menial" jobs or "dead-end" jobs. Those kinds of jobs kept me alive for years, before I scraped together enough money to go to college. Moreover, what I learned in the process continues to help me to this day. In my research on racial and ethnic groups around the world, I discovered again and again that groups who are hung up over "menial" work get overtaken and left behind by groups who consider a job a job. That is as true in Latin America and southeast Asia as it is here. Japan is one of the few industrial nations that does not have to import foreigners to do low-level work, because its own people have no hesitation about taking such jobs.

Please forgive the length of this letter, but this is something I feel very strongly about. If our younger generation doesn't make it, it isn't going to matter how many people my age have professorships or cabinet appointments or anything else.

I can only hope that your position on this issue indicates a new awareness of what is at stake, among black leadership in general.

Among the unexpected letters I received from time to time was one from former Senator Sam Ervin, best known for his role in exposing the Watergate scandal that forced President Richard Nixon to resign.

June 18, 1984

Dear Senator Ervin:

When I returned from some travels recently, it was a special pleasure and honor to find your letter in the mail. It immediately took me back to a time when you epitomized the values and the human decency people so much longed to see in the wake of Watergate. I hope that history will preserve for the benefit of later generations the significance of your role at this critical juncture in American history.

I must confess that the only time I ever found myself angry

at President Ford was when I heard on the radio of his pardon of his predecessor. I had to pull the car off the road until I calmed down, because of the dangers of driving when agitated. President Ford may have made his decision for the most high-minded reasons, but it seems to me profoundly wrong to grant leniency to those in high places, who have more responsibility and less excuse than others.

On a happier note, I am of course very gratified at your generous comment on *Civil Rights*. As you can imagine, such generosity is not universal. It was a painful book to write, but other Americans have done more painful things than that, or none of us would be here, living in freedom today. My dues were small.

Your comments on the threat from good people, rather than evil ones, are all too true. Currently I am researching preferential treatment programs in other countries and find striking parallels in the counterproductive consequences. The truly disadvantaged seldom benefit but nevertheless become targets of resentment. Violence against untouchables doubled in less than a decade in India, amid resentment of benefits most of them never actually receive.

Harvard professor Martin Kilson submitted an article to *National Review* magazine, criticizing an article by another Harvard professor, Harvey

Mansfield. Upon having his article rejected, Professor Kilson then wrote an indignant note to the magazine's founder, William F. Buckley, and Bill passed a copy on to me.

August 29, 1984

Dear Bill:

Thanks for the copy of Kilson's letter. It provided much-needed comic relief on a hectic day.

You may think that you have seen Kilson at his silliest and most pompous, but I can assure you from experience that you have not.

Although I had published an international study of racial and ethnic groups (*The Economics and Politics of Race*) in 1982, scarcely had this book been written—and even before it was published—when I began to think that its expansive thesis required a much larger sample from countries around the world. Eventually this led me to seek to have the Hoover Institution sponsor an international trip that would take me literally around the world to study racial and cultural issues in a wide variety of societies. In September 1984, Mary and I began that trip. While I was busy collecting data and publications, interviewing scholars, journalists and officials, Mary was enjoying life as a tourist.

We flew first to England, then to Israel, Greece, India, Hong Kong, Singapore, Australia (stopping in Perth, Melbourne, and Sydney), and then home by way of Fiji and Honolulu. Among those to whom I wrote while away was a colleague at the Hoover Institution.

September 26, 1984

Dear Jack:

We are now in Greece, recuperating from Israel. Actually, we had a very good time in Israel, both professionally and as tourists. However, "security" going to, coming from, and remaining in Israel is something else. Nor is it necessarily excessive relative to the situation. One day a hand grenade exploded in the old walled city of Jerusalem, not too far from where we entered—in fact, not far *enough* from where we entered. But we only learned about it the next day, in the newspaper. Personally, I am not a stickler for first-hand information.

I was somewhat surprised at how relaxed and informal ordinary one-on-one discussions are between Jews and Arabs in Israel. It is not at all uncommon to see a lone Jew walking through an Arab neighborhood or an Arab (even with camel) going through a Jewish part of town. Now that I have seen a camel, by the way, I know that I would never walk a mile for one.

On a more mundane note, I am still puzzled by the practice in foreign hotels of giving husband and wife separate beds. I call the space between these beds "the gender gap." I am even more anxious than Ronald Reagan to eliminate it.

By the time you get this, I will probably be in India—or Hong Kong, depending on how bad the mail is.

Upon returning home, I found the expected backlog of correspondence to catch up on. One was with a colleague at Duke University.

November 21, 1984

Dear Joel:

I have been overseas for a couple of months, so I am belatedly replying to your gratifying letter of September 6th.

The views I have held before have been much reinforced by my observations from Israel to Singapore. It is truly remarkable that highly educated people have racked their brains for the causes of poverty and income differences, when in many cases they are blatant to the casual observer. Anyone who has seen the Malays and the Chinese in action in Malaysia or Singapore can hardly be surprised that the latter earn far more money. Ditto for the Fijians and the Indians in Fiji. Perhaps intellectuals find it hard to accept the obvious.

Israel was the real surprise of my trip. As one who once worked in New York's garment district, I was wholly unprepared for inefficiency in Israel, or for discovering that its average income is below that of Italy. It is the first instance I have ever discovered of Jews making less than Italians. Apparently their political system has more to do with such results than their heavy military obligations, which are offset by government and private aid from the U.S.A. Jews thus join the peoples of China and India as groups who prosper all over the world—except in their homelands. Stifling policies and bureaucracies seem to be the common denominator in all three cases.

1986

After years of collecting material and taping interviews for the book *New Black Voices*, I began to have doubts about publishing it—and those doubts were reinforced by others with whom I discussed the book. These doubts were expressed in a letter to Glenn Loury, one of the people I planned to interview.

January 24, 1986

Dear Glenn:

Many thanks for agreeing to be interviewed for *New Black Voices* and for sending your vita. Incidentally, it was very reassuring to see that your many efforts on the racial front have not kept you from publishing in the top scholarly journals. Too many black academics have been set back professionally because of the time taken up by their interest in racial issues.

Since writing you, I have talked with my wife and my editor about the book, with the net result that I have decided to back off my plan to wrap it up quickly in February. I found these stories fascinating, largely because I dealt with the people in the flesh and caught the nuances of what they were saying. But it is by no means clear that I have conveyed that to the reader on the printed page. More time is going to be needed for some re-thinking and re-writing, so I have resigned myself to seeing publication

> postponed until next year.

Publication was not simply postponed. I eventually decided not to publish it at all. I didn't think that my writing had done justice to the stories or that my style of writing was likely to. It would not have been fair to the people interviewed, to the readers, or to myself, to publish something that failed to convey what these people were all about.

Within the Reagan administration, there were those who were trying to get the President to rescind the Executive Orders from Presidents Johnson and Nixon which had created "affirmative action." Some were optimistic that this would be done and I flew to Washington to talk with a number of people in various parts of the administration to make the arguments that I had been making for many years that preferences and quotas were both wrong and counterproductive. One of the people I saw during my visit, and to whom I wrote after returning to California, was Assistant Attorney General William Bradford Reynolds.

January 27, 1986

Dear Brad:

Travel and the Christmas holidays have kept me from properly thanking you for being so generous with your time when I was in Washington. It was very gratifying to meet you, to have you introduce me to Michael Horowitz, and to have both of you be so candid in giving me your insights into Washington politics. When you are out this way, I hope you will allow me to try to reciprocate your hospitality.

As to so-called "affirmative action," which has preoccupied each of us in very different ways, I am old-fashioned enough to be against it simply because it is wrong. Having been forced by birth to be on the receiving end of discrimination for many years, I cannot find the cleverness to justify discrimination now, either to others or to myself. And if I now reduce this issue to a pragmatic question of whose ox is gored, then what right did I have to be morally indignant before?

My research findings on the counterproductive effects of affirmative action—here and in other countries—simply tell me that this is a dangerous social madness, in addition to being immoral. In the context of American history, preferential policies seem to be part of a much larger set of tendencies sent in motion during the 1960s and 1970s, and amounting altogether to a program for the gradual repeal of the American Revolution. The great significance of the emergence of this country in world history was its unprecedented opportunities for the common man—for his personal freedom and for his voice in the running of the nation. The historic significance of the civil rights era was that it completed the American Revolution by making it apply to *all* people.

All too soon, however, the achievements of the civil rights era fell victim to other powerful political currents—aimed not at the freedom of the common man but at the concentration of power in the hands of the morally self-anointed. Some call them "the new elite," "the new class," or by other names but, under whatever name, they can be seen indefatigably at work across the whole spectrum of American life—from environmental extremists to Naderites to the tragically misnamed "peace movement." The common denominator of their efforts is the substitution of their presumed superiority for the freedom and power of the common man. They of course phrase it differently.

Many of us have hoped that the 1980s would see the American Revolution restored and continued. "Affirmative action" is a crucial battleground in that effort, for the fundamental issue here is whether the anointed shall *assign* people to their "places" by birth. If that fundamentally un-American notion remains intact, then it is not going to matter whether the numbers used are called "goals" or "quotas" or whether words like "voluntary" are salted and peppered here and there.

I am old enough to remember when housing advertisements in Washington newspapers said "white" and "colored." I resented it. But what I truly hated and despised was the chicanery and hypocrisy of federal employment practices under the pretense of equal opportunity. That not only damaged me, but insulted me, and dishonored the country in which I lived. I hear echoes of those feelings in complaints I receive from people cheated out of jobs or promotions in order to make numbers look good to third parties.

Chicanery and hypocrisy have been central to the whole evolution of "affirmative action." The fact that big business, like other bureaucracies, has learned to live with it is beside the point. . . .

There is no way to produce anything resembling an even distribution of groups in employment, housing, or anywhere else, except by suppressing the rights of ordinary people to make their own decisions and transferring that power to third parties. People do not distribute themselves evenly anywhere. Even on the little island of Curaçao, Sephardic Jews have historically lived separate lives from Ashkenazic Jews. They have lived separate lives for centuries in Europe and America, and today in Israel. Even in a "melting pot" nation like Brazil, the Japanese whose ancestors came from Okinawa marry other Okinawans, not people from Tokyo, much less Brazilians at random. Examples could be multiplied to fill volumes. Nevertheless, the dogma prevails that non-random patterns must be due to institutional decisions. Once that crucial assumption is accepted, it is vain to resist its corollaries, much less to try to do so by a verbal retouching of "affirmative action" policies.

Please forgive the length of this letter. Partly it is because of the long-run importance of this issue. Partly it is because you mentioned hearing interpretations of my views from others. I speak for no one else and no one else speaks for me.

I also wrote in a similar vein to Clarence Thomas, then head of the Equal Employment Opportunity Commission, and to President Reagan. But it was all in vain. I was told that the fact that big business preferred to stick with affirmative action, rather than face the legal uncertainties that its rescinding might produce, was a reason that the Reagan administration did nothing, despite the people within its own ranks who wanted the previous Executive Orders rescinded. I have no hard evidence to substantiate that but it was the only explanation I heard that sounded plausible to me.

My objections to affirmative action in college admissions, on grounds that it mismatches black students with colleges, causing needless failures among students perfectly capable of succeeding in colleges geared to students of their own individual academic achievement, were repeated in a collection of essays that I sent to David Riesman. His reply included his conclusions that similar results occur with other groups admitted to college on bases other than academic achievement.

> 4 March 1986
>
> Dear Tom:
>
> Harvard College remains very hard to navigate for unsophisticated white students brought here for their athletic prowess, their geographic rarity, the judgment of an alumni interviewer that the person—usually male—is a really good guy, and a potential leader who does not stumble and suffer in terms of self-esteem; everybody gets through in the absence of a real effort to fail, but many who would have found invitations to learning in less pressureful environments are scarred.
>
> > Sincerely,
> >
> > David

———————————

Writers have no way of knowing who will read what they write, so I was surprised to receive a hand-written letter from tennis star Arthur Ashe, inviting me to a meeting.

---

20 May

Dear Dr. Sowell,

Forgive the informality—I just wanted to get this note off to you.

Your presence at this 2nd Black Leadership Retreat would provide valuable insight to the usual content of conversation of our established and traditional leaders. The Retreat has no formal organization—there is no chairman, or president, etc. A group of us just decided that the Black American opinion leaders needed to get to know one another better without a formal agenda hanging over their heads.

As I said, I've been a fan of yours for quite some time and your *The Economics And Politics Of Race* has been a pivotal work for me. Your views about a host of things need to be heard by the more traditionally-minded Black leader.

I am asking if you can free yourself to attend the Retreat on July 24-27. Please try. As an invitee your expenses would be paid.

The first Retreat was extremely successful and I am sure you would both enjoy the camaraderie and have your point of view heard.

Please get back to me at your earliest convenience.

Thanks,

Arthur

(212) 249-1627

288-9614

While the *Harvard Crimson* is the official student newspaper at the college, and has followed the usual liberal-left line, the *Harvard Salient* has been the unofficial conservative student newspaper there. A fund-raising letter from the *Harvard Salient* caused me to make a small contribution and to write a long letter.

May 28, 1986

Dear Sirs:

For some time I have felt ambivalent about Harvard's fund-raising campaigns. Because Harvard played an important role in my life, I felt that I should make whatever small contribution I can to keeping such opportunities alive for others. Yet the general drift of Harvard over the past quarter of a century—from its shameful capitulations in the 1960s to preventing Nicaraguan refugees from speaking today—make me unwilling to be an accessory to a trend whose cumulative effect can only be disastrous to the academic world and ultimately to this nation.

The fund-raising letter from the *Harvard Salient* offered me a way out of this dilemma. Now I can put my drop in a different bucket and feel that I am contributing to Harvard in a way it needs—to fight for a diversity of ideas and against capitulation to ideological intolerance and coercion. When I was a student at Harvard, I was a Marxist, and very much out of step with prevailing views there at that time, but no one found it necessary to mark me down, put me down, or shout me down. These were things people debated. One of my indelible memories is of arguing outside Kirkland House with a classmate as the Housemaster passed by on his way to dinner—and on his way back from dinner.

I hope that others, who have more substantial contributions to make, will likewise redirect their efforts toward rescuing Harvard rather than subsidizing its current drift. Whatever lofty talk issues from university officials, academic pragmatism remains the dominant feature on most campuses. What this boils down to is that the noisy, self-righteous, and coercive fringe will be indulged as long as it doesn't stop the money from coming in from outside. Only when they start hurting in the pocketbook will the academic pragmatists start re-evaluating their strategy. If university administrators are going to follow the path of least resistance, then it is up to others to see that that path is directed toward a freer, more open and more diverse institution.

The *Harvard Salient* is to be congratulated, not only for the quality of its product, but also for contributing to a diversity of ideas that has become all too rare on all too many campuses. While you are arguing for your particular ideas, as I argued for my own very different ideas 30 years ago, in the larger scheme of things it not a particular view but the clash of ideas which makes the greatest contribution to individual understanding, to a great university, and to the never-ending quest for a better destiny for mankind.

After giving a talk at a free-market think tank in Jamaica, I wrote back to one of my hosts.

May 6, 1987

Dear Hu:

The basic problem of many Third World countries, it seems to me, is that those citizens who have the know-how and drive to increase the national output are—and must be—depicted as parasites by those who lack such talents, but who have academic credentials which impress both others and themselves. Perhaps it is the poverty of my imagination, but I cannot imagine how it

> could be otherwise, given the circumstances and the incentives those circumstances create. That does not make it less galling, of course.

The academic practice of pre-emptive surrender to disruptive campus elements was exemplified by Harvard dean Michael Spence's decision to curtail the number of "controversial" outside speakers allowed on campus. Since no one on the left was likely to be disrupted when giving a talk at the university, what this meant in practice was that the storm trooper tactics of the student left would keep away those that they disapproved of. Michael Spence was also an economist, best known for his theory of "market signalling," to which I referred obliquely in this letter.

> May 13, 1987
>
> Dear Dean Spence:
>
> A recent issue of the *Harvard Salient* says that you have publicly declared that the university should reduce the number of "controversial" lecturers speaking on campus, in order to save on security expenses. Is this a fair summary of your position—or is there some other version I should read?
>
> If this version is even approximately correct, it raises disturbing questions. Surely maintaining a free market of ideas is not one of the lesser concerns of a university. I would not presume to tell you about the importance of signalling. On the contrary, I would appreciate any enlightenment you can provide as to what this policy is intended to signal.

Leanita McClain was a young black writer for the *Chicago Tribune* whose anguished essay that I read in *Newsweek* magazine in 1980 told of her sense of being pulled in all directions by the racial expectations of both blacks and whites. This struck me as symbolic of the needless pressures put on many young blacks by the racial hype of our times. More urgently, it struck me as a sign of a very distressed young woman, and I thought that I should write a letter to her, in hopes of saying something that might help relieve some of that distress. But, with the distractions of many other things, that letter never got written—and a few years later I learned that Leanita McClain had committed suicide. Had I written her, my letter might not have made any difference to her, but it would have made a difference to me to know that I had done what I could. I was painfully reminded of all this when a friend in Chicago sent me a book containing a collection of her writings, now three years after her death.

May 19, 1987

Dear André:

Many thanks for sending me the essays of Leanita McClain, though they have saddened me for several days. It is not just the shame of a bright talent, snuffed out before it could mature—she would undoubtedly have been a very wise woman at 60—but, more important, the sense that there are other young black people out there, going through what she went through. It also reminded me of another suicide a couple of years ago—Fred "Doc" Holliday, a black superintendent of schools in Cleveland, and a dedicated educator. We just don't have people like this to throw away.

The most I could do now was to write a column, as a substitute for the letter that I wished I had written, and in hopes of having some effect, somewhere, that might prevent another young black person from feeling the same pressures that proved fatal to Leanita McClain.

RACIAL HYPE

by Thomas Sowell

Few books have saddened me so much as a recently-published collection of essays by the late Leanita McClain. She was a talented young black writer for the *Chicago Tribune* who took her own life in 1984.

Leanita McClain's writings are full of the pain of having to run a gauntlet of criticism and innuendo from fellow blacks because of her success and independence—and then having to run another gauntlet of hostility or condescension from the whites her success put her in touch with. "I am a rope in a tug of war," she said.

Nothing can be done for Leanita McClain now. But something can be done for many other young blacks who live under similar pressures, especially on college and university campuses.

Racial hype is a big source of this pressure. On campuses, as elsewhere, there are "leaders," organizations, hustlers, and messiahs who depend on racial hype for whatever significance they have. Their program is to get black students enrolled in segregated organizations, living a segregated life-style, scavenging for grievances, issuing manifestoes, and otherwise pouring their energies into the time-consuming activities of campus politics.

There are, of course, also campus organizations for white busybodies, exhibitionists, and saviors. But there are some important differences.

Black students, who often come to college with serious deficiencies in their educational backgrounds, are less able to afford the time for such distractions from their studies. Black students are often also more emotionally vulnerable to charges that they are "betraying" their people or have "sold out" to whitey if they don't fall in step with the prescribed black lifestyle and parrot the pre-packaged ideology.

For some 18-year-old kid from the ghetto, trying to adjust to a whole new world on a white campus, it can be heavy stuff to be told that you have "forgotten where you came from" or that you "think you are white" if you don't go along. Hustlers and messiahs know how to play on their vulnerabilities.

All too often, college officials are accessories to all this. Many times it is they who first deliver the new black students to the campus black establishment. Unlike white students, who can choose whether to seek membership in this or that campus organization, activity, or movement, black students are delivered.

This delivery can start even before the student applies to college. Black students are labelled as high school seniors and their names put on nationwide, computerized mailing lists. They are also identified from application form photographs and in other ways. These names are then routed to the local black organizations on campuses, often with neither their [the students'] knowledge nor permission.

Bates College, for example, has a special weekend excursion for black high school students separately, under the auspices of the Black Students Union at Bates. This is by no means unique. At some schools, the unsuspecting black student learns that he or she has been racially labelled and segregated only after arriving at the planned festivities.

White students and faculty may be blissfully unaware of all this. On some campuses, they may wonder why black students keep to themselves so much—but there is always some easy answer from pop psychology. The cold fact, however, is that black students were treated more like individuals on many campuses 30 years ago than they are today.

The Harvard class of 1958 elected a black student as class [marshall]—and nobody thought it was any big deal, or had any racial symbolism. He just happened to be a popular guy. Neither he nor the other black students there at the time clumped together in a corner.

Back in those days, black students had far more obstacles to overcome when they went out to begin a career after graduation. But they were more confident that they would overcome them. Today's black student often seems to lack the same easy confidence that he will take the hurdles in stride and keep moving.

Today, the combination of racial hype, sociological whining, and the doom-and-gloom rhetoric that has become standard from civil rights "leaders" have succeeded only in undermining the confidence of many black youngsters. Whites increasingly tune it out—or even become hostile to blacks in general. Some of the ugliest campus attacks on blacks have occurred in places where nothing like that happened a generation ago, before racial hype poisoned the atmosphere.

Fortunately, not all colleges and universities are like that, by any means. On some campuses, black students are as free to be individuals as any other students, are widely accepted and are academically competitive. Often these are places where there has been no lowering of standards to increase the minority body count and no black studies establishment to promote campus politics.

It is too late to help Leanita McClain. But it is not too late to help other young blacks find personal peace in this life and fulfillment of their talents.

Forbes magazine did a flattering profile of me as someone who came out of Harlem and went on to leading universities and a professional career. This brought a letter from a lawyer who had also grown up in Harlem.

September 10, 1987

Dear Dr. Sowell:

A write up in Forbes is not bad. But by no means are you "a man alone," not the way Forbes means it.

I grew up at 143rd and Amsterdam, not far from your neighborhood and lived in a 5-story walk-up tenement. From just that one building came a college president, an M.D., two engineers, a lawyer, a college professor, a high school teacher and a Jesuit priest.

From our viewpoint you do not attack economic orthodoxy, you express its reality.

Very truly yours,

Albert J. Forn

The story of the tenement in which Mr. Forn grew up is one whose reality remains largely unknown, even among supposedly well-informed people today, and whose wider implications are almost completely lost on people across the political spectrum. The five-story walk-up tenement in which I lived was just three blocks from the one where he lived and the schools available to both of us had far higher academic and behavioral standards than the schools in Harlem today. It was by no means miraculous for someone to come out of those schools and go on to good colleges and professional careers. Most did not but the ones who wanted to could. I am neither the best known nor the most financially successful of the blacks who grew up in that neighborhood. There was more racial discrimination back in those days but we were equipped both educationally and in terms of attitudes to overcome such barriers. The reduction of external barriers since then has too often been accompanied by increasing internal barriers that are harder to overcome, including excuses, paranoia, dependency, lower behavioral standards, and a mindless tribalism that condemns black kids who work hard to get an education as "acting white."

––––––––––––––

One of my many ideas that failed to come to fruition over the years was a plan—really a hope—to get some publisher to reprint a book titled *In Search of Peace* by Britain's ill-fated Prime Minister Neville Chamberlain. The book was published in 1939, so 1989 would be its 50th anniversary and an appropriate occasion for republishing it. My plan was to write a long introduction to the re-issued book, explaining that (1) Chamberlain's ideas on how to promote peace led instead to the most terrible war in history and that (2) today's "peace" movements were echoing precisely the same kinds of ideas that Chamberlain had expressed, often in the very words and phrases that Chamberlain had used. Because of a need to get started early if I wanted to see the book published in 1989, I wrote to my friend and former editor Midge Decter, whose reply hit the nail on the head.

December 30, 1987

Dear Tom:

It was great to hear from you. Naturally, no publisher would touch your idea; it's too expensive a gesture.

I myself don't think your idea is hare-brained, but I do have one problem with it: I'm afraid you over-estimate the public, especially the media public. They would not get the point. They never heard of Neville Chamberlain and would celebrate him as a past martyr to noble principle.

Best,

Midge

The 1990s

Sometime during the early 1990s, I was coming out of a post office in Palo Alto, when a motorist driving out of the adjoining parking lot stopped and honked a horn at me. Figuring that it was someone who wanted directions, I walked over to the car and said, "Can I help you?"

"You don't remember me," she said softly. I took a closer look and then said, "Audrey!" I had not seen her in more than 20 years.

She got out of the car and hugged me. The only emotion I felt was embarrassment. For both of us.

We talked briefly. She now lived in Palo Alto and was still on the left politically. She recalled being with a group of her friends watching me on television as I was testifying during the Bork confirmation hearings. Her friends were incensed at my testimony and asked her: "What do you think about this Thomas Sowell?"

To which she replied: "Thomas who?"

Ironically, Audrey was head of some local community legal project and their activities included raising legal challenges to the expulsions of hoodlums from schools in the nearby black community. This was ironic in at least two senses—first, that she was defending kids who were making it impossible for other black kids to get a decent education and, second, in that role her organization was often opposed by my wife Mary, an attorney representing the school district.

Some time later I encountered Audrey at a filling station where she and I were putting gas into our cars. She apparently wanted to exchange pleasantries but, when I thought of what she was doing to destroy black kids' education, I could not bring myself to join in. I hope I did not seem curt or rude but cannot be sure.

If you live long enough, I suppose fate will have its little cruel jokes on you, as it did by having me encounter Audrey after all these years.

1991

Back in 1982, when Clarence Thomas was nominated to be head of the Equal Employment Opportunity Commission, my name was dragged into the confirmation hearings by Senators who expressed apprehensions because he had commented favorably on some of my writings. Now, after he was nominated to the Supreme Court, I was determined that I would do everything I could to prevent me or my work from being made a distraction in the media.

I left strict instructions at the office that no phone calls were to be answered by anybody, lest the calls be from reporters. My conviction was that the only thing the media couldn't quote out of context was silence. I also notified people who handled media relations at the Hoover Institution, who seemed somewhat taken aback that I was refusing opportunities for publicity for myself and the institution, despite requests they were receiving for me to be interviewed. But this nomination was too big for me to allow myself to become even a peripheral distraction in the media, knowing that any effect that might have on the nomination could only be negative.

As it turned out, I was no distraction but sensationalized charges against Clarence by Anita Hill at the eleventh hour put his confirmation in jeopardy.

October 12, 1991

Dear Walter,

Just today, I finally sent off to the publisher the book I began writing nine years ago: *Race and Culture: A World View*. It is my valedictory on this subject. Just the fact that I can still stand to read it, after all this time, makes me hopeful that the public will like it. However, I would sooner bet the rent money on a long-shot than try to predict book sales. Another piece of good news is that *Ethnic America* is now being translated into Russian and Chinese.

With all this good news, this would be one of the happiest times of my life, if it were not for the horror that Clarence Thomas is being dragged through. This stuff makes the Bork hearings look like the good old days. Clarence is still young enough to be shocked at being knifed in the back by someone he went out of his way to help, but I have all kinds of scars between my shoulder blades.

> My theory is that Clarence's problem arose precisely because he did *not* sexually harass Anita Hill. You know the mean-spiritedness of some of our women, especially when they see white women walking off with some of the few black men available at their social and professional level. Add to that her disappointment at discovering that following Clarence to E.E.O.C. did not mean that her own career would follow the same upward trajectory as his. And to come out of Yale and end up in Oklahoma is not necessarily everyone's idea of the American Dream. Now it appears that there are also ideological differences. Those Senators who are wringing their hands about finding a motive don't seem to be able to see the woods for the trees.
>
> As for Clarence, he has done himself proud in the way he has handled this thing.

Now that Clarence Thomas was under attack before the Senate Judiciary Committee and in the media, I reversed myself on giving media interviews and agreed to talk to virtually anybody at any time, hoping to add whatever small weight I had on his side of the scales. What carried far more weight than anything I said, however, and what may well have been what saved his nomination, was the parade of women he had worked with over the years who appeared in the televised hearings before the Senate Judiciary Committee and gave him their strongest endorsement, with at least one of these women also adding her devastating account of what she had observed of Anita Hill when both of them were working at E.E.O.C.

Some of these were women I recognized from having seen them in passing when visiting Clarence when he was head of E.E.O.C. Now their testimony on his behalf brought me to the verge of tears as I realized how people who once seemed to be just part of the background had become crucial to his fate and his reputation. This was also a fitting repayment for the considerate way he treated people.

One of the things I had always admired about Clarence Thomas was his human touch and his respect for other people, in whatever walk of life they might be. His chauffeur at E.E.O.C. was an elderly black man whom the staffers called by his first name before Clarence became chairman. But after Clarence arrived and began addressing his chauffeur as "Mr. Randall," the staffers began to address him in the same fashion. When riding in the car with the two of them, I was struck by their considerate politeness toward each other. To listen to the way they spoke to one another, you would have no clue as to who was the chauffeur and who was the head of the agency.

The testimony of women who had been his employees in the past revealed a side of Clarence Thomas that had never come out in the media. One of the reporters who interviewed me was a young black woman who expressed her surprise at the people who spoke of him as a concerned, respectful, and compassionate person.

"You thought he kicked old ladies out of his way as he walked down the halls of the E.E.O.C.?" I asked.

"Well, sort of," she admitted. It was a sad reminder of how many people think of those they disagree with politically as lacking human decency.

Knowing how exhausting and draining the confirmation hearings must have been for Clarence, I avoided phoning him and adding to his fatigue. However, after making his defiant statement to the Senate Judiciary Committee on television, Clarence phoned me and we had a long conversation. He was clearly relaxed after having gotten things off his chest and, even though the Senators had not yet voted on his confirmation, it was obvious that he was not sweating how the vote would come out.

After Clarence was confirmed as a Justice of the Supreme Court, I had a local shop make up a plaque that said, "Please do not emanate into the penumbra"—a facetious reference to Justice William O. Douglas' opinion in *Griswold v. Connecticut*—and sent it to him. He later told me that his clerks at the Supreme Court got a laugh out of it. He had his own gallows humor about the confirmation episode, which I passed on in a letter to my son.

November 5, 1991

Dear John,

I heard from Clarence Thomas recently. He said: "If anybody phones you and says, 'I want to nom—' *hang up on him right there.*"

My old mentor, Professor George J. Stigler of the University of Chicago, died and I sent a letter of condolence to his son.

December 3, 1991

Dear Stephen,

Please let me add my words of condolence to those of others, though I know too well that there are no words for times like these, except perhaps words that recall earlier and better times.

As a former student of your father, I was of course hard hit by the news of his passing. He had a profound influence on my life and career, beginning even before I met him or saw the University of Chicago. One article of his, on Ricardo, in the June 1952 JPE[1] not only turned my interest toward the history of ideas but also made me determined to do my graduate work under him. Ironically, I turned down my largest fellowship offer, from the University of Chicago, to go to Columbia to study under him— only to discover upon arrival that he had just left for Chicago. The next year, I followed him there.

In addition to all the great intellectual qualities of George Stigler which are so widely known, I discovered moral and human qualities which were no less valuable. What he said of Frank Knight seems equally to apply to himself:

---

1. *Journal of Political Economy.*

...he did not seek a place in the popular press. He conducted himself as if the pursuit of academic knowledge was a worthy full-time career for a first-class mind.

It seems to me that this was a moral choice, not just a personal taste.

One of the virtues for which I never thought your father received enough credit was patience. It is true that he didn't suffer fools gladly, but in retrospect I realize now that I must have been a trial when I was a student. Indeed, he indicated as much at the time. However, he gave me great amounts of his time, by mail as well as when I was in residence—and all this despite our continuing disagreements over the interpretation of Say's Law. Last month I was very pleasantly surprised, while going through old correspondence files, to discover a letter he wrote me thirty years ago on that subject. It was a special find then, and of course more special than ever now.

Peace be with you.

While Professor Stigler was still alive, I had written an essay on my experiences as a student of his but, since it included criticisms as well as praise, I cancelled plans to publish it, now that Stigler was no longer here to defend himself. However, when I mentioned this to Milton Friedman, he asked to see the manuscript and, after reading it, urged me to allow it to be published in a special issue of the *Journal of Political Economy* devoted to commemorating Stigler's work and influence. No one else could have convinced me to publish that essay but Milton had been a close friend of George, as well as someone whose wisdom I respected—indeed, one of the few people with both genius and wisdom. My essay appeared in the commemorative issue (October 1993) and, what was even more gratifying, brought a letter of appreciation from Stigler's son. Only then was I convinced that I had done the right thing.

1992

After nearly half a century, I still heard from time to time from my friend and mentor from my days as a student at Howard University, Mrs. Gadsden.

January 20, 1992

Dear Mrs. G,

It was such a nice warm feeling to see your familiar handwriting again. I am especially nostalgic lately, as a result of writing some autobiographical sketches. You are of course featured in the episode involving a young African woman who was having trouble in my economics class at Howard.[2]

Incidentally, one of the letters I came across in going back through my records was one I wrote to some organization, urging them to sponsor your writing *your* memoirs. I hope that worked out and that we can look forward to seeing what must be a fascinating story.

Looking back over my life, I can see enormous amounts of good fortune at critical junctures, including the good fortune of encountering someone like you. In all the blatant and superficial

---

2. *A Personal Odyssey*, pp. 155-157.

things that economists and sociologists can measure, I was of course "disadvantaged," but the measurable things are not the crucial things. If I had been raised in a home with twice the money and half the attention, I would have been far worse off. Had the ghetto schools been as bad then as they are now, the situation would have been virtually hopeless.

Last year was an emotional roller coaster in a number of ways. If one day can epitomize what it was like, it would be the day that I learned that *Ethnic America* was going to be translated into Russian and Chinese—producing a happiness that lasted only a couple of hours, until I learned of Anita Hill's charges against my friend Clarence Thomas. For the next couple of weeks, I was emotionally wrung out by the hearings. What was merely implausible to others was to me impossible to believe, though I did not know how anyone could possibly defend against such charges—until those ladies from the E.E.O.C. testified and saved the day.

More than once in my life, I have gotten a knife in the back from someone I went out of my way to help, so I know how Clarence felt.

Because Anita Hill's charges were impossible for me to believe, I did not examine them closely enough at the time to see a fatal flaw in them that I should have noted and written about, so that others would see through those charges. She asked at first that Clarence Thomas be confronted with her charges without revealing the source. That made sense only if the charges were false. If the charges were true, and pertained to things that were said when only two people were present, he would automatically know the identity of the person from whom the charges came.

Although I make it a point to avoid discussing any case pending before the Supreme Court with Clarence Thomas, I sometimes commented after a decision.

July 7, 1992

Dear Clarence:

I have just finished forcing myself to read all the way through all the opinions in *Planned Parenthood vs. Casey* (partly in order to reassure myself that there were not more than nine opinions) and the conclusion I reach is this: The motto "Equal Justice under Law" should be removed from the facade of the Supreme Court building and replaced with: "Brevity is the soul of wit." Just reading this opinion is an "undue burden."

Scalia's dissent was like a great dessert after a bad meal. I burst out laughing in several places, as he punctured the hot air balloons. Yet it was also a quietly eloquent and very moving statement that reminded me of some of Holmes' dissents or of Harlan's dissent in *Plessy*.

Circuit Court judge Laurence H. Silberman made a speech before the Federalist Society, suggesting that judges were influenced by media comments on their decisions. Since I knew him, I wrote to him about it.

June 23, 1992

Dear Larry,

What you said very much needed to be said, and was of course said well, though I was depressed to hear you confirm my worst fear, that judges allow themselves to be influenced by the media. Psychologically, however, I still find it utterly baffling that people who are well-insulated from any serious consequences nevertheless bend with the winds of fashion. When I think of the firemen who go into burning buildings, or the policemen who put their lives on the line in many other ways, I find it hard to be charitable toward comfortable old men with lifetime tenure who cannot summon up enough courage to brave a few words on an editorial page.

Another point which seems to me so basic that it is hard to grasp why there should be any argument is that law is virtually meaningless unless its principles are known in advance and can be relied on. Do judges have any sense of the amount of uncertainty and hesitation they create among decision-makers in all kinds of institutions, all across the country, when they ad-lib their decisions? People hesitate to expel hoodlums from school, to fire incompetents from work, or to do a thousand other things that need to be done, because nobody knows how some judge will apply the "evolving standards" of a "living constitution."

> Even if every case decided by a judicial activist led to a better result than if the law were adhered to, the damage done throughout the society can still completely outweigh those better results in the particular cases decided.

As my book *Inside American Education* was being written, I commented to various people on what my research was uncovering.

> July 9, 1992
>
> Dear Mrs. Mueller:
>
> I would never have believed that the schools were so bad before this. My research assistant told me that she had trouble sleeping at night after watching more than twenty movies that are shown to children in the public schools.

I never cease to be amazed by people who think that Supreme Court decisions should be judged by whether the policy that emerges is one that they agree with.

> July 27, 1992
>
> Dear Mr. Fischer:
>
> Thank you for your kind comments on my writings in general, though I must have failed in this case if you thought my objection to *Planned Parenthood v. Casey* was based on policy

preferences. As I said in my newspaper column on the same subject: "It is none of the court's business which policy is better."

My objection to *Roe*, as to *Griswold* before it and *Planned Parenthood v. Casey* after it, is that it represents judicial usurpation of power through the dishonest pretense of interpreting the Constitution. That is far more important, and far more dangerous, than one policy versus another on abortion.

The arguments you make about abortion policy would be relevant to a legislative decision. They do not deal with the broader and ultimately crucial question of judicial integrity and the rule of law in a self-governing democracy.

One of the relatively few hardy souls in academia who still defends the rule of law against judicial activism is Professor Lino Graglia at the University of Texas law school.

July 28, 1992

Dear Lino:

Thank you very much for sending me a copy of your recent article in the *Stanford Law Review*. As usual, I immediately began reading it, and as usual found it thoroughly convincing....

Coincidentally, I received in the same mail a letter from a reader of my *Forbes* column, who takes me to task for having let my "anti-abortion" bias cloud my judgment of *Planned Parenthood v. Casey*. The very possibility that my criticism of that case was about judicial activism, rather than the policy decision, seems not to have crossed his mind. In reality, I am one of the few people in America who does not have "the answer" on abortion policy.

The discussion of *Brown v. Board* in your article also led me to melancholy thoughts. What do we have to show for all the sound and fury, and all the bitter divisiveness of busing? Indeed, does anyone even care about the substance, as distinguished from the symbolism? There is no question in my mind that a kid growing up in Harlem today, where I went to school half a century ago, does not receive nearly as good an education as I received. A recent article by David Armor cites empirical evidence which throws into question the assumption that black students do better academically in desegregated schools. Some of the more unthinking statistical comparisons in the literature fail to take account of the self-selection factor in many desegregated schools. Again going back to my childhood, the black kids I knew who went on to predominantly white junior high schools were better than average academic performers *before* they ever set foot in a white school. If the *post hoc* fallacy were banned—perhaps by being ruled unconstitutional—that would destroy at least half of all so-called social science research.

Someone ought to expand on the point made in your article that phrases like "due process" had a long history before they first appeared in the Constitution of the United States. We don't have to guess what the founders could possibly have meant by "freedom of speech" or "an establishment of religion"—or, more to the point, give their words "contemporary meaning," because their meaning was already pretty clear from the outset, though clever people can always think up hypothetical conundrums.

These are very discouraging times on a number of fronts. . . . Recently I have been reading some correspondence of Edmund Burke, written at a time when he was very discouraged about the future of his society. Somewhere he said that at least he could go down to defeat in the company of brave and honorable comrades. That is how I felt after reading your article.

Here and there, other brave people were fighting the good fight on other fronts, including the issue of women in the military.

July 27, 1992

Dear Ms. Smith:

Your recently televised discussion of women in the military was very enlightening. . . .

While your part of the discussion was enlightening, I was appalled by some of the other statements that seemed to presuppose that all that mattered was individuals, as if individuals could even survive infancy without society and social norms, and as if "men" and "women" were just arbitrary designations. . . .

One of the strongest arguments for keeping women out of military combat is one that can hardly be breathed, in these politically correct times: Women's lives are more valuable to society—a fact recognized in practice, though not in words, by even male chauvinist societies. Population losses are quickly made up after a war because fewer women than men die in wars. There is also a qualitative dimension: Do trained killers make the best mothers?

Despite many discouraging trends in many aspects of contemporary society, I tried to keep my pessimism from turning to despair.

September 12, 1992

Dear Mr. and Mrs. Jurvis:

Thank you for your kind remarks and for sharing some of your experiences with me.

At times, I too get depressed about the future of this great country. However, more than two hundred years ago, Adam Smith wisely observed: "There is much ruin in a nation." Once I asked Friedrich Hayek if he were optimistic or pessimistic about the future. "Optimistic!" he said, with great surprise at the question, and recalled that when *The Road to Serfdom* was published back in 1944 his was a lonely voice in the wilderness, while people and publications with similar ideas have since proliferated around the world. I have in fact visited free market think tanks from Jamaica to Australia.

Think too of all those brave souls who bucked the intellectual tide by opposing Communism during all the decades when it enjoyed all kinds of sympathy and support among the Western intelligentsia. I was so happy that Sidney Hook, for example, lived to see the collapse of the system and movement he opposed for half a century, despite suffering all sorts of attacks, smears, and ridicule.

Few things are more discouraging than the American public school system, as I have learned from research for a book on education that will be published early next year. . . . However, the battle goes on, even on this front. Things may look bad at times, but it's not over until it's over.

As to why I have not been involved in politics, that is partly a matter of temperament. However, I have also long believed that whatever influence ideas have on Washington is likely to be indirect, by influencing the voting public. Ronald Reagan, after all, was elected on very much the same ideas with which Barry Goldwater was defeated 16 years earlier. What happened in between was a spread of ideas by people like Milton Friedman, preparing the way for a changing climate of opinion that made political change possible.

David Riesman was one of the people with whom I continued to correspond—in this case, about the pitfalls of projecting our feelings onto other people.

October 30, 1992

Dear David:

As I look back over my early life, in the segregated south of the 1930s, I find it hard to take seriously the notion expressed in *Brown vs. Board of Education* that separating black children from white children in school so affected the black students psychologically as to impair their ability to learn. I cannot recall anyone who even commented on the absence of white children in our schools, much less anyone who was preoccupied with it. There were no white kids in our neighborhood, in our churches, or on our playgrounds. If we had found them in our schools, we would have wondered what was going on. None of this is an argument for racial segregation—just for talking sense.

The arbitrary psychological projections in *Brown* no doubt accurately reflect what a middle class white man would feel if magically transformed into a black child and sent off to public school. This same kind of bogus projection seems to underlie the efforts of some writers to tell the story of Columbus from the standpoint of the American Indians, when in fact they are telling it from the standpoint of a 20th century white American magically transformed into a 15th century Indian. It seems highly unlikely that our 20th century perception that conquest and enslavement were wrong per se was the view of 15th century Indians, who would probably have been quite happy to have conquered and enslaved Europeans (or anyone else) if they could have.

A reader who questioned the labeling of blacks who disagree with the civil rights establishment as "Uncle Toms" prompted me to respond.

November 24, 1992

Dear Mr. * * * * *:

No one seems to have noticed that Clarence Thomas' net worth—all that he has accumulated over a lifetime—is less than half of what some "leaders" in the black civil rights establishment make in one year. Surely no one believes that people sell out to the lowest bidder.

Back in the early days of the Reagan administration, when the illusion flourished that I was going to become a member of that administration, one of the black "leaders" invited me to lunch in his hotel suite in San Francisco. I had never seen such a suite before, complete with a spiral staircase leading to the upstairs rooms.

1993

While traveling, I happened to run into Charles Murray in Dulles Airport and asked what he was doing these days. He mentioned that he was working on a book about mental tests, prompting this letter. That book, of course, turned out to be *The Bell Curve*.

January 25, 1993

Dear Charles:

I wish we had had more time to talk more when our paths crossed at Dulles airport. In view of your interest in the I.Q. controversy, I wonder if you are familiar with the work of James R. Flynn, an American expatriate who teaches at the University of Otago in New Zealand. Though a professor of political science and politically to the left of center, Jim Flynn is not only a man of integrity but also an old-fashioned scholar who goes all the way back to the original data—and has found some of it fatally flawed.

Incidentally, my mentor in economics, the late Nobel Laureate George Stigler, once suggested that anyone who spent an afternoon in a library checking up on footnote citations was likely to find the experience disillusioning. Years later, when I had occasion to follow the trail of a footnote on a familiar proposition in labor economics, I found that the evidence for it

> collapsed like a house of cards. My wife, an attorney, says that she has had similar experiences when following up on citations in court cases.

Although Jim Flynn's work was later discussed in *The Bell Curve*, I have no way of knowing whether my mentioning it to Charles Murray was the reason, especially since *The Bell Curve* so thoroughly covered other research on the subject.

I passed along to Shelby Steele an excerpt from a letter from a professor at one of the Ivy League colleges, revealing one of the many painful and sordid aspects of contemporary academia.

> February 19, 1993
>
> Dear Shelby,
>
> Thought you might be interested in the following passage in a letter written by a professor at an elite eastern college:
>
> > Two years ago I suggested to * * * * * * that we make an offer to Shelby Steele. * * * * * * said it would be vetoed by the black caucus.
> > "Wait a minute," I said, "I meant an appointment in the *English* Department, not Black Studies. Steele is an *English* professor."
> > No go. Evidently the black caucus has a veto over appointments in the *English* Dept.! Wow.

The loss was not Shelby's. He is doing quite well. The real loss is that of the students at that college—black and white alike—who may never hear a different perspective that he could bring that goes beyond the narrow confines of the politically correct education that so many of them get.

I met for the first time with one of the few media people for whom I have real respect.

April 13, 1993

Dear Joe,

Had dinner with Rush Limbaugh the other evening. In person, he is really a very gentle and gracious man. He told me that when he first set out with his program, and with his particular strategy for marketing the program, people said that it couldn't be done. But now that he has done it, the story is that *anybody* could do it.

When my son graduated from college with a degree in statistics and computer science, I wrote a column about his late talking and how that had led many people to consider him mentally retarded, even though he later turned out to be, among other things, a math whiz. Little did I suspect what this column would lead to—a flood of letters from parents of very similar children, some of whom asked me for explanations or advice. I was surprised to receive the first few letters, little suspecting how many more would be received in the months and years ahead. One of these letters was from a colleague and friend who wrote to me about her son, who was both late in talking and adopted.

June 22, 1993

Dear * * * * * * :

As regards the question of adopted children knowing about their parents or the various other "rights" mentioned by the "experts," I am by no means convinced. I am grateful to my sister for having sought me out, as a young adult, despite efforts to keep me from knowing that I was adopted. However, I am by no means sure that I would have been better off knowing this, and trying to come to grips with it, at an earlier age. As it was, I probably had the best of both worlds, growing up as an only child and later discovering a sister and brothers.

Among the letters I found after returning home from a vacation in Europe was one from Mrs. Gadsden.

June 25, 1993

Dear Mrs. G,

Your letter arrived while I was overseas and I have just gotten back.

I was very saddened to learn of the passing of Mr. Gadsden. What I remember most about him was dry humor and good nature. While I remembered that he was in photography, I had no idea of what all was involved until I read the obituary you sent me.

There are no words for times like these, except to say that my heart is with you. I hope that your biographical writings will engage your attention and feelings enough to help you through this terrible time. I will of course be happy to read and critique whatever you wish to send me.

There was a certain irony now in my critiquing the writing of someone who had taught me freshman English but life is full of role reversals. All we can do is do the best we can to play the role we have at the time when we have it.

The year began with my granting permission to have one of my favorite columns translated into German.

January 1, 1995

FAX TO: Peter Lutz

FROM: Thomas Sowell

SUBJECT: Permission to Reprint "Grasshopper and Ant"

Thank you for passing along the request for permission to reprint "Grasshopper and Ant" and for offering to supply a translation.

Here is the column:

GRASSHOPPER   AND   ANT

Just as the "Rocky" and "Star Wars" movies had their sequels, so should the old classic fables. Here is the sequel to a well-known fable.

Once upon a time, a grasshopper and an ant lived in a field.

All summer long, the grasshopper romped and played, while the ant worked hard under the boiling sun to store up food for the winter.

When winter came, the grasshopper was hungry. One cold and rainy day, he went to ask the ant for some food.

"What are you, crazy?" the ant said. "I've been breaking my back all summer long while you ran around hopping and laughing at me for missing all the fun in life."

"Did I do that?" the grasshopper asked meekly.

"Yes! You said I was one of those old-fashioned clods who had missed the whole point of the modern self-realization philosophy."

"Gee, I'm sorry about that," the grasshopper said. "I didn't realize you were so sensitive. But surely you are not going to hold that against me at a time like this."

"Well, I don't hold a grudge—but I do have a long memory."

Just then another ant came along.

"Hi, Lefty," the first ant said.

"Hi, George."

"Lefty, do you know what this grasshopper wants me to do? He wants me to give him some of the food I worked for all summer, under the blazing sun."

"I would have thought you would already have volunteered

to share with him, without being asked," Lefty said.

"What!!"

"When we have disparate shares in the bounty of nature, the least we can do is try to correct the inequity."

"Nature's bounty, my foot," George said. "I had to tote this stuff uphill and cross a stream on a log—all the while looking out for ant-eaters. Why couldn't this lazy bum gather his own food and store it?"

"Now, now, George," Lefty soothed. "Nobody uses the word 'bum' anymore. We say 'the homeless'."

"I say 'bum'. Anyone who is too lazy to put a roof over his head, who prefers to stand out in this cold rain to doing a little work—"

The grasshopper broke in: "I didn't know it was going to rain like this. The weather forecast said 'fair and warmer'."

"Fair and warmer?" George sniffed. "That's what the forecasters told Noah!"

Lefty looked pained. "I'm surprised at your callousness, George—your selfishness, your greed."

"Have you gone crazy, Lefty?"

"No. On the contrary, I have become educated."

"Sometimes that's worse, these days."

"Last summer, I followed a trail of cookie crumbs left by some students. It led to a classroom at Ivy University."

"You've been to college? No wonder you come back here with all these big words and dumb ideas."

"I disdain to answer that," Lefty said. "Anyway, it was Professor Murky's course on Social Justice. He explained how the world's benefits are unequally distributed."

"The world's benefits?" George repeated. "The world didn't carry this food uphill. The world didn't cross the water on a log. The world isn't going to be eaten by any ant-eater."

"That's the narrow way of looking at it," Lefty said.

"If you're so generous, why don't you feed this grasshopper?"

"I will," Lefty replied. Then, turning to the grasshopper, he said: "Follow me. I will take you to the government's shelter, where there will be food and a dry place to sleep."

George gasped. "You're working for the government now?"

"I'm in *public service*," Lefty said loftily. "I want to 'make a difference' in this world."

"You really have been to college," George said. "But if you're such a friend of the grasshopper, why don't you teach him how to work during the summer and save something for the winter?"

"We have no right to change his lifestyle and try to make him like us. That would be cultural imperialism."

George was too stunned to answer.

Lefty not only won the argument, he continued to expand his program of shelters for grasshoppers. As word spread, grasshoppers came from miles around. Eventually, some of the younger ants decided to adopt the grasshopper lifestyle.

As the older generation of ants passed from the scene, more and more ants joined the grasshoppers, romping and playing in the fields. Finally, all the ants and all the grasshoppers spent all their time enjoying the carefree lifestyle and lived happily ever after—all summer long. Then the winter came.

Justice Clarence Thomas is a Dallas Cowboys fan, as I am as well. So I wrote to him after the Cowboys' defeat at the hands of the Forty-Niners.

January 16, 1995

Dear Fellow Sufferer,

During the Dallas-San Francisco game, I kept repeating my favorite misquote from Robinson Crusoe: "I don't like this atoll." The Cowboys may have lost this game a year earlier, when they fired Jimmy Johnson. It is hard to imagine his making the kind of dumb moves that Barry Switzer made, including getting a 15-yard penalty for bumping an official. . . .

I keep reading in the papers that you are a recluse but, every time I turn on television, there you are making a speech someplace else. Since there is only a limited demand for black

> conservative speakers, I regard this as another example of government competing with private enterprise.

Clarence knew that I didn't like going on the lecture circuit, so he wouldn't take seriously my complaint that he was cutting into my market. As for what I read in the newspapers about him, I didn't take any of that seriously. The media liked to depict him as a withdrawn and embittered man but I knew that he was one of the most upbeat people around, with a great sense of humor. Whenever I was on the phone a long time and was laughing a lot, Mary would almost invariably ask me afterwards, "Was that Clarence?" Usually it was.

———————

A painful reminder of how narrow and dogmatic many people had become on racial issues came when I learned of a situation involving a young black boy in California who had been raised since early childhood by white foster parents, who were the only parents he knew. When they sought permission from the local social service agency to take him with them when they moved across state lines into Oregon, the agency not only denied permission, they sought to remove the boy from their home—based on the notion that black children should not be raised by white parents. I wrote a column about this but what created a real controversy was my discussing the case with Walter Williams, when Walter was a guest-host on the Rush Limbaugh program, with its audience of millions of people across the country.

> January 19, 1995
>
> Dear Walter:
>
> The black youngster we talked about on the Rush Limbaugh show was spared. The boy's attorney tells me that the commissioner sitting as judge gave the social service agency short shrift. I gather that the agency was deluged with phone calls, including death threats. But the honcho in charge of the division that handled this case apparently still doesn't get it. He

said that all this would never have happened if the child had been in his agency's jurisdiction from the beginning—i.e., he would never have been allowed to go into the home in which he has thrived.

The late-talking children project is growing out of control. At last count, there were 36 families in the group with 5 or 6 more ready to join. In addition, I am constantly discovering new people who talked late. This may be one of those widespread but invisible phenomena, in the sense that any given parent going through the experience does not know of anyone else who has ever faced a similar situation. In my case, I had no idea that my college room mate had also talked late. That I learned a couple of weeks ago.

When Walter Williams mentioned my project to his mother, she told him that he too had talked late!

The first break in my attempt to get some qualified professional interested in this subject and this group came very unexpectedly and involved the renowned neuroscientist Steven Pinker of M.I.T.

April 27, 1995

Dear Professor Pinker:

In what I hope will prove to be a Providential event, I stumbled across one of your books—as yet unread—while straightening out my bookshelves a few minutes ago and discovered from the advertising copy that you specialize in an area that is very relevant to something else that I have stumbled into and become very concerned about.

Let me begin at the beginning. In May 1993 I wrote a newspaper column on the occasion of my son's graduation from college, devoting most of that column to the fact that he did not talk until he was almost four years old. From around the country came letters from other parents whose children talked late—and who exhibited some of the other characteristics of my son. One mother said that she burst into tears upon reading the column because her son was also named John, also talked late, and also majored in computer science in college. Many other quite moving letters came in, most from parents still going through the anxiety of waiting for a child to talk.

As you can imagine, these parents wanted answers and I had none. However, I had some computer searches done in the scientific and medical literature—and still had no answers. There was plenty written on late-talking children in general, but my assistants and I found nothing on late-talking children who had normal and above-normal ability. Some of the late-talking children in our group seemed to have truly extraordinary ability in some respects, as my son did at an early age. To make a long story short, I ended up writing a memo to those who had written me, telling them that I had come up empty and suggesting that the best I could do was to put them in touch with one another—including some parents whose children were now grown and doing fine. Thus began an informal group which has now grown to more than 40 families spread over more than 20 states.

From the letters and phone calls that went back and forth over a period of months, I began to think—with incredible slowness, now that I look back on it—that there might be some sort of pattern among these children. To find out, I sent out a questionnaire, which about half the parents filled out and sent back. What staggered me most was that more than half of these children had a close relative who was an engineer—especially since my brother is an engineer and so are two of his sons. Among those who did not have an engineer in their nuclear family or among their grandparents, uncles or aunts, most had a mathematician, scientist, pilot, physician, or other such analytical person among their close relatives. About half had a close relative who played a musical instrument, either professionally or for recreation. Some of these families were loaded down with both analytical people and musicians. About ninety percent of the children were boys but the first grown girl I heard about seemed very similar to the boys. She graduated 13th in a high school class of 700 students and went off to college planning to become an engineer—like her father. She is not part of our group but, like some other late-talking children I have encountered or learned about outside the group, her family pattern is much like that of most of the children within the group.

> Since my only professional training is in economics, what I most hope to do this year is to find someone with a scientific or medical background who will take over research on this group, both for the sake of these parents and their children and for the sake of other such parents and children elsewhere, now and in the future.
>
> The parents themselves share this goal, not only to learn more about their own children, but also to contribute to an understanding of this whole phenomenon for others. If you would be at all interested in looking into this, please let me know. If you phone, please do not be put off by the forbidding message that my assistant has put on the answering machine. I always respond as soon as possible to anything connected with the late-talking children.

Although I had tried in vain to get other specialists interested in my group, Steven Pinker began to discuss the issues with me and suggested scientific literature that might be relevant, even if there was still nothing directly dealing with bright children who talk late. I had thought before that I just might not have been looking in the right places, but Professor Pinker generously had his own research assistants canvass the scientific literature and they could find nothing directly on point either. Although Pinker would not take over the project as I had hoped, he gave me invaluable help in trying to understand the issues myself. The fact that his assistants had found nothing in the literature on exceptionally bright children who were also exceptionally late in beginning to speak made me realize that, by default, I would have to be the one to write the first book on that subject.

Despite the fact that most of my relatives live on the east coast, I tried to keep in touch and offer what help or advice I could. One of the children of my niece in New York had come through serious medical problems and was now going to college.

May 22, 1995

Dear Rachel,

I wish I knew what things you are interested in. Perhaps I have some books on the subject I could send you. In difficult times like these, something you have developed a real interest in can be very good to get yourself absorbed in, whether it is stamp collecting or sky diving or anything in between. There have been difficult times in my life when my work has been my salvation. . . .

You mentioned in your letter not being able to repay me. *All* of us owe much to people we can never repay. The best we can do is to remember that and pass it on to someone else later, when the time comes. I am sure that time will eventually come for you. It could be someone in your family or someone you meet in later years. Maybe it will be one of my children after I am gone. Or it might be me. Who knows whether I will end up someday ill and alone, perhaps not fully aware of what is going on around me, and you might be the only one around to keep me from being mistreated. Life has many huge changes in people's fortunes and misfortunes.

Among the letters I found upon returning from a vacation in Europe was one from neuroscientist Steven Pinker.

September 9, 1995

Dear Steve:

It was good finding your letter when I returned from overseas and especially good to learn that you will be in Santa Barbara this coming academic year, which may make it easier for us to get together to talk about our group of late-talking children.

Your view that late talking may be a result of competition for resources in the brain was very welcome . . . as a professional's buttress to my layman's assessment, which might otherwise have been considered just an economist's natural tendency to say that there is no free lunch in the brain. The incidence of allergies among high I.Q. people seems to lend further support to the competition-for-resources view. However, as you indicate, this is all at the level of preliminary speculation and something as serious as this will need some empirical work. It may even need research that lasts much longer than a 65-year-old man may last.

An autopsy of Einstein's brain had shown that the area of the brain that handles analytical thinking was enlarged and spilled over into the area that normally controls speech. Whether that was why he and the children in my group were highly analytical and slow to begin talking only future research by scientists could determine. But it was interesting that Steven Pinker thought such competition for resources within the brain was at least a plausible possibility for explaining this and other problems peculiar to people with high

IQs.

_____

Back in 1980, then New York City mayor Edward Koch wrote to me, saying, "I would love to have an opportunity to chat with you over lunch or dinner," and asked me to phone him the next time I was in New York City. For one reason or another, we never actually got together until 1995, after even his long term as mayor was over.

September 27, 1995

Dear Ed:

It was a pleasure to finally meet you after all these years, especially because we have both accumulated a lot of scars in the ideological battles of these times.

When you speak of my "dismissal" of affirmative action programs, you use the word in the way described in the chapter on "The Vocabulary of the Anointed" in my recent book.[3] In no ordinary sense of the word have I dismissed affirmative action. When you study something for more than 20 years, travel literally around the world to learn about it in other countries, and then analyze it in numerous articles and books, that is not a dismissal. That is simply reaching a conclusion different from that of other people. In this context, the word "dismiss" is itself a way of dismissing all this. . . .

The idea of giving criminals "a second chance" has been tried in many ways and at enormous cost to those victimized by

_____

3. *The Vision of the Anointed.*

them. The only thing I know that works is putting criminals behind bars and keeping them there. A few years ago, East Palo Alto was the murder capital of the nation, in proportion to its population. In just one year, murder and other serious crimes declined sharply after stepped up police activity put more hard-core criminals behind bars. There is no reason to suppose that East Palo Alto has found those elusive "root causes" of crime.

As I noted in *The Vision of the Anointed*, the "root causes" argument might make some sense if human beings were born into the world already civilized, for then we would have to explain why some do barbaric things. But with every human being still being born into the world today as barbaric as the children of the cave man, there is no mystery in the fact that those who are not properly raised remain barbarians.

Justice Clarence Thomas is not the only public figure who pays no attention to the media, as I mentioned to him.

October 9, 1995

Dear Clarence,

You seem to be getting a lot of good press lately, perhaps because the critics have exhausted all their powers of denunciation and a few others have actually gotten around to reading some of your opinions. Incidentally, Margaret Thatcher was guest of honor at a recent Hoover luncheon and mentioned in passing that she doesn't read the papers. Just think, if everybody were like the two of you, the press would become extinct. You would become the first Justice to destroy the free press, in violation of the first amendment—in addition to being the youngest and the cruelest!

All the best.

The facetious remark at the end grew out of a charge in the media that Clarence Thomas was "the youngest and cruelest justice" because of his dissenting opinion in a case involving a handcuffed prisoner who had been beaten by prison guards. Although Justice Thomas' opinion stated explicitly that the abused prisoner had a right to sue under various laws, the Constitutional ban on "cruel and unusual punishment" was not one of them, because the illegal behavior of the guards was not punishment imposed by any court. Many in the media seem not to understand that things that are immoral, or even illegal, are not necessarily unconstitutional. Assassinating the President of the United States is not unconstitutional and, for most of our history, it was not even a federal crime. The reason that the Dallas police, rather than the F.B.I., had custody of Lee Harvey Oswald was because Oswald had committed no federal crime when he shot President Kennedy.

The whole point here is simply that different laws cover different things and a judicial opinion that a particular law is not applicable to the case at hand does not mean that the case is not covered by other laws. Despite Justice Thomas' going out of his way to point out that other laws were available to the abused prisoner, many in the media—including people who should have known better—tried to make it look as if he was just being "cruel" or uncaring, as if he approved of the beating or was refusing to let the prisoner have a right to sue. How much of this represented sheer ignorance on the part of journalists and how much represented malicious bias is hard to know, since so many journalists have both ignorance and bias.

———————

As the year came to an end, I made a sober decision about the upcoming new year and communicated it to James W. Michaels, the editor of *Forbes* magazine.

December 27, 1995

Dear Jim:

As I begin planning what I am going to do in the upcoming year—and, at age 65, with the rest of my life—it is painfully clear that I am stretched very thin and that maintaining my physical health, as well as the quality of my work, requires some changes. With great reluctance, I have decided to include my column in *Forbes* among the things I am taking off the agenda.

Writing that column has been a very good experience for me and I believe that my best columns have been the ones published in *Forbes*. I know vividly about the people it reaches, for many of them had dinner with my wife and me during a Baltic cruise last summer, even though we knew no one on the ship except people who introduced themselves because they had seen my column in *Forbes*. Whether in writing or in other aspects of life, it is better to leave while the audience wants more rather than continue on like some athletes or other performers who decline until they become parodies of their former selves.

Writing the column has gotten a little tougher recently and I hope that has not meant a decline in the quality of the final product. In any event, my top priority has to be completing a huge manuscript that I began writing back in 1982 and which has thus far produced two books—*Race and Culture* and *Migrations and Cultures*—and will produce a third, *Conquests and Cultures*, in a couple of years. This international cultural history seems to me to be not only the most important thing I can leave behind me, but also one of the most urgently needed things, at a time when the Balkanization and polarization of this country are truly dangerous prospects.

Let me thank you for the courtesies and considerations I have received and please let me know if you are ever travelling out this way, so that we can reciprocate the hospitality you showed to my wife and me.

1 9 9 6

I brought my niece up to date on how things were going.

April 1, 1996

Dear Ruthellen,

I am much more relaxed now that I have stopped writing for *Forbes* magazine. It was just one thing too many. All the letters and phone calls I have received from readers saying how much they will miss me are very gratifying. The editor of *Forbes* says that there have been only half a dozen times in the 35 years he

> has been at the magazine that there has been as much reader response as there was to my farewell column. My tax accountant will be happier too. With my income going down, I won't have as much to pay in taxes. That seems to be the way he looks at the world.

After I stopped writing regularly for *Forbes* magazine, Jim Michaels suggested that I simply send them something when I felt like it, thereby getting rid of the deadline pressure and I proceeded to do so. However, a resumption of writing "guest columns" meant having to cope with copy-editors that Jim had largely kept off my back before. After I complained to him, he sent out an unequivocal memorandum:

TO: Betty Franklin, Copy Desk, Proofreaders

June 4, 1996

Re: Thomas Sowell

Under no circumstances are changes to be made in copy submitted by Dr. Thomas Sowell. I've asked for this in the past but my request hasn't been strictly observed. Please—not a comma, not a hyphen and never mind our style book. As he writes it so shall it be printed.

Jim Michaels

That was the end of that problem at *Forbes* magazine and made writing for them a special pleasure as long as Jim remained editor. I was told by a friend in New York that one of the copy-editors at *Forbes* complained bitterly about me at some social gathering. It was music to my ears.

1997

More depressing to me than people who have views that I consider mistaken are people who say things that have no logical or empirical meaning but which are fraught with insinuations that they confuse with meaningful conclusions. Some such people publish articles and books and some write letters to me.

January 31, 1997

Dear Mr. * * * * * *:

It is not nearly as surprising that different people have different opinions as it is that some opinions refuse to subject themselves to the test of empirical evidence. A clear example is your statement: "Even those societies which make an effort to achieve social justice and fail are far better off than those societies which do not even try." If this is not simply an arbitrary definition—a tautology—then the whole twentieth century is full of painful, if not horrifying, evidence to the contrary.

How do you suppose Communist movements built up the followings needed for eventual success in achieving power in Russia, China, Cambodia, etc., except by tapping the idealism of people who were seeking "social justice"? Do you regard the actual consequences—the millions slaughtered by Stalin, Mao, Pol Pot—as making these societies "far better off"? As a former Marxist, I felt betrayed when I saw St. Petersburg a couple of years ago and have been sickened by the stories of what has happened to orphans under the Ceausescu regime in Romania.

Those people whose idealistic quest for "social justice" provided the political support in the Communists' drive for power—the "useful idiots"—without whom such horrors would not have been possible may be counted as representing "righteousness" by you, but not by anyone who sees politics as something more than an arena for moral preening. I believe it was Pascal who said that the first moral duty is to think clearly. At the very least, one can look at the evidence. Communism is only the most blatant evidence but by no means the only evidence.

While I was on the book tour for *Late-Talking Children*, a specialist in the study and treatment of late-talking children heard me on a radio talk show and wrote to me to offer to help in any way that he could. He was Professor Stephen Camarata of Vanderbilt University.

July 28, 1997

Dear Professor Camarata:

Your interest in our group is very much appreciated and I would like to talk with you at a time that would be convenient to you. I have no schedule, but only a large backlog of work, so I can be flexible as to particular times. Quite frankly, both the group and the book turned out to be more time-consuming, more

> exhausting, and more emotionally draining than I would have dreamed going in. As a result, now that the book is done, my feeling is one of "I gave at the office."

I wanted out and Professor Camarata was a boon to me in providing a way out. Now that my group of parents of late-talking children was being publicized as part of the book promotion, protecting their individual privacy became even more of a concern than before, so I closed the group to any additional people who might want to join, partly because I feared the group's being infiltrated by someone from the media and partly because I wanted to phase out my involvement with this work.

Since Camarata now set up his own support group of parents of late-talking children, I could refer new parents to him and his group. Moreover, as I continued to get letters from people who sought my advice on what to do with their late-talking children, I could at last offer them some help by referring them to Professor Camarata, who had years of clinical practice with late-talking children. Parents who took their children to Camarata for evaluation or treatment sang his praises to me and I also met him in person and we visited each other from time to time, so I got to know him and to realize how enormously conscientious he was. I also learned that he had himself been late in talking.

The first person I wrote in the new year was my niece in Harlem.

> January 3, 1998
>
> Dear Ruthellen,
>
> I hope that this will really turn out to be a happy new year for you. It can happen. Just the other day, I received a phone call

from my former travel agent, who has been through all kinds of problems with her health, her children, and her former husband. She was phoning to tell me that her son is now in college and is on the dean's list, while she has another job. I think she has turned the corner and will not have to look back—and I think that time can come for you as well.

What you did during your brief career at Columbia [University] confirmed my feeling that you are capable of far more than you seemed to think you were. That it turned sour later on does not change that. . . .

Incidentally, it was 50 years ago this month that I left home with all my worldly belongings in a little cardboard suitcase. It was a tough start in life but it was more valuable to me than if someone had filled that suitcase with dollar bills.

Although going on a lecture tour was exhausting, sometimes there were interesting experiences, one of which I passed on to the lady who booked my speaking engagements.

April 7, 1998

Dear Ruth:

The people treated me extremely well in Detroit. Also heard a touching story from the chief of police, who was master of ceremonies. It seems that he was driving home one evening when he saw a woman out on a bridge and realized that she was about to jump. He did a U-turn, called out to her, got out, and started toward her. While trying to climb over a railing, he banged his knee against an iron grate and bent over in pain. Then he limped on over to her. Her first words were: "Are you all right?"

He said, "Yes. Are *you* all right?"

She said "Yes" and they both wept and put their arms around each other.

Letters from school teachers almost invariably blame the poor quality of our public schools on things outside the schools. But the behavior of the teachers' unions suggests that they are determined to avoid having such claims put to the test.

April 9, 1998

Dear Ms. * * * * * :

If the educational deficiencies are caused by all the things you say, why then the desperate, multi-million dollar campaigns to prevent the excuses to be tested empirically by allowing some of these same children, from the same families and with all the other social handicaps, to be educated by someone else through vouchers?

There is more than enough blame to go around—including blame for parents, students, and the general culture of the times—but teachers and teachers' unions are determined that nothing that goes wrong in the schools could possibly be their fault.

After years of researching and writing about affirmative action, I would like nothing better than to forget about it. But others keep making it an issue—and keep saying things that I know to be false and believe to be harmful to the very people who are supposed to be helped by preferences and quotas. Advocates of affirmative action often criticize the Scholastic Aptitude Test (SAT) and other criteria which make individual qualifications the basis for college admissions. One such critic of the SAT was Hugh Price, president of the Urban League.

May 29, 1998

Dear Mr. Price:

It may not surprise you that I disagree with your recent op-ed piece in the *New York Times* about the SAT. However, I think we agree sufficiently on the ultimate goal—the best education for black students—that it may be worth discussing our differences on the means toward that end.

The kinds of objections you make to the SAT could be made against the medical use of thermometers. Surely no one considers thermometers to be either infallible predictors or the be-all and end-all of medical practice. Undoubtedly there may be people who will die today whose temperature is a perfect 98.6 and others who are healthy and flourishing whose temperatures have been dangerously high. But, when all that has been said, no one wants any doctor or hospital to get rid of thermometers. And no one denies that a temperature of 104 is a very important warning sign.

Your essay begins by describing your debates about affirmative action. But it seems to me that we are long overdue to change from seeing issues in terms of debating points against whites and that there is a need to refocus on what will in fact advance blacks most. If you have serious reservations about the predictive validity of the SAT or other tests, or of academic criteria in general, then there is a large and solid body of evidence on this subject. . . .

This is ultimately an empirical question whose answer makes all the difference in its consequences for black students. If large test score differences are a warning sign, like a 104 temperature, then getting rid of these tests can do more damage to black students than to anyone else. In recent times, rising numbers of black students on the Berkeley campus led to declining numbers of black graduates. Who did that benefit, other than academic administrators, who were able to boast about racial body count ("diversity") while over-matched students went down the tubes?

One of my bitterest duties when I taught at UCLA was talking to black students who had flunked out of the school by having failed my course—after obviously having failed other courses before. Without exception, these were students who should never have been admitted in the first place, even though most of them could have succeeded in most other colleges.

I understand why administrators find it politically expedient to sacrifice black students' future for the sake of institutional image and protection against having federal dollars cut off or delayed. What I cannot understand is why blacks in responsible positions are trying to perpetuate double standards of admissions that produce horrendous dropout and flunk-out rates. Minority students who meet the same standards as other students already graduate at a far higher rate than those admitted under various "special" programs. I have no doubt that the redistribution of black students within the University of California system will likewise lead to higher graduation rates throughout the system. To me the bottom line is not how many black students go into the system but how many come out of it with an education.

I would hate to see this constant crusade of black leaders and spokesmen against tests and standards convince people that blacks simply cannot meet the same criteria as others. . . . Blacks do not need to be scoring miles behind whites on standardized tests, as they are today. Attacks should be directed against the school system and the cultural vogues of the day that create such disasters, not the test scores that are messengers bringing the bad news.

Former Judge Robert Bork and I had the rare experience of being on opposite sides of a public issue—in this case, the antitrust lawsuit against

Microsoft. He was representing one of those who filed complaints against Microsoft. Bork was kind enough to give me some material on his side of the issue while I was passing through Washington and visiting the American Enterprise Institute, where he was one of the scholars in residence.

June 4, 1998

Dear Bob,

After looking over the material you gave me when I was at AEI, it seems to me that my real quarrel is not with your legal argument but with antitrust law itself. The attached column sketches some of those objections. . . .

Antitrust law seems to me to have anticipated by decades one of the most disturbing aspects of civil rights laws—shifting the burden of proof to the accused after a very flimsy prima facie case. The Robinson-Patman act did this long before "disparate impact" law came along. But the Sherman Act is hardly a model of clarity either. Some years ago, you suggested that courts declare the Robinson-Patman Act "void for vagueness," as I recall. Is not the incredible length of time taken by antitrust cases, especially when the essential facts are not seriously disputed, an indication of a lack of clarity in the law itself? Some would argue that it is not law, in the full sense of rules known in advance, if neither attorneys nor Circuit Courts of Appeal can confidently say beforehand what will or will not be permitted.

Here is the column that I attached to this e-mail:

FAST COMPUTERS AND SLOW ANTITRUST
by Thomas Sowell

Few things develop as fast as technological change in the computer industry. And few things are as slow as antitrust cases. So an antitrust case against a computer software company like Microsoft is about as big a combination of opposites as you can find.

Five years is breakneck speed for completion of a major antitrust case and it is not unknown for a decade or more to elapse before the appellate courts say the last word on one of these cases. Five years is at least two generations when it comes to computers. A decade ago, laptops were a novelty of the rich.

The idea of slowing down innovation in the computer industry to the glacial pace of the legal system is grotesque. Yet that is what the Justice Department's Antitrust Division tried to do when it asked the courts to stop the recent introduction of Microsoft's new Windows 98 operating system until the legal fine points could be argued out.

Antitrust law is so full of ambiguous phrases, mushy concepts and elusive definitions that it cannot really be considered law. Laws are supposed to tell you in advance what you can and cannot do, not just allow government officials to nail you when they don't like what you are doing or want you to do it their way.

Antitrust cases can involve years of wrangling in the courts and many millions of dollars in legal fees, even when the plain facts of the case are not in serious dispute. That is because the terms used have no clear and consistent meaning.

Microsoft is accused of being a "monopoly" that uses its "power" to prevent rival software producers from being able to compete. The Justice Department claims to be trying to protect "competition" by reining in Microsoft's ability to exclude other companies' software from its Windows operating system.

Let's begin at square one: Is Microsoft a "monopoly"? By the plain dictionary definition—one seller—it is not. Apple computers have a different operating system, for example. By an economic concept of monopoly—a firm able to prevent other firms from engaging in the same activity—it is likewise not a monopoly.

In antitrust law, however, numbers and percentages can be used to claim that a particular company "controls" a certain share of the existing market. If that share is very high, then the firm may be considered to be a rough equivalent of a monopoly.

Slippery words like "controls" insinuate what can seldom be plainly stated and proved. If a high percentage of the customers buy your product, that statistic after the fact does not prove that you controlled anything before the fact.

Those same customers can change their minds tomorrow and you will be history. That is why Microsoft keeps updating its operating system and adding new features. If it really controlled the market, it could relax and let the good times roll, instead of constantly scrambling to stay ahead of its rivals and potential rivals.

While the Justice Department's Antitrust Division claims to be trying to protect "competition," it is in fact trying to protect competitors. Competition, like monopoly, is a set of conditions in the market. It cannot be reduced to an outcome like percentages of sales.

There is competition in boxing when the champion agrees to fight the leading challenger—even if the champ knocks him out in the first round. Competition is about a set of initial conditions, not about outcomes.

The Antitrust Division wants to prescribe outcomes by asking the courts to force Microsoft to include rival Netscape's Internet software in its own Windows system. Some in the media have spread the disinformation that Microsoft makes it impossible to put non-Microsoft software in its system or on the Windows screen.

My own computer came with non-Microsoft software, including Netscape, on the Windows 95 screen—and I didn't even order Netscape. The computer manufacturer put it there.

Moreover, Windows is set up so that the consumer can easily install all sorts of other software. Why some media people don't bother to check out the simplest facts is beyond me.

Some media pundits have been calling Microsoft founder Bill Gates "arrogant" for dismissing the Justice Department's arguments as nonsense. But Gates' real problem may be that he is not a lawyer, and so does not realize that much nonsense is already an established part of antitrust law and precedents.

When I read that Ward Connerly, a black regent of the University of California, was thinking about having ethnic studies programs evaluated, I took the liberty of writing him, in hopes of clarifying some things that someone from outside academia might not fully understand.

June 19, 1998

Dear Mr. Connerly:

Press accounts say that you are considering a re-evaluation of ethnic studies programs. If so, it is long overdue but is almost certain to be met with claims that non-academics are meddling in academic affairs. However, one way to meet this objection might be to poll the faculty, *using a secret ballot*, to determine how they evaluate various kinds of programs, including feminist studies and other trendy ventures.

To maintain the objectivity of the voting, it might be useful to send the ballots only to professors in departments other than those being evaluated, in order to find out whether professors in solid fields such as mathematics, science, and engineering regard these other programs as intellectually respectable. I strongly suspect that they do not.

Needless to say, the secrecy of the ballot would be crucial, given the level of courage (or lack thereof) among academics. I recall some issue at Berkeley a few years ago where there was a bitter battle over whether there should be open voting or a secret ballot, since both sides understood that this might well determine which way the faculty voted. If a vote were taken by mailed ballots, it would also be important to make the ballot one that could not be Xeroxed for purposes of stuffing the ballot box. This might be done by the use of an authentication seal printed in a color and/or with a raised surface that a Xerox machine cannot reproduce.

Resistance to evaluating—much less ending—ethnic studies programs may be much more desperate than resistance to ending admissions quotas. The threat is much more direct to people already in place on campus, who include people without any comparable employment opportunities in other fields. They are not like engineers or economists, who can always go to work in private industry, probably at higher salaries than in academia.

One of the perennial arguments in favor of affirmative action is that there has been a history of racism and discrimination, and therefore we need preferences and quotas until the last vestiges of racism and discrimination are gone. A reader repeated that argument in a letter to me, citing examples.

June 23, 1998

Dear Mr. * * * * *:

While I appreciate your sincerity in presenting an argument that I have heard many times over the years, that argument does not make the case that Policy A is better than Policy B—which is an argument about future consequences, not past history.

To say that any policy should exist until human beings stop committing some particular sin amounts to the same thing as saying that the policy should exist for eternity. You could use such an argument to defend almost any policy on almost any subject. In some countries, people who steal have their hands cut off. Should that policy continue until no one steals any more? Should Prohibition be brought back, because some people still drink too much and others suffer because of it? In other words, should we consider only the bad effects of drinking and not the bad effects of Prohibition itself?

As Churchill once said: "If the past sits in judgment on the present, the future will be lost." We cannot keep fighting the last war and we cannot keep crossing that bridge into Selma.

There are many issues on which facts have had to take a back seat to fashionable dogmas. One of them was mentioned in a letter to *National Review* writer Kate O'Beirne.

July 28, 1998

Dear Ms. O'Beirne:

Belated bravos for your essay on boys back in the May issue of *National Review*. Growing scientific research on innate differences between the sexes—even in the womb—has not made a dent on the unisex dogmas of the feminists. My little book on late-talking children (87 percent boys) led me to some of the literature on MRIs showing the different ways that male and female brains respond.

I have a lot of skepticism about conspiracy theories, for reasons I explained to a reader who had asked me about one.

August 26, 1998

Dear Mr. * * * * * * :

Conspiracies are hard to keep secret. After all, people even squeal on mafia dons, hazardous as that must be. The Watergate cover-up failed despite the fact that Nixon had control of the FBI, the CIA, a huge slush fund with which to buy people's silence, and the power of pardoning any federal crime. If a conspiracy cannot succeed under those conditions, it is hard to see how it can succeed very often under less promising conditions.

The idea that a President of the United States can "run the country" or "grow the economy" is one that seems almost childish to me, for reasons I expressed to a reader who had written to me, pointing out the widespread belief of people in such notions.

October 1, 1998

Dear Mr. * * * * * *:

As for what Clinton did that has people thinking that he is "running the country" well, he was at the right place at the right time, just as Herbert Hoover was at the wrong place at the wrong time. If presidents could make the economy prosper, the economy would always be booming at election time.

For Christmas, I sent Milton Friedman a couple of scenic photographs of mine and a note.

Dear Milton,

In view of all that I have learned from you, both as your student and later, sometimes I have thought that, in a truly just world, I would have to share my royalties with you. Fortunately, it is not a truly just world, so I get away with just a couple of tokens of appreciation!

I had some overdue news to announce to the people in the support group of parents of late-talking children.

March 16, 1999

TO: MEMBERS OF LATE-TALKING CHILDREN GROUP

FROM: THOMAS SOWELL

I have just been notified that "Dateline NBC" is finally going to broadcast tonight the segment on late-talking children for which some of us were interviewed as far back as August 1997. However, a previously scheduled broadcast of it was cancelled because of some news event. Let's hope that no one gets assassinated and no war starts today.

The broadcast went on as scheduled and one of the members of our group was featured. Since she had agreed to be publicly identified, she is the only member of our group whose name I have not kept secret.

March 18, 1999

Dear Mrs. Gage:

You were wonderful on "Dateline NBC"—very genuine and very effective. It was also very gratifying to learn of your son's progress. When you admitted that you still worry, you gave the lie to those "experts" who claim that parents will just assume that their kids are geniuses instead of getting help, as a result of what I have said. Most parents are going to worry long after the danger has passed.

A well-connected friend in Washington wanted me to meet with a rising political star.

April 26, 1999

Dear Chris:

While I appreciate your efforts to have me meet Governor George W. Bush and remain very willing to do so, it has occurred to me that perhaps I should give you the same warning that I gave to someone who wanted me to meet with his father when the elder Bush was in the White House: It would do him no good politically to be known to be talking with me.

From time to time I offered advice to younger relatives, though it is hard to know how much good any of it did.

June 1, 1999

Dear * * * * * *,

I am glad you asked about mentioning my name when applying for a job at *Forbes*. It would be a bad idea. Obviously I know nothing about your work and the very fact that you would try to bring in someone who is irrelevant to the job you are applying for could be a negative factor.

If there is any advice I would offer you, not only for this situation but for life, it would be this: DON'T PLAY ANGLES. Playing angles may get you some little things here and there—but at the cost of big things over all. Most people who are influential enough for you to want to influence them are usually old enough that they have seen angles being played longer than you have been in the world.

Immigration seems to be one of the intractable problems of our time. Actually, it is not necessarily immigration per se, but the context in which it occurs, that seems to be the biggest problem, as I mentioned to a former colleague at UCLA in a letter about a lot of current issues.

July 2, 1999

Dear Bill:

The cultural impact of bringing Mexico to California is hard to quantify, but that doesn't make it negligible, except perhaps to mathematical economists. In a different time, when both social and legal norms were more seriously enforced, the net effect might be more clearly positive. But, in an era when upholding norms is equated with repression, if not racism, the negative factors carry more weight, especially when there are vocal movements determined to keep foreigners foreign and supply them with grievances. One of the most ferociously militant Hispanic movements is far better supported by the Ford Foundation than by Hispanics themselves. The militants tacitly recognize this by trying to cut Hispanic parents out of the loop when it comes to decisions about bilingual education, since these parents usually want their children taught in English.

At a personal level, I must say I am impressed by the fact that it is far easier to find black or white "sturdy beggars" on the streets than to find a Mexican beggar—if I have ever seen one. . . . But my generally favorable views of Mexican Americans must be tempered by the fact that I do not come in contact with Latino gangs or other ruffian elements. . . .

One of the most serious problems of sub-Saharan Africa, which does not lack for serious problems, is that it is so thinly populated—about one-tenth the population density of Japan— that the per capita costs of supplying electricity, piped water, sewage lines, and medical care to the hinterlands is far higher than it would be in many other parts of the world.

After the death of Julian Simon, I went to my bookshelf to take another look at one of his books before writing an obituary. As I opened the book, out fell a letter from Simon that I had never seen before. In it, he said that Kuznets had told him that he (Kuznets) believed that a larger world population might be a plus economically, but that voicing such a view would risk undermining his own credibility in general. Julian Simon said that he understood such prudence, but that he also understood the larger negative implications of such prudence. Perhaps for that reason, I especially value those who are not so prudent, including of course one W. R. Allen. Can you and Fran come up this way this summer?

Kuznets was a Nobel-Prizewinning economist, while most of those promoting "overpopulation" hysteria were uninformed or misinformed. It was a painful irony that knowledge could be silenced by ignorance, like that of far too many people to whom our educational system has given "self esteem" instead of either knowledge or a sense of logic.

September 3, 1999

Dear Mr. Daniel:

You are quite right that wealth buys insulation from the realities of life. For some, it also provides a need to escape a sense of undeserved bounty by championing the "have nots." I have suggested that rich people who feel guilty should see a psychiatrist at their own expense, rather than make public policy at other people's expense.

Thank heaven I grew up in a more hard-hearted time, when my teachers in Harlem did not consider it "unfair" to expect me to learn what kids in affluent neighborhoods were learning. If

> they had the present mushy thinking and pandered to my "disadvantages," where would I be today? Uneducated and undisciplined, I might well have ended up in some half-way house somewhere—if I were lucky. But the "humanitarians" would have felt good about themselves.

I addressed a question about the Soviet economy to Condoleezza Rice who, at this point, had finished a term as provost of Stanford University. Though not yet widely known to the general public, she was a scholar specializing in the study of the Soviet Union and spoke Russian.

December 9, 1999

TO: Condoleezza Rice

FROM: Tom Sowell

1. BOOK: I am currently writing a little introductory economics book for the general public and have found some very interesting stuff about the Soviet economy in a 1989 book by a couple of Soviet economists named Shmelev and Popov. Do you happen to know of any more recent books or articles on the Soviet economy that I ought to read?

2. NOW IT CAN BE TOLD: My wife has long been a fan of yours. However, when she first heard that you were

going to become provost, her response was: "What's a nice girl like her doing in a place like that?" My own reaction was equally stereotypical: "I don't trust anyone under forty." However, all's well that ends well!

The 2000s

2 0 0 0

When my little memoir, *A Personal Odyssey*, was published, I of course sent a copy to my niece from the family in which I grew up in Harlem. The early chapters re-living my childhood evoked a re-living of her own childhood, for in later years she and her parents lived in the same apartment that I had once lived in at 504 West 145 Street, and she had an even worse time with the aunt who had raised me, who was her grandmother. Her brother Jimmy lived in the same little room in the back where I had once lived and the public library across the street was also a place to which she escaped. She wrote to me immediately after receiving the book.

9/6/00

My dear Uncle Tommy,

The book arrived yesterday and I've completed the first four chapters.

It is truly a good read from the acknowledgment on. I picked it up and had to force myself to put it down.

I'm writing you because I'm afraid I'd become a simpering mess, once I heard your voice, but I'll call you when I've completed your odyssey.

That same library was my refuge also when things became ugly in 504. That small room off the kitchen was my brother's. Such a tiny place it never looked well kept. Although he did make use of the fire escape day or night.

I also enjoy the way you tie up things at the end of each

thought. Which I'll do now.

I love you,

Ruthellen

An attempt to order books from Malaysia for my research caused me to comment to my research assistant about my experiences when visiting that country some years earlier.

June 7, 2000

FAX TO: Na

FROM: Tom

You are quite right about the slow pace in Malaysia. However, it is the Malays who are slow, not the Chinese or the Indians there, and I would be surprised if the Kuala Lumpur Publishing Company is run by Malays, unless it is part of some government largess to the "sons of the soil." Does the company have an e-mail address? That might be better for international transactions.

After our first visit to Kuala Lumpur, where Mary and I suffered from the slow and inaccurate service by the Malays in the hotel restaurant where we were staying, our next stop was Singapore, where I was absolutely startled by a Chinese waitress who suddenly appeared at our table with our meal, shortly after we ordered it. It was an almost equal shock to discover that it was exactly what we had ordered. It always amazes me that people who have traveled more extensively than I have cannot seem to figure out why some groups have higher incomes than others, without getting into esoteric theories about exploitation and the like.

From time to time, some kind and generous reader urges me to run for public office—sometimes for President—and I respond when I have time.

June 27, 2000

Dear Mr. * * * * *:

As for my running for public office, I appreciate the spirit of your offer to support me. However, if I ever do announce my candidacy, you would do me a bigger favor if you would contact the proper authorities to have my sanity tested.

2 0 0 1

A reader raised some questions about psychology and psychiatry.

May 13, 2001

Dear Mr. * * * * *:

As far as I am concerned, the American Psychological Association and the American Psychiatric Association are faith-based organizations. There seems to be no test of what they believe except that they all believe it. What baffles me is why law enforcement officials do not keep a record of what psychologists and psychiatrists say about particular criminals, in court or elsewhere, so that the next time they testify with such confidence, their previous record can be brought out—how many criminals released on their say-so have committed how many violent crimes, costing how many lives, etc.

The terrorist attacks of September 11th left me in a state of shock. I sent e-mails to friends and family back east to make sure that they were all right. Among these was Norman Podhoretz, whose wife Midge Decter had sent me a copy of a recently published book of hers.

September 12, 2001

Dear Norman,

Midge's book got me through the day yesterday. The events themselves were too overwhelming for me to also subject myself to the inanities of the media, so I turned the TV off and sat in an easy chair, reading her book. So I can only hope that nobody said that we should offer bin Laden land for peace.

Today, as I read the various statements that have been made in Washington, I am disquieted by references to "justice" and "tragedy." It is as if they want to make this a legal case, with perhaps bin Laden ending up at the International Court of Justice in the Hague and getting so many hours of community service. As for Colin Powell's reference to "tragedy," the bubonic plague was a tragedy but Pearl Harbor was an outrage. Maybe these are just semantic quibbles but I fear the official statements betray a mindset in Washington that is not good.

From time to time, I hear from some professor who insists on being honest with black students and maintaining academic standards, as distinguished from going along with current academic fads. Often such professors are resented by black students and/or other faculty members who try to be "friends" of black students.

December 18, 2001

Dear Professor * * * * *:

It is heartening to know that outposts of courage and honesty still survive on campus, even in this corrupt and canting age. What David Riesman has called "affirmative grading" is part of a truly despicable fraud that sends minority students out into the world unprepared to meet the inescapable challenges of life. It is like sending half-trained soldiers into battle to be slaughtered, as green American troops were at the Kasserine Pass in the early days of World War II.

You deserve the thanks of anyone who has the best interests of black students at heart. Eventually some of them may come to realize that, though perhaps not until after they get out of this artificial campus atmosphere and into the real world. Their "friends" among the faculty and in the administration are friends only in the sense that Iago was a friend to Othello by feeding his paranoia. In any event, you have a clear conscience and that is one of life's most precious possessions.

I continued to keep in touch with my niece in Harlem.

December 20, 2001

Dear Ruthellen,

Good to hear from you and hope that your health is on the mend. . . .

My health seems to be all right, so long as I remember not to push things. A couple of weeks ago, I forgot my limitations and ended up spending the weekend on crutches. As I have said before, women lie about their age to others, but men lie about their age to themselves. Whenever I wake up in the morning feeling like I am 19 again, that usually ends up with my body reminding me that I am not.

The other day, in my local bank, a radio was playing "O Little Town of Bethlehem" and it recalled a melancholy time back in 1948 when I heard that song at Christmas time, right after I had been laid off and had no idea what the future held. The young tellers, looking at my bank balance on the screen in front of them, probably could not have imagined what I had been through. My little room back then was less than half the size of my bathroom today. The sadness I felt while hearing the song that reminded me of those days reinforced my suspicion that shrinks who have people dredge up the past are probably not doing all of them some good. Recently, I read somewhere that a study indicated that as well.

Not all memories of the past are sad, however. Whenever I play a CD of Liszt's preludes—a passage of which used to be played on "The Lone Ranger," in addition to the "William Tell overture" with which the program began—it recalls happy times when I had first arrived in New York and first listened to this program.

Mary and I live a quiet life, but we like it. My main contacts besides her are through faxes to and from my assistant at the Hoover Institution and mail, mostly e-mail, forwarded in bundles from the syndicate that sells my column to newspapers around the country. The truly touching messages are from parents of late-talking children. . . .

> Merry Christmas to all.

Sweeping statements by obviously uninformed people are a painful reminder of how far we have gone in the wrong direction—and how much farther we may go in the future.

January 8, 2002

Dear Mr. * * * * * *:

The idea that the United States needs to be rehabilitated in the eyes of Africans because of slavery is staggering because (1) slavery still exists in parts of Africa to this very moment, and (2) where it has been stamped out in Africa, it was stamped out by Western colonial powers, over the opposition of Africans, who sought to retain this institution, which had existed there before the first white man appeared on the scene.

Misconceptions were common on other subjects, as I explained to an academic in England.

January 25, 2002

Dear Ms. Osler:

On this side of the Atlantic, the "role models" dogma has been repeated incessantly without a speck of evidence to support it. In reality, the Irish Catholic immigrant children who went to school in New York in the nineteenth century were usually taught by Protestant American teachers, the Jewish immigrant children who later went to school there were usually taught by Irish Catholic teachers, and when I went to school in Harlem in the 1940s, black kids were usually taught by Jewish teachers. On page 43 of the enclosed book, the data show that these black kids did a lot better than black students today—and just as well as the white kids on the working-class lower east side of Manhattan.

An e-mail from Walter Williams likewise compared the past with the present, as a test of popular beliefs today.

Date: Saturday, February 16, 2002 4:36 AM

Tom:

Last week I was watching a PBS show having a title something like Duke Ellington's Washington. The academic excellence of Dunbar High, as well as Armstrong High, was mentioned. It showed file footage of the streets where ordinary blacks lived, stores they patronized and theatres attended, etc. This was around 1910, 1920, 1930 and following years. There were interviews with elderly blacks who lived in those neighborhoods at the time talking about: kids being kicked off the swim team if they didn't keep up grades, keeping up appearances, working hard and all those parental, teacher, family admonishments that you and I might have heard when we were young.

As I watched the show, one thought dominated my mind. Here was a time when blacks weren't a century out of slavery, encountered gross discrimination and were mostly poor yet I saw no graffiti, neither neighborhood stores nor homes had iron bars on the windows and the old interviewees weren't speaking Ebonics. I wondered whether those who claim today's pathology [is] the inevitable result (legacy) of slavery and discrimination ever question their premise in light of historical facts, or do they not know or do they know and make some lame explanation like "that was a different era"?

Walter's comments caused me to look back to earlier times as well.

Date: Sun, 17 Feb 2002 09:51:28

Dear Walter,

I am afraid that there are people who just want to say what is in vogue, so that their words become shibboleths—like the original "shibboleth" in Biblical times, which served as a password to show whose side you were on, since one group could pronounce it and their enemies couldn't. At a higher level, the "leaders" have purely pragmatic goals. If putting a guilt trip on whites produces benefits, then they will run that play until the defense figures out how to stop it.

Did you know about the poem on the walls of Dunbar High School that was written by Paul Laurence Dunbar? It said:

> Keep a-pluggin' away.
> Perseverance still is king.
> Time its sure reward will bring.
> Work and wait unwearying.
> Keep a-pluggin' away.
>
> Keep a-pluggin' away.
> From the greatest to the least,
> None are from the rule released,
> Be thou toiler, poet, priest.
> Keep a-pluggin' away.

How such a philosophy would be sneered at by today's sophisticates! And yet this was written in 1916 and put on the walls of a segregated black school in a Jim Crow city, during a period of a resurgence of the Ku Klux Klan—and it worked! That is the bottom line that all the clever people do not recognize as the ultimate test.

Dunbar High School had an outstanding academic record during those decades. Most of its graduates went on to college when that was rare for white as well as black high school graduates. At one time the school's reputation was such that its graduates could get into Harvard without taking an entrance exam. While there were many racial barriers, Dunbar alumni were often those who first broke through those barriers, becoming "the first black who" did many things, ranging from the first black man to graduate from Annapolis to the first black federal judge, the first black general, and the first black cabinet member. Dunbar's distinguished alumni also included the doctor who pioneered the use of blood plasma and Duke Ellington.

From time to time, someone suggests that I have an exhibition of my photographs or else publish them in a book. I have never had the time or energy to devote to either of these things. The best I can do is display the pictures on the walls of my home, so that visitors can see them. Shelby Steele has been one of those visitors and he has taken copies of a couple of my photos to hang in his own home.

Date: Sun, 31 Mar 2002 03:54:59

Dear Shelby,

Since the last time you were out here, I have added more photos on the walls and had some lighting installed to show them off. Hope you and Rita stop by to see them when you are up this way some time. . . .

Did I ever mention a book titled "Life at the Bottom" to you? It is about the lifestyle in a white slum in Britain—which is a perfect match for the ghetto lifestyle over here—right down to beating up kids who try to do well academically.

Although race is not the key factor there, the British intelligentsia has been pushing the "unfairness of society" and "the hopelessness of the prospects of the poor" even longer and more insistently than American intellectuals. The net result is the same illiteracy and innumeracy found among those attending many ghetto schools over here. In both cases, why be a chump and play the man's game, if it has already been rigged for you to lose?

Many of those who peddle this line to the poor probably think of themselves as friends or allies of the poor whereas, in terms of consequences, they are in fact among their worst enemies.

―――――――――

Walter Williams and I were becoming more aware of our advancing ages.

Date: Monday, April 01, 2002 6:07 AM

Tom: I hope you're still doing well or at least making gains in that direction. Yesterday, was my 66th year. I'm not looking for congratulations but sympathy.

Walter

Date: Mon, 1 Apr 2002 09:46:29

Dear Walter:

First of all, you young whippersnappers will get no sympathy from me. . . .

Recently I have taken up bicycling and it has done wonders for my arthritic knee, which had me on crutches a couple of years ago. Not long ago, I walked up the tallest hill in San Francisco. Fortunately, I remembered to take a cab back down. Walking down that hill also had me on crutches a couple of years ago. As the Pennsylvania Dutch say: "We are old too soon and wise too late."

―――――――――

One of the hazards of writing a syndicated column is that you cannot keep track of how various local newspaper editors around the country have edited what you wrote. Worse yet, sometimes editors slip up and put your name and picture on someone else's column. Some of the most favorable mail I have received arrived after an editor mistakenly put my name and picture on a column written by Cal Thomas. At other times, however, the results are negative, as I learned after receiving an e-mail from a reader, to whom I replied.

Date: Sun, 5 May 2002 11:00:46

I have NEVER criticized Rush Limbaugh. However, from time to time, the wrong columnist's name is put on someone else's column, and I assume that this is what happened here. I would appreciate it if you would send me a copy of the column where I supposedly criticized Rush or tell me when and where it appeared.

It always amazes me how few people see a connection between "open space" policies that make large amounts of land off-limits to building and the fact that the remaining land rises in price, driving up housing prices. Nowhere is this carried to more extremes than in parts of California. I noted this in an e-mail to Walter Williams.

Date: Thu, 30 May 2002

I have been riled up lately about the incessant expansion of "open space" and the skyrocketing land and housing prices it produces. A recent ad in a local paper listed a house in Palo Alto with 3 bedrooms and one bath, 1300 square feet, built in the 1920s, for an asking price of $1,095,000. In any other part of the country, "asking prices" are usually the top price expected. In these parts, it is common for asking prices to be bid up higher. . . .

It really burns me up when huge burdens are put on families for very modest homes, all so that a relative handful of environmental cultists can feel puffed up about themselves.

It is not unheard of in parts of California for rent or mortgage payments to take half of people's income. Meanwhile, "open space" zealots like to picture themselves as trying to save the last few patches of greenery from being paved over—when in fact forests alone cover more American territory than all the cities and towns in the country combined, and over 90 percent of the land area of the United States is undeveloped.

Among the many signs of the mushy thinking of our times are people who seem to think that courts are supposed to decide cases on the basis of whether the policy involved is good or bad.

July 22, 2002

Dear Mr. * * * * * * :

I never cease to be amazed at people who refuse to make a distinction between a policy issue and a Constitutional issue. Whether it is or is not good policy to enable children to attend religious schools with a voucher is not the question before an appellate court. The question before the court is whether such an arrangement is or is not a violation of the Constitution's ban against an "establishment of religion."

An "establishment of religion" is not an esoteric phrase

requiring tortured exegesis. It was a very common phrase when the Constitution was written by people who had lived under an established church and who knew very well what it meant. Judges who twist and strain these words two centuries later are simply legislating from the bench. If judges are going to settle policy issues, why do we need a Congress and a President? More to the point, there are few things more dangerous than having unelected legislators. The separation of powers is at the heart of our Constitution and a crucial bulwark against tyranny. But the much-touted "separation of church and state" is nowhere stated or implied in the Constitution. That is why there are chaplains in the military and in Congress. Neither is there an amalgamation of church and state. All that there is in the Constitution is a prohibition against an establishment of religion like the Anglican church. If you want more, then convince your fellow Americans to amend the Constitution—but don't have judges do it with verbal sleight of hand.

The demonization of the pharmaceutical industry in the media has led many people to express the idea that the high prices of some medications are caused by "too much" advertising.

August 14, 2002

Dear Ms. * * * * *:

Contrary to a popular view that advertising costs are simply added to the price of a product, when advertising increases the sales of a product—and that of course is the whole purpose—then economies of scale may permit that product to be produced at lower costs per unit. If automobiles were *not* advertised and had lower sales, that would almost certainly result in much higher prices, since the high fixed costs of producing cars would have to be shared among a smaller number of buyers. Whether advertising adds to or subtracts from the price of pharmaceutical drugs depends on its effects on sales and on production costs. However, since fixed costs are an even higher percentage of total costs of production for these drugs, it seems likely that advertising lowers their cost as well.

As to how much advertising is enough, it astonishes me that people with neither expertise nor experience in this industry imagine that they can determine that off the top of their head. A drug that remains unknown is like the proverbial tree falling in an empty forest. My life happens to have been improved greatly by a sample of a new drug that my doctor received and passed on to me. What in the world would lead you to think that you know how much of this should go on in an industry for which you have neither the training nor the experience? The only rational

> explanation I can think of is that our educational system encourages people to have and voice opinions on things that they know little or nothing about.

Among the people with whom I shared memories of earlier times was my niece in Harlem.

October 6, 2002

Dear Ruthellen,

Hope things are going well with you. I am feeling much better after a change in medication and adding a little exercise to my routine. Mary Frances worries about someone my age being out riding a bicycle but I worry because she is not riding one. . . .

While going through old files today, I came across the enclosed genealogy that I did years ago, and which I send along in case I didn't send it before. One of the other things I came across were letters to and from my college room mate, Norton, with whom I have kept in touch all these years. It was he who said to me during my first semester at Harvard: "When are you going to stop goofing off and get some work done?" I was shocked because I thought I was raising hell. But, when the first grades came out, it became painfully clear that I hadn't done nearly enough. Without Norton's harsh criticism, I might never have lasted out the year. But a black student in a similar situation today is unlikely to get the same advice because everyone is so "sensitive."

Although I was no longer in the academic world, but worked at home despite being on the Stanford payroll, my friend Walter Williams kept me informed about what was going on in academia.

October 21, 2002

Dear Walter:

The young lady from Princeton whom you mentioned is a symptom of a really tragic situation for students of all races. When you said that she had "never heard the other sides" of a whole range of issues, that is the real tragedy, regardless of which side she might have heard or the relative merits of each side. Turning out generation after generation of people who do not know what it is to weigh opposing arguments is producing intellectual couch potatoes who know only how to repeat whatever they have been indoctrinated with. They are precisely the kind of gullible people that the Nazis targeted in their years of struggle for power. I think it was Jefferson who said that freedom and ignorance cannot co-exist indefinitely.

The other aspect of this that is very disturbing is how supinely parents and others accept teachers at all levels taking advantage of students' immaturity and vulnerability to

> indoctrinate them. There was a time when indoctrinating students behind their parents' backs would have been considered dishonorable and cowardly. But so many of the parents themselves were so indoctrinated when they were in school that they would not say anything so judgmental.

One of many issues on which many people have heard only one side is gun control—and that one side is often based on faulty "studies," as I mentioned in an e-mail to Greg Lindsay, a friend who runs a think tank in Australia.

> Date: Fri, 6 Dec 2002 21:30:59
>
> Dear Greg,
>
> Last week I did three columns on gun control myths (www.tsowell.com) and in one of them I predicted that a discredited study by a professor who has resigned from Emory University would continue to be cited by gun control advocates. This week that study was cited in a decision by the 9th Circuit Court of Appeals!

One of many reasons for courts to restrict themselves to deciding questions of law, but not policy, is that there is no way that judges can keep themselves informed about the vast range of policies involved in the cases that come before them. The Ninth Circuit's misinformation about the effect of gun control laws only highlights a more general problem—that judges are not equipped to decide cases on the basis of what they think the effect of a policy would be. That is a subject on which they have no special expertise. What they are supposed to have expertise about are legal principles, which is why that is what they should stick to.

2003

A quarter of a century after the Supreme Court's *Bakke* decision, another major affirmative action case, *Grutter v. Bollinger*, was on its docket as the new year began. In an e-mail to Walter Williams, I mentioned a young black writer named John McWhorter, who was one of the few to put his finger on a key point, that racial quotas made it harder to get black students to meet academic standards.

Date: Sat, 4 Jan 2003 02:23:09

Dear Walter,

As a triumph of hope over experience, I still have some residual hope that the Supreme Court will finally bite the bullet on quotas, instead of going through verbal sleight of hand as they did in the Bakke case 25 years ago.

I think McWhorter is right, that ending preferences and quotas is necessary if you want to get black students to do their best. There is no point having standards if the students know that they don't have to meet them.

As it turned out, even my small amount of hope was excessive. The Supreme Court majority gave an even more muddled decision in *Grutter v. Bollinger* than it had in *Bakke* and dissenting opinions by Justices Clarence Thomas and Antonin Scalia made mincemeat of the rationales for that decision. My forlorn hope was that, if the courts could ever bring themselves to issue a clear-cut statement that racial quotas and preferences were illegal, the next day teachers across the country, at all levels from elementary school to graduate school, could confront black students with a need to meet standards or else. But, if that ever happens, it will probably not be within my lifetime. Meanwhile, supporters of quotas and preferences can congratulate themselves on being friends of blacks, while in fact retarding their progress.

When Clarence Thomas signed a contract to write a book, some in the media seemed upset that he had apparently received the kind of large advance that public figures usually get for writing books. Since he ignores much of the media, I thought I would let him know some of their reactions.

> January 10, 2003
>
> Dear Clarence,
>
> First of all, congratulations on the book deal. It could not have happened to a better or more deserving person.
>
> You might be amused by some of the hand-wringing concerns of media deep thinkers. But, fortunately, you don't have to read or listen to this stuff, while I have to, in order to keep up for the sake of my column. (Talk about injustices!) None of these great concerns seemed to bother them when the Clintons got their advances for their books.
>
> Whatever your advance, I suspect that the publisher will make it back—although I hasten to add that predicting book sales is so hazardous that I never include royalties in my budget. . . .
>
> This has been a good week for me. In addition to hearing about your book contract, I learned that my niece, who was believed to have cancer, does *not*. If I fall down the stairs and break my leg today, it will still be a good week.

Arguments for and against gun control often get bogged down over conflicting interpretations of the Second Amendment to the Constitution. But that controversy seems to me tangential.

January 13, 2003

Dear Mr. * * * * *:

My arguments about gun control are not based on the Second Amendment. If I thought gun control was a good idea and likely to save more lives than allowing citizens to carry guns, I would then advocate repeal of the Second Amendment. The facts, however, are just the opposite and it is these facts on which I base my opposition to gun control.

I was surprised to learn that President Bush was going to award me the Humanities Medal. The infirmities of age had made flying across the country to receive it at the White House too much stress to subject myself to. Fortunately, Clarence Thomas went to the White House in my place and accepted the medal for me. This was a bittersweet time for me because my niece in Harlem died suddenly and unexpectedly, after having been given a clean bill of health not long before. I wrote to my sister Mary Frances about both these events, including a newspaper column that I had written about my niece.

March 11, 2003

Dear Sis,

Thanks for your advice on the column about Ruth Ellen. Something like this depends so much on personal judgments that I would not have sent it out without hearing what you and Mary thought about its suitability. . . .

On a happier note, I enclose a copy of a document that accompanied a medal awarded to me recently by President Bush. I of course could not travel to Washington to get it but Clarence Thomas went in my place to accept the award for me. I would have liked you or some other member of the family to have accepted it for me but it would just not have been worth bringing the media into your lives.

Given Clarence's heavy responsibilities, at home as well as at work, I was very reluctant to impose on him but Mary and Walter Williams urged me to do so. Even after I warned him that the ceremonies and activities might take all day, he replied, "Well, it will just take all day!" Actually he also attended the White House dinner that evening for those receiving the awards. He is truly a gem and I only hope that someday that fact will become more widely known.

In addition to his heavy load of work on the court, Clarence was raising a young nephew and that was taking up a lot of his time. Nor was this the first young relative he had taken into his home over the years.

There was an on-going controversy because Pete Rose was banned from baseball for violating rules about gambling, and was ineligible to go into the Baseball Hall of Fame, though his career achievements would ordinarily have led to that. This was not the first time that an otherwise qualified player had been kept out of the Baseball Hall of Fame. Shoeless Joe Jackson, with a lifetime batting average of .356—12 points higher than Ted Williams'—was also ineligible for the Hall of Fame as a result of being banned from baseball after the gambling scandal surrounding the deliberate throwing of the 1919

World Series.

The Pete Rose controversy seemed to me to have wider implications, as I tried to explain to a reader who thought that wrong-doing in Pete Rose's personal life should not keep him out of the Baseball Hall of Fame.

March 25, 2003

Dear Mr. * * * * *:

I am truly frightened by the fact that so many people today seem unable or unwilling to think beyond particular individuals and their particular acts to the larger issues involved in preserving frameworks on which many other people depend, because this goes far beyond baseball.

The issue in Pete Rose's case is not his "personal life wrongdoings." It is his violating an explicit *rule*, with explicit penalties, that were put in place to preserve major league baseball itself. It is not someone's "personal" act when that act jeopardizes the whole framework in which he and many other people operate. That framework is what made possible both Shoeless Joe Jackson's career and that of Pete Rose—as well as the careers of hundreds of others before and since. If Jackson and his team mates had not paid a high price for what they did, there might not have been the same opportunities remaining for Pete Rose to have his career because major league baseball itself might not have regained the public trust and support on which its prosperity—and perhaps its existence—depends.

We will never know but we weigh probabilities in life every

day—and we don't usually give more weight to one person than to vast numbers of others whose prospects can be jeopardized by that one person's irresponsibility, or the similar irresponsibility that others may engage in if he doesn't have to pay the penalty that was prescribed in advance.

The same principle—and the same myopia—was involved in the impeachment of Bill Clinton. The question was not his moral culpability for his cheap encounters with an intern. The issue was what it does to the whole framework of law and government when any President of the United States can commit perjury and obstruction of justice with impunity. Anyone who has read the history of the decline and fall of the Roman Empire must have some sense of how internal erosions of intangibles can destroy even a great civilization. It doesn't happen all at once but it does happen, especially when people refuse to look beyond what is immediately in front of their eyes.

With friends such as Walter Williams I often discussed personal things that had nothing to do with public issues.

April 2, 2003

Dear Walter:

To this day I get cold chills thinking about some of the things I did while I was growing up—and, if the truth be known, after I was grown. Once, when Mary and I were in New York, I took her up to Harlem to show her where I used to live. She shuddered when I showed her a gap between two buildings that I used to jump across. Afterwards, whenever I did something that she considered risky, she would say, "Well, what would you expect from somebody who would jump between buildings?"

My dear friend Mrs. Gadsden was now in a home for the elderly but we still kept in touch.

May 2, 2003

Dear Mrs. G,

I have not forgotten your birthday. I have just been "feeling poorly," as they say, for the past week or so. Nothing serious, just mildly miserable. But now I seem to be well on the way to recovery.

It reminds me of a time, a few years ago, when I was recovering from something and I could hear my wife talking on the phone to my research assistant, saying with mock horror: "Oh, Na. Tom is back to *normal*!" They have lunch together occasionally and I can only imagine who they gossip about.

Recently I had lunch in a group that included Milton Friedman, who is still going strong in his 90th year—so please don't think of yourself as old! Incidentally, in going through my collection of photographs recently, I came across a picture I took of you back in the 1950s. My wife exclaimed "She's beautiful!" and then gave me one of those sidelong looks that wives give.

People who think that Canada's government-run medical system is a model that the United States should follow seldom show the slightest interest in the actual consequences of that program. Even some Canadians proceed like this, though by no means all.

May 30, 2003

TO: ***** *****

FROM: Thomas Sowell

What a shame that other Canadians do not seem to share your sense of humor nor "cherish" the health care system as you do. See poll published in the Toronto Star of May 6th. The news story begins: "Canadians with health problems are more likely than ailing residents of four other countries to say that the health care system has deteriorated and that they have had difficulty getting a doctor or a hospital bed."

Although I have a generally high regard for the British magazine *The Economist*, I am sometimes disappointed even with them, especially when it comes to careless and misleading uses of statistics, as I explained in a letter to the editor.

September 15, 2003

Sir:

Why do people who write about income inequality[1] keep talking about *household* income and income *brackets*—instead of discussing *people*? Are we interested in flesh-and-blood human beings or in statistical categories?

Households differ by huge amounts in the number of people in them. They differ even more in the amount of work done by those people. For example, in the year 2000, the top 20 percent of American households contained 19 million heads of households who worked, compared to fewer than 8 million heads of households who worked in the bottom 20 percent of households. When it comes to working full-time the year around, even the top 5 percent of households contained more heads of household who worked full-time for 50 or more weeks than did the bottom 20 percent. That is, there were more heads of household *in absolute numbers*—3.9 million versus 3.3 million—working full-time and year-around in the top 5 percent of households compared to the bottom 20 percent.

As for income brackets, most Americans do not stay in the bottom income bracket for even a decade. An absolute majority of those Americans who were in the bottom 20 percent in income

---

1. "Would you like your class war shaken or stirred, sir?" *The Economist*, September 6, 2003, p. 28.

> in 1975 were also in the top [40] percent at some point over the next 16 years.
>
> An individual always means the same thing—one person—but households vary from time to time, from group to group, and from country to country, making international comparisons such as those in your September 6th issue highly questionable, if not meaningless.

The statistics cited have long been publicly available but widely ignored, as so many other facts are ignored when they do not fit prevailing notions. These data are all mentioned in Chapter 9 of my *Basic Economics* and the sources are listed in the back of that book.

I was surprised to receive a phone call from the Bradley Foundation, saying that I had been selected to be one of the recipients of a new prize that they had created. Knowing nothing about any of this, I asked if I had to be present in Washington in order to receive the award, since I had not taken a plane in a few years, in order to avoid stress. It turned out that I would have to be present in person for the award—but it also turned out that (1) the award included a quarter of a million dollars and (2) one of the foundation officials would pay half the cost of a charter jet to fly me there. It was an offer I couldn't refuse.

Another offer I couldn't refuse was an invitation to a state dinner at the White House the day before the Bradley Foundation award ceremony. In the past, during other administrations, I had turned down other invitations to White House state dinners but now there was no decent way to decline, since I would be in town the next day. Taking a charter jet was far less stressful than going through airport security and all the other hassles and delays of traveling by commercial airlines.

There was a certain irony when I thought back on all the years when I worked like a dog for incomes that, put together, would not add up to what was now being given to me without my even applying for it. However, this was one of life's ironies that I was willing to cope with.

I later described the experience to my old college room mate, Norton.

November 10, 2003

Dear Norton,

Last month I ventured outside California for the first time in several years. The Bradley Foundation gave me an award in Washington and, when I said that I was reluctant to take on the stress of commercial air travel, they arranged a charter jet flight for Mary and me. Sometimes I have wondered what—if anything—I would do differently if I were rich. Now I know that I would travel by charter jet, so the money wouldn't go completely to waste.

Mary and I also attended a state dinner at the White House. In the past, I have turned down White House invitations to state dinners. But, since so many people knew that I was going to be in Washington for the award, there was no decent way to decline this time. The Bushes are very decent and down-to-earth people, but being in a mob of more than a hundred strangers with whom I have nothing in common was not my idea of the best way to spend an evening—especially since it made me miss a playoff game.

Mary really enjoyed herself, however. She was seated at the next table and got into it with some Democratic Congressman who claimed that California's problems are due to Proposition 13, which kept politicians from taxing homeowners even more outrageously than they do. Mary lit into the Congressman, with a certain humor but not without a certain sting as well. Colin Powell was seated at her table and afterwards came over to me with a big grin and said: "Your wife has disgraced us all!"

At Christmas time, I included a message in the cards I sent.

To Family and Friends: This has been quite a year. First of all, it has been a year when I was not once taken to a hospital emergency room, when I was able to give hour-long interviews for the first time in several years, and when my crutches gathered dust in the closet while I was out biking or swimming. I was sufficiently emboldened to refer to myself as "a former old man." Part of this was due to one of those much-lamented samples of new medications given to doctors by those much-deplored pharmaceutical companies. Part was due to just a moderate amount of exercise. For years, I had not even exercised discretion.

Clarence Thomas was one of the few people with whom I could share my enthusiasm for the work of Justice Oliver Wendell Holmes.

Dear Clarence,

Recently I have been re-reading the *Holmes-Laski Letters* and the *Holmes-Pollock Letters*. Do you have either set? I find both to be full of Holmes' wisdom and insights. I skipped most of Laski's letters this time around, partly because he has been shown to have been an inveterate liar, but perhaps also because I realize what a tragedy it was that so many future third-world leaders studied under Laski and later tried to apply his half-baked ideas in their own countries, using their own people as guinea pigs for testing the left-wing vision. Nowhere was this more catastrophic than in sub-Saharan Africa.

It has been fashionable to downplay the effect of any single individual on history but it could have made a huge difference to vast numbers of people in the third world if their future leaders had studied under Peter Bauer at the London School of Economics, instead of under Laski at the same institution. But Laski was there first and was a bigger name in his time. Despite Laski's erudition and basically decent instincts—and above all his willingness to continue to write to Holmes in the latter's last days, after the good justice was no longer capable of replying—it seems to me that the world would have been a better place had Laski never been born.

The sad story of Holmes' resignation from the High Court in

his nineties, at the request of the Chief Justice, speaking on behalf of his colleagues, reminds me to use what abilities I have left while I still have them to finish up the writings that remain unfinished in my computer. Fortunately, I have my computer chess game to help me monitor any decline. A losing streak a while back, playing at my usual intermediate level, had me wondering. But, since then, I won four straight at the expert level, so I was able to relax. Perhaps I had been reading too many *New York Times* editorials before and that undermined my ability to think rationally.

Incidentally, the recent passing of Bob Bartley reminded me that here too was one man who made a real difference by making the editorial page of the *Wall Street Journal* a counterweight to the nonsense pouring out of most of the elite media. Often, when reading the morning newspapers, I thought that going from the editorial page of the *New York Times* to the editorial page of the *Wall Street Journal* was like going from adolescence to adulthood.

As I expected, there was a note of dismay in my tax accountant's voice when I phoned him a few days ago and told him of the money I had received from the Bradley Foundation award. Since he seems to regard the minimization of taxes as the purpose of life, he did not congratulate me as others have, but at least he didn't say "You poor devil," which I suspect is what he felt. Every occupation seems to have its own myopic way of looking at the world.

2 0 0 4

One of the mysteries of our time is why Republicans are so inept in trying to get more of the black vote, as I noted in a letter to David Horowitz.

January 21, 2004

Dear David:

Today, I am told, the government is issuing a Paul Robeson stamp. Earlier, the Bush administration proclaimed Kwanzaa. For reasons unknown and utterly baffling to me, the Republicans seem to think that the way to make inroads into the black vote is to approach from the left. Nor is this the first time that this approach has been taken—witness Senator Lott's going on Black Entertainment TV and Jack Kemp's urging him to schmooze with Kweisi Mfume and the like.

Those black voters whom the Republicans have the best chance of detaching from the Democrats are unlikely to be thrilled by Kwanzaa or Paul Robeson and some may be repelled.

Rap music was one of the cultural phenomena of our times, which some among the intelligentsia celebrated. I was not one of them, as indicated by my reply to a parent who had written me.

February 16, 2004

Dear Mr. Brown:

You asked me for "a few words of wisdom" for your teenage son, who has apparently been drawn into the counterproductive world of rap and the like. It breaks my heart that a whole generation of black youngsters may throw away their own chances in this world because of this corrupt silliness. I am afraid that the words that come to my mind are not words of wisdom nor even words that could be repeated in polite society. What I would do to those who are pushing this self-destructive stuff on the young would not be permitted by the Geneva Convention.

Much as I like to test theories against hard data, I am also aware of the limitations and pitfalls of statistics, as I indicated in a letter to social scientist David Armor.

February 23, 2004

Dear David:

Your concern about family characteristics as a factor in academic achievement is one that hits home with me especially. I was adopted and raised in a family where no one before me had reached the seventh grade. In fact, I was quite surprised by what a big to-do they made when I reached that level, telling me, "You have gone further than any of us." As with many other things, however, "family characteristics" cannot be restricted to things on which sociological statistics can be collected. Some years ago, I interviewed a number of black professionals for a book that was never written, but the most striking thing to me was how many of them credited illiterate or semi-literate parents for pointing them—and sometimes pushing them—in the direction of higher education.

In my own case, looking back I am amazed at how much my family gave me in this regard, and others, considering how little they had. I was taught to read before ever setting foot in a school. Moreover, even before I moved to New York at age eight, family members who were already living in Harlem had picked out a boy from a well-educated family that they wanted me to meet, since he could tell me things that they could not. You can't buy that and you can't measure it in statistics. Much later, when I had children of my own, I asked one of the family members how old I was when I started walking. "Oh, nobody knows when you could walk, Tommy," she said. "Somebody was always carrying you." You can't buy that either. People on welfare today have a higher standard of living than we did. But what good does that do them?

None of this is peculiar to blacks. Many of the immigrant children who came out of places like the lower east side of New York and went on to have professional careers likewise came from families with poorly educated parents, some of whom could barely speak English. None of this is meant to denigrate statistics. I have been guilty of collecting statistics myself.

The idea of planning our lives from an early age sounds good but is seldom what happens, as I mentioned in a letter to my sister.

March 24, 2004

Dear Sis,

Looking back on my life, I realize that most of my ambitions were unfulfilled—playing centerfield at Yankee Stadium, for example—but the things that I never expected to get more than made up for them. It is so foolish for our schools to be asking high school students to choose careers and plan their lives. When I was in high school, I didn't know what an economist or a think tank was, yet I have been an economist at a think tank longer than I have been anything else.

I also did some reminiscing with my former room mate, Norton.

July 8, 2004

Dear Norton,

From time to time I think back to my first month at Harvard, when a letter from Washington arrived at Apley Court, offering me a job as photographer in the government. Since the late 1960s, especially, I have wondered whether my life would have been happier if I had left Harvard and taken that job. When I received my Ph.D. in 1968, there was a sense of bitter irony that years of struggle had paid off in a ticket to a career in academia, for which I had lost all respect. During the 1970s, I escaped the campus for a couple of years in Washington and another year and a half as a scholar in residence at the Center for Advanced Study and the Hoover Institution, but I did not escape permanently until 1980, when I became a Senior Fellow at Hoover. There were attempts, in the early 1980s especially, to draw me into the larger Stanford community but I let all those "opportunities" pass.

2005

Syndicated columnist Mona Charen sent me a note to thank me for recommending her book *Do-Gooders* in my column but I did not think that thanks were in order.

April 17, 2005

Dear Ms. Charen:

I was doing a favor to my readers when I recommended your book. Although it was an outstanding work, the first part was particularly painful for me to read because I am closer to your parents' generation than to yours and remember all too well what New York was like in the late 1930s and early 1940s, as compared to later times.

Once, when I was talking with students at a high school in Harlem, I mentioned that I used to walk my dog in the park across the street—and looks of horror passed over the students' faces. That very day, the principal warned them against walking across that park—a distance of one long crosstown block in New York—to the nearest subway station, even in groups of six, and recommended walking ten blocks away, where they could reach the next subway station without crossing the park. In my day, I was a kid weighing maybe a hundred pounds and walking a little cocker spaniel the length of the park, which was about ten blocks.

Earlier, in the 1930s, my sister and her husband used to sleep in that park on hot summer nights, as people slept in parks all over New York on such nights, in the era before air conditioning. Relatives of mine in Washington slept down on Haines Point where, I am told, people are no longer allowed after dark today.

Let me stop, since I am now at that stage of life that Disraeli called "anecdotage." Since I don't do much traveling these days, I would especially appreciate it if you would let me know when you are out this way, so that my wife and I—both fans of yours—could invite you to lunch or dinner.

Later, when Ms. Charen was traveling in California, we had the pleasure of her company for dinner.

In May, my latest book, *Black Rednecks and White Liberals*, was published. In it, I challenged most of the assumptions about race in America, including the role of slavery in shaping the cultures of blacks and whites in the South. In the title essay, I documented from history what was wrong with the prevailing views on this subject, which went all the way back to the early nineteenth century, when de Tocqueville expressed the views that have been echoed by many other distinguished writers since then. This was more than an exercise in history, however, because misunderstandings of the past have led to misconceptions of the present and policies with counterproductive repercussions extending into the future.

In addition to this title essay, the book also had long essays dealing with misconceptions about Jews and antisemitism, about the Germans and Nazism, about the worldwide history of slavery, and about the history of black education at all levels. Knowing how much many people had at stake in these misconceptions, I documented my case to the hilt with hundreds of citations, anticipating criticisms from those with existing views. But the criticisms never came. In contrast to the widespread media attention received by *Ethnic America* back in 1981, *Black Rednecks and White Liberals* was not reviewed in any of the biggest publications in the country—and was reviewed by fewer than ten publications of any kind.[2] Yet it was praised in the highest terms in comments from some respected scholars and the general public alike, and it sold 50,000

---

2. Mona Charen reviewed it in her column but I counted that as one review, even though her column appeared in many newspapers across the country.

copies in less than a year, almost half of what *Ethnic America* has sold during a quarter of a century.

In retrospect, I should not have been surprised by any of this. Many of my controversial writings over the years have received little or no real criticism, as distinguished from whatever name-calling they might provoke. People with a vested interest in certain beliefs were following their best strategy for preserving the influence of those beliefs, when they could not answer what I said, by simply acting as if I had never said it and continuing to repeat their own message. It was, however, odd that most leading conservative, as well as liberal, publications did not review *Black Rednecks*, maybe because it was too explosive. Still, I could not complain about the sales or the royalties, though it was sobering to realize how the marketplace of ideas had contracted over the years.

Collecting these letters caused me to write to Walter Williams.

January 7, 2006

Dear Walter,

Currently I am going through four file cabinets full of old letters in my garage, throwing most of them out, but excerpting some of them for a book of letters, though I am not sure at this point who would want to publish them. Among other things, these letters show that, back in earlier years, you and I were both pretty pessimistic as to whether what we were writing would make any impact—especially since the two of us seemed to be the only ones saying what we were saying. Today at least we know that there are lots of other blacks writing and saying similar things—more than I can keep track of, in fact—and many of them are sufficiently younger that we know there will be good people carrying on the fight after we are gone.

Index of People

Index of Subjects